S0-BDL-785

Arctic Zone

Hudsonian

Canadian

Transition

Upper Austral

Austral

Lower

Tropical

Groma Grass-Antelope Biome (Grassland)

Oak-Wild Turkey Biome (Deciduous Forest)

Palm Forest

Scrub and Palmetto Forest

Tropical Savanna (Areas of Tropical Deciduous Forest)

WEST LONGITUDE

DOUBLEDAY NATURE GUIDES SERIES

Audubon Land Bird Guide

Small Land Birds of Eastern & Central North America
from Southern Texas to Central Greenland

by Richard H. Pough

*With illustrations in color
of every species
by Don Eckelberry*

SPONSORED BY

National Audubon Society

DOUBLEDAY & COMPANY, INC.
GARDEN CITY, NEW YORK

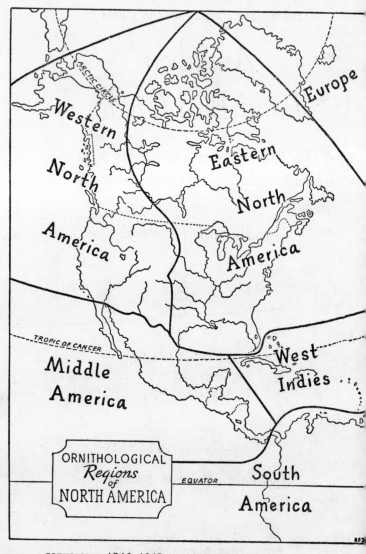

ORNITHOLOGICAL *Regions* of NORTH AMERICA

Western North America

Eastern North America

Europe

Middle America

West Indies

South America

ARCTIC CIRCLE

TROPIC OF CANCER

EQUATOR

*To my mother and father who initiated
me into the happy fraternity of
naturalists.*

Contents

CONTENTS

STANDARD ABBREVIATIONS USED IN TEXT

♂	Male	e.	eastern
♀	Female	w.	western
Im.	Immature	c.	central
Jv.	Juvenile	m.	middle
n.	northern	mts.	mountains
s.	southern	*	Sexes similar

L. Over-all length in inches
T. Length of tail in inches
W. Wingspread in inches
B. Length of bill in inches
R. Permanent residents, i.e., non-migratory
M. Migratory
P.M. Partially migratory
E.W. Erratic wanderers
(1.25 x 1.06) Egg length and maximum diameter in inches
✳ Color plate number

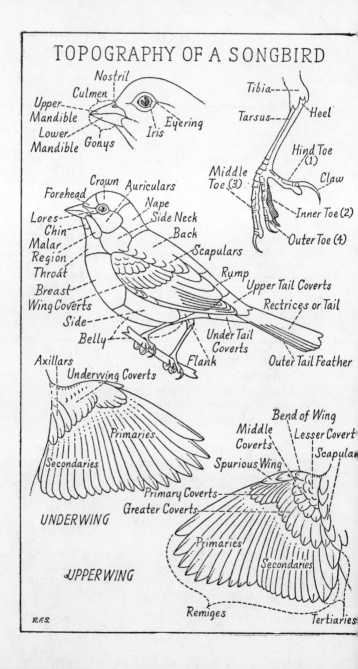

TOPOGRAPHY OF A SONGBIRD

Foreword

THE study of birds is much more interesting if you know certain general facts. This Foreword proposes to give you some of these facts and to show you how to use this book to the best advantage.

AREA: The area covered (some five million square miles) is eastern North America north of Mexico, excluding East Greenland. The line dividing eastern from western North America is taken as the eastern edge of the semi-arid Great Plains, where the tall-grass prairie country meets the drier, short-grass plains. In the United States it corresponds approximately with the one hundredth meridian running north through central Texas, western Oklahoma and Kansas, central Nebraska, and the Dakotas. In the Prairie Provinces of Canada, where the Great Plains end at the edge of the Hudsonian Forest, it swings sharply west and closely parallels the eastern side of the Rocky Mountain system almost to Alaska. The line roughly marks the westward range limit of many of the most typical birds of the humid East, but is far enough east to exclude most of the distinctly Western birds, except for species that roam far out across the grass-covered lowlands in winter.

SCOPE: All birds are classified in a systematic series. The position of any bird in the general scheme is determined by its degree of specialization. Fossil remains show that birds were originally less highly specialized than they are now. Some water birds are still relatively simple, but most land birds are exceedingly complex. The standard classification begins with the more primitive birds like loons and grebes and ends with the most highly specialized—the sparrows.

The first and broadest of the groupings are called orders. Within the orders, closer relationship is expressed by the term family. Families are divided into genera and genera into species. The species describes the individual bird. It is a natural biological unit. It reproduces its own kind and, no matter how much two birds may look alike, they are not of the same species if they live in the same area and do not interbreed. This book follows the sequence of orders, families, genera, and species established by the American Ornithologists Union in their check-list (fourth edition).

The birds (estimated as between twelve and fifteen billion) that regularly spend at least part of the year on the American continent north of Mexico, frequent its coastal waters, or appear as occasional visitors are currently divided into 700 species, of which 525 occur more or less regularly in eastern North America. Many of these also occur in western North America, in addition to the 175 species confined to that area. Of those found in eastern North America, 275 are the land birds—our common song and insectivorous birds—with which this book is concerned. They belong to the last eight orders of the A.O.U. check-list, some 228 of them (83 per cent) to the last order (passerine or perching birds), which includes more species than all other orders put together.

BIRD NAMES: Every bird has a scientific name formed of Latin and Greek terms. The name of a species consists of two words. The first, which is capitalized, is its generic or group name and is the same for all species in a genus. The second, which is not capitalized, is the bird's specific name; each species has its own.

Most species in North America also have an English name agreed upon by the A.O.U. and published as part of its check-list, but other common names are often popular in different sections of the country. Those in widespread use are listed in the Index with a reference to the bird's standard A.O.U. name.

Since this book is concerned only with species, it is unnecessary to do more than point out in passing that many species are now being subdivided geographically into subspecies or races. In most cases the differences are so minute as to have no significance in the field, and in some instances the question of whether to regard two similar but geographically separated bird populations as two distinct species becomes a matter of judgment. (See Ipswich and Savannah sparrows.)

Unfortunately, ornithologists themselves have further confused bird nomenclature by giving some of the subspecies English names which make them appear to be full species. In some cases the subspecies are specifically designated while the species itself is left without a distinctive name. Where this is true the author has chosen a name (he hopes a logical one) for the species as a whole. In a few cases where the A.O.U. name makes the bird seem a member of a race when it is actually a member of a full species, the name has been modified or changed for the sake of clarity. To avoid any possible confusion, where more than one species bears the same name, as with the crows, each is given a distinctive first name.

VARIATIONS IN APPEARANCE: It is important to remember that a bird may not look the same the year round and that male and female may not look alike. Where sexes have virtually the same appearance, the bird's name is followed by an asterisk (*).

A young bird may not look like either parent, but if there is a difference between the sexes it usually resembles the female.

Newly hatched birds may have more or less natal down. This is quickly replaced by fluffy body feathers, referred to as *juvenile* plumage; in this they leave the nest. By the time it is fully developed the bird has achieved full growth; it is as large as it will ever be.

Shortly after they are able to fly most species molt all juvenile plumage except wing and tail feathers. The next plumage, which they wear until the end of their first winter, is called the *first winter* plumage. In this the young again may or may not look like their parents. To add perplexity, males and females are often alike in this plumage even when they become quite different as adults. This and subsequent plumages which are different from adult plumage are referred to as *immature,* and the birds themselves are called *immatures.* In their first spring immatures go through another molt of varying completeness. This gives them their *first nuptial plumage.* In some species, e.g., orioles, the male's first nuptial plumage is not as brilliant as in its second, third, and fourth years.

After it becomes adult the average bird has two molts a year—a late-summer post-nuptial molt in which all feathers are renewed, and a pre-nuptial molt in late winter or early spring. The latter is highly variable, only a few birds undergoing complete change, including wing and tail feathers. Most birds change only the body plumage, and in some species, like the English sparrow, all brightening is due to the wearing off of dull feather tips.

Freak birds with white or paler-than-usual feathers are not uncommon, and complete albinos are occasionally found. A rarer variation is *melanism,* in which darker feathers replace those of normal color. A few birds, like the screech owl, occur in two colors or phases, irrespective of age or sex.

COLOR PLATES: The color plates in this book are a key to the birds. Every distinct plumage is illustrated except the juvenile. During the short period it is worn the birds are best identified by their close association with their parents. Usually the plumage extremes of any species are represented by the adult spring male and the immature female.

If other plumages are so close to one of these as to be un-mistakable, they are not shown. Figures not labeled as to season may be assumed to be in spring plumage. If not labeled as to sex, adults can be assumed to be virtually alike. If there is a marked difference between sexes in immature plumage, the duller female is usually shown and so labeled. All birds on a plate, except the crow-jay plate, are drawn to the same scale.

Familiarity with the color plates will greatly increase the usefulness of this book. To add further value, it is suggested that you go over it species by species, checking the ranges as you go along, and mark in some way the birds apt to be in your locality. A convenient way is to underline the birds you may expect, using a distinctive color for each seasonal group: red for permanent local resident; green for summer resident; blue for migrant; brown for winter visitor; and some other color for acci-dental visitors driven in by storm or other disturbance. Check-lists of local birds are available for most areas and can usually be obtained in a public library. If not, write to the National Audubon Society, 1130 Fifth Avenue, New York 28, New York.

MEASUREMENTS: In making an identification it is important to note the bird's general size. Keep in mind a few standard lengths: house wren 5 inches; English sparrow 6 inches; robin 10 inches; blue jay 12 inches; crow 20 inches. In the text the average length from tip of bill to end of tail (L.) is given. Where the ratio of tail length to over-all length has a decided effect upon the bird's appearance, the tail length in inches (T.) is given. If a bird is most com-monly seen in the air the spread from wing tip to wing tip (W.) is given. Egg measurements are in inches, the maximum long diameter or axis by the maximum short diameter or thickness. All dimensions are average.

VOICE AND SONG: Many land birds are more frequently heard than seen, and a knowledge of their songs is of the utmost value. In most cases songs are as diagnostic as appearance and in a few cases, as with the small flycatchers, more so. Unfortunately, songs are hard to set down in print. Aretas A. Saunders has been more successful than anyone else to date in *A Guide to Bird Songs*, a work to which the author of this book is much indebted.

Actual bird songs are available on phonograph records. These are very useful if you wish to memorize a few songs before going afield or to refresh your memory on songs you have forgotten, but the best way of all is to listen to the bird itself. When you hear an unfamiliar song, run the bird down until you have identified it by sight. Then listen to its song for twenty-five or even fifty repetitions. It sometimes helps if in the cadence you can detect the rhythm of words, like the barred owl's *Who cooks for you, who cooks for you all?* or the white-throated sparrow's *Old Sam Peabody, Peabody*.

PSYCHOLOGY AND BEHAVIOR: The study of birds has been greatly handicapped by a tendency to interpret their behavior according to human standards. This is a mistake. Birds are creatures of instinct, and the whole pattern of their lives is determined in advance by their inheritance. They have no power of thought as we understand it.

Apparently a newly hatched bird inherits everything it needs to carry out every step in its life cycle, even when it includes long migration flights, elaborate nest building, or any one of hundreds of other equally complex performances. These potentialities may be likened to coiled springs. The spring is motionless until it is released, but once released by some stimulus the bird is under an almost irresistible compulsion to continue the chain of action to the end. Some birds, for example, as soon as incubation is well under way, will sit on almost any object that may be substituted for its eggs.

Birds are no less fascinating because they act like automatons; that is, like birds instead of people. If anything,

they are much more so. On their own level their lives are
endlessly amazing.

ENJOYING BIRDS: Birds are our most conspicuous and most
readily observed form of wildlife. Everyone is aware of
them in the spring when their bright colors, lively movements, and chorus of song render them inescapable, but
some birds are present at all seasons. Making the acquaint-
ance of the common varieties in your neighborhood is an
excellent way to establish a closer bond with nature. It
will give you an understanding of that feeling of kinship
with the denizens of the wild, so characteristic of primitive
peoples, and you will gain an awareness of the order in
the world of living things and a perspective on human
problems and concerns that are beyond price. It is no acci-
dent that so many of our great men have been keen stu-
dents of wild birds. Few forms of outdoor recreation have
so much to offer.

The search for species that are new to you can become
an absorbing pastime. Learning to recognize by sight and
sound the birds in your immediate vicinity will give you
many pleasant hours out of doors. It is unnecessary, even
undesirable, to try to cover as much ground as possible
in order to see a great many different species. One of the
best methods is to pick out a comfortable place in an interesting habitat and sit quietly. If you make no sudden
movements the birds will soon be oblivious of your presence.

Your study of birds can be valuable to science as well
as delightful to you. There is so much we still do not know
that anyone with a little time can make worth-while con-
tributions to the sum total of our ornithological knowledge.
Probably the greatest need is for intensive behavior studies
of our common birds. These can be made wherever birds
are found. There is also need for more careful and more
detailed censuses of bird populations throughout the year
in relatively small areas, especially areas representing a

single, homogeneous type of wild plant and animal life. A
yearly calendar of the comings and goings of migrant
species is always interesting.

SEEING BIRDS: Birds are elusive, but there are many ways of
overcoming their shyness. They have excellent eyesight
and hearing but little or no sense of smell. A strange object in their vicinity often causes fright or resentment, but
if the object remains stationary they soon ignore it. Slow,
deliberate movements are generally overlooked, but quick
movements always attract attention. Be still if you can. If
you must move, do it slowly while the bird is feeding or
otherwise distracted.

Sounds, especially if loud, may startle birds momen-
tarily, and a loud clap of the hands as you cross an open
meadow or marsh will often flush into view birds that were
hidden in the grass. However, the ordinary reaction to
sound seems to be curiosity. Some birds will investigate
any strange sound, but certain sounds are more effective
than others in bringing them near. One is a squeak or a
squeaky kiss made by sucking air thorough closely pursed
lips, preferably with the lips against the back of the hand.
Another is an imitation of the screech owl. This is made
by blowing air out in a low whistle through saliva cupped
on the fore part of your tongue. If you throw your head
back slightly the air bubbling through the saliva will produce the characteristic quavering of the call. In many instances the best lure is an imitation, no matter how crude,
of the bird's own call. Success depends upon the accuracy
of your imitation and the degree of stillness you can
maintain.

Birds will come back again and again to a given spot
for food and water. These can be just outside your window or in a place you visit regularly for observation or
photography. The food to offer depends upon the birds.
For seedeaters, foxtail millet (*Setaria italica*), also known
as German or Hungarian millet, is good. Beef suet is a

favorite with insect eaters, and many birds relish sunflower seeds, peanuts, peanut butter, and stale doughnut
crumbs. Fruit eaters will usually come for raisins, dried
apples, and bananas. Some birds, especially the Northern
finches, seem to crave salt and will be attracted by salty
foods.

In providing water for drinking and bathing, use a
shallow container with a rough bottom and a gently sloping
edge, and remember that some birds will use a raised
birdbath while others will not. Whether level with the
ground or raised, it should be near a shrub in which the
bird can sit to dry off after its bath. Water dripping
into a pool from a can or faucet will attract many more
birds than still water.

Many birds can be encouraged to nest if you put up
suitable boxes or otherwise fill their special nesting requirements. Particulars are given in the paragraphs on
habits.

BINOCULARS: For serious field work a binocular is almost in-
dispensable. This will be your major tool and should be
chosen with the utmost care. A good one is expensive, but
it is a lifetime investment and worth every penny of its
cost.

Not every binocular is suited to bird work. To bring the
bird close enough for a really good look you need at least
a six-, if not an eight-, nine-, or ten-power glass. A six-
power glass means that the distance between you and the
bird is divided by six; if the bird is thirty feet away it will
appear to be only five feet away. Eight-, nine-, and ten-
power glasses further decrease the apparent distance (di-
vide the actual distance by eight, nine, and ten respectively), but the higher-powered glasses are more difficult to hold steady. Every slight motion of the observer
makes the bird appear to move six, eight, nine, or ten
times as much, depending upon the power of the binocular.

The bird must not only appear to be close, it must be well

illuminated. If it is in full sunlight almost any binocular will do, but if it is in deep shade or the sky is overcast you need a glass that collects as much light as your eye can use. For all-around use on dark as well as sunny days, your binocular should have "objectives" (front lenses that collect light) with a diameter in millimeters about five times the power of the glass. Thus, a 6-power binocular should have an "objective" 30 millimeters in diameter. An 8 x 40 magnifies eight times and has an "objective" 40 millimeters in diameter.

A third important factor in choosing a binocular is the "field of view." The greater the field, the greater the area (a flock of birds or a whole treetop, for instance) you can watch without moving the glasses. A large field of view makes a glass easier to handle, since the observer need not be so accurate in his aim. The field is broad enough to include the bird, though it may not be in the exact center. Breadth of field is determined by the optics of the binocular and bears no fixed relation to the size of the objectives or the power of the glass, but in general the greater the power, the narrower the field. With an eight-power glass you cannot expect a breadth of field of more than 15 feet at a distance of 100 feet. An unusually fine glass may have a 20-foot field of view, but only in a low-power model. The manufacturer often expresses the field of view as 150 feet at a distance of 1,000 feet or 450 feet at 1,000 yards. The ratio is the same.

For the sake of your eyes, buy a good binocular. Be sure that it has a center focus wheel to focus both eyepieces simultaneously. Make certain that it is in alignment, that the center of the field of each of the two sides falls upon the same point. Your eye muscles can pull the fields together, but it is a strain. If you wear spectacles have the eyecups of the binocular cut down until they permit the lenses of your spectacles almost to touch the lenses of the binocular. Otherwise you lose part of the field of view you should be getting.

REGIONAL BIRD DISTRIBUTION: Everyone knows that different species of plants and animals live in different parts of the country. Some fifty years ago Dr. C. H. Merriam advanced the theory that these differences were largely the result of differences in average temperatures and proposed that seven broad east-west life zones be recognized in North America, beginning with the Tropical Zone in southern Florida and continuing through the Lower Austral, Upper Austral, Transition, Canadian, and Hudsonian zones to the Arctic Zone. According to his theory, the average temperatures at the edges of the zones represented the critical temperature limits beyond which the zone's characteristic animals could not survive. It is becoming increasingly clear, however, that the apparent conformity of many bird species to these life zones is based less upon temperature sensitivity than upon their affinity for communities where certain types of plant life are dominant. Often plants of the same life form, e.g., grassland, forest, etc., are inhabited by the same birds even when they are in widely separated temperature zones.

More recently a proposal has been made that the continent be divided into natural units based upon the vegetation with which nature finally clothes undisturbed land, the vegetation which no other plant species can dislodge. Such a climax growth may be a deciduous or coniferous forest, a grassland, or open tundra. The word "biome" was coined for these units, and individual biomes are given names based upon their most characteristic plants and their most distinctive resident animal. The distribution of some birds coincides quite closely with the extent of a biome unit, but not of all birds. The value of both concepts—life zones and biomes—is that they help to show that bird distribution is not haphazard but subject to controlling factors. (See end paper map.)

LOCAL BIRD DISTRIBUTION: The modern biologist considers all the plants and animals living together in a certain spot as members of a wildlife community. The simplest way of of designating a community is to call it by its dominant plant life—grassland, forest, marsh, or swamp. In any region there are usually many different types, depending upon differences in soil, wetness or dryness, and the degree of disturbance by man, fire, or flood. Generally each type has its characteristic birds, and these may or may not have a relation to the life zone or biome in which it lies.

The trend of any community is always toward the climax vegetation, which is usually forest or grassland. Not every forest or grassland represents a climax community, but the Northern spruce-fir forest and, somewhat farther south, the forest of beech and sugar maple are the ultimates for their respective areas; west of the beech-maple country, in a region of limited rainfall, lie the natural grasslands.

All communities except those at climax are subject to change unless man stabilizes them. Most of our native birds are therefore members of unstable communities. Over this they have no control; they simply expand or contract their populations according to the prevalence of the community they require, and the bird life of any area may change completely within a very short time.

The natural succession of plant life on abandoned ground in the once-forested East begins when the bare ground is clothed with weeds. Weeds frequently give way to grass. Shrubs and young trees shade out both, and a brushy stage appears, then a dense stand of young trees and finally a mature woodland. The first forest on abandoned land is invariably composed of trees with sun-loving seedlings, the second (often the climax) of those with shade-tolerant seedlings. Often the natural succession is retarded by lack of sufficient soil, by dryness, or by a water table too close to the surface, as with a swamp forest, but each successive plant stage, whatever it may be, has its characteristic bird life.

The paragraphs on habits in this book define as closely as possible the kind of wildlife community in which each species can be expected; they should also enable you to judge how permanent a bird is likely to be as the resident species of a given area and to predict what other birds are likely to come in as the plant succession advances. Clear cutting of forests, fire, overgrazing, soil erosion, and other forms of land abuse, though bad in terms of human economy, often increase certain species of wildlife since they provide community types that would otherwise seldom be encountered. Today it is probably safe to say that for every land bird that is less abundant than it was when the Pilgrims landed, five or six are more abundant.

"HABITAT" REQUIREMENTS: Every species of animal inherits certain habits, instincts, and abilities which admirably adapt it for life in a certain community. These attributes change little from generation to generation, and they are usually so highly specialized that the animal is not able to survive for long in any other type of community. When a bird's range is given in this book it is not implied that it occurs everywhere, or even widely, within the specified area, but only where its special community requirements are met. The older way of expressing this restriction was to speak of the bird's "habitat," but this tended to ignore the mutual interdependence of the bird and the other members of the wildlife community.

"Habitat" requirements are most critical during the breeding season. In winter most birds retain community preference but are more readily lured elsewhere by an abundant supply of attractive food. In migration they seldom have a choice. Most land birds migrate at night and drop to earth wherever daybreak overtakes them. They select the nearest spot that makes them feel at home and gives them food enough to continue their flight.

TERRITORIAL NEEDS: During the breeding season most song-birds require a territory over which the resident pair has undisputed ownership against others of its kind. Generally no attention is paid to members of other species (but see house wren). This habit may have arisen as a means of assuring an ample food supply for a nestful of hungry young, but today it seems largely instinctive and entirely without reference to the food supply. Territorial defense is primarily the male's job, but the female sometimes assists. The song that delights our ear during the breeding season, poets to the contrary, appears to be a proclamation of ownership and a warning to other males not to trespass.

Once a pair has proved its claim to a territory, it shows a strong attachment for it. In the case of very sedentary species the birds may remain in it the rest of their lives. In the case of migrants the male commonly returns to his old territory and defends it against newcomers. The female returns also, but if a rival appears ahead of her she may have to look for another mate. A bird's territorial attachment is so strong that if it is captured during the breeding season and taken some distance away before it is released, it will "home" with amazing speed. Often a bird will remain even after its territory is so drastically altered by lumbering, clearing, or building as to be no longer a very suitable habitat, the particular individual or pair coming back as long as they live.

The size of the defended territory varies from species to species, and there are minor variations in the acreage any given pair tries to claim. During the breeding season a pair of red-shouldered hawks needs about one square mile while a pair of ovenbirds needs only about an acre. Thus ovenbirds would not be abundant unless there were approximately 640 pairs per square mile, while red-shouldered hawks would be abundant if there were one pair within the area.

OTHER SPECIAL REQUIREMENTS: Food is seldom the only or even the most important factor limiting a bird to a particular community. The many detailed studies that have been made of the foods of various species reveal a fairly wide choice within certain categories—insects, seed, or fish.

Birds do seek variety sometimes, but in general they take from a wide range of acceptable items whatever is at the moment easiest to get. Thus, their food may vary greatly from day to day, season to season, and place to place.

The crucial habitat need may be for a very special kind of nest site or nesting material, for a suitable lookout or singing perch, a night roost, or a patch of escape cover. As these vary to the point of being unique with each species, they are discussed under the individual bird in the main body of the book. Their special interest lies in the fact that man is often responsible for their presence or absence.

SEASONAL MOVEMENTS: Some birds remain in one locality throughout their lives. Others migrate in winter to areas far south of their breeding grounds. The first are generally spoken of as residents, noted in this book by (R.), the second as migrants (M.). Many species fail to give such clean-cut examples. Migrants may be summer or winter residents, depending upon the location. Often a bird appears to be a migrant only in the northern part of its range and a more or less permanent resident farther south. Often it is difficult to know whether this indicates a southward shift of the whole population or whether there are two population groups, one migratory, one sedentary. At any rate, breeding birds appear south of the normal range, and there are species where the most northerly breeders are the ones that winter farthest south. Such species are referred to in this book as partially migratory (P.M.).

A few species wander erratically except during the breeding season, pausing wherever they find suitable food. As the majority of these erratic wanderers (E.W.) belong to the North, most of us see them only in winter. Because of their irregularity in any given locality they are often called winter visitors rather than winter residents. Another group of erratic wanderers are Southern species, chiefly herons, which breed early and come North during the summer in numbers that vary greatly from year to year.

In the section on range, if a bird is a permanent resident, its over-all range is given. If it is a migrant, its breeding range is given first, followed by its winter range, in which case it can be assumed that it is a migrant between the two. Only where breeding and wintering ranges are widely separated and the birds follow a rather well-defined route between the two is the route specified. For dates of arrival and departure one should consult a local check-list or, preferably, make one's own.

ECONOMIC RELATIONS: In books of an earlier period birds were often arbitrarily classified as good or bad, beneficial or harmful, according to their feeding habits. Such designations are valid only where man's economic interests are directly involved. A great horned owl, for example, is "bad" when it takes a chicken from its roost, "good" when it removes a woodchuck from your garden. The truth is that a bird or any other animal in the wild is one of the many cogs in a beautifully balanced, smoothly running assemblage of wild creatures. Every member of the group must be present if the population equilibrium necessary to the health of the community is to be maintained.

A wildlife community begins with plants. Plants create organic material, the foodstuff of life. They take a gas (carbon dioxide) from the air, water and minerals from the soil, and, using the energy of the sun, combine them in organic compounds. From these compounds, in their original or in altered form, comes the substance from which all plant and animal tissue is made. A food chain begins when a plant is eaten by an animal, keeps on when that animal is eaten by another, the second by a third, and so on until the body-building, energy-supplying foodstuffs are transmitted to many members of the wildlife community.

This chain which binds the community together is called predation. Unpleasant as it may seem, the relation of predator to prey, eater to eaten, is perfectly natural. Without it there would be no wildlife except plants and no wildlife communities. In community terms there are no good or bad birds, but simply wild birds, each living according to the behavior pattern of its kind, a pattern which evolved as the species evolved, in response to the laws of nature.

The science which deals with plant-animal relationships is called ecology. A newcomer among sciences, it has only recently begun to reveal the inner workings of wildlife communities and to explode some of our misconceptions. Once, for example, the claim was popular that man had irretrievably upset the balance of nature; a simple calculation can prove its absurdity. Take any common bird or other animal, figure out its theoretical rate of reproduction, and count the descendants it would have in ten years if normal mortality was absent. In the case of the fairly long-lived, two-brooded robin the astounding total is 3,906,250 birds! Obviously (though from year to year there are minor variations in the robin population) the general level is maintained by such balancing factors as predation, disease, and starvation.

In a healthy wildlife community each animal lives upon the surplus produced by the species upon which it feeds; i.e., upon individuals which in the absence of predation would die of starvation, starvation-induced disease, or inter-species strife. Once the surplus is removed, a law of diminishing returns begins to act against the predator. The death rate of the prey-population becomes extremely low, and some of the predators become surplus and suffer the fate of all animals that exist in greater numbers than their food supply can support. The predator becomes prey.

Popular belief to the contrary, no predator ever seriously threatens the survival of the species upon which it preys. The normal population of insect-eating birds, for example, helps keep insects down to normal levels, but the birds must allow some insects to mature as breeding stock or doom themselves to starvation during the next season.

In towns and villages dogs and cats kill large numbers

of birds just out of the nest and some adults, but many
naturalists doubt if their toll exceeds, or even equals,
that of wild predators in remote sections where dogs and
cats are not a factor. Seldom do wild and domestic predators prey on the same population, since wild predators
generally avoid the thickly settled areas where dogs and
cats are abundant.

CONSERVATION: Man with his guns, traps, hooks, nets, and
poison has proved himself a most efficient killer of wildlife. The decimation of species after species during the last
century shows what happens when he is not restrained.
Many bird species, once valued for food, eggs, or plumage,
exist today only because an aroused public opinion finally
brought about the enactment of protective laws and the
will to support them.

Many birds have been persecuted because of damage to
crops or livestock. The only parrot native to eastern North
America, the beautiful Carolina parakeet, was exterminated
because it raided crop fields and was easy to kill. Most of
our hawks and owls take quantities of rodents and in some
cases insects as well, but because certain species nab an
occasional chicken, all are condemned and destroyed by
those who know not what they do.

The least excusable threat to bird life is wanton shooting for the sake of a live target, a practice that is hard to
condone on any grounds. In the old days travelers stood for
hours at the rails of river steamers to shoot passing birds
"for the sport of it." Such destruction was not confined to
riverbanks, and a few of our birds have never recovered
from it. One is our handsome bald eagle, our national
emblem, which is now protected by Federal law. Another
is the graceful swallow-tail kite, which is gone from 95
per cent of its former range, though it is a perfectly gentle
species. Fortunately, this type of hunting is largely a thing
of the past, but there are still people who carry loaded guns
in their automobiles to shoot hawks off telephone poles

along the highway, and there are still irresponsible hunters and unthinking boys who take a shot at any bird that happens to fly within range.

Much more threatening to bird life than willful destruction of non-game birds and reckless overhunting of game species are the changes incidental to modern industry and agriculture. Some that have received the most publicity are probably the least serious. Water birds, as every newspaper reader knows, are especially vulnerable to floating oil sludge. Lighthouses, highways, and tall buildings levy an annual toll, but up to the present these losses seem to have been offset by the surplus produced during the breeding season. This is not stated to minimize the danger. Every reasonable precaution should be taken. At any moment these losses, coupled with the normal losses from other causes, may be great enough to imperil the survival of the species.

For many birds the gravest threat is destruction of the only type of wildlife community in which they can live. Every year extensive areas of fresh- and salt-water marshes are drained, flooded, or ditched for mosquito control. When the marshes vanish our shore birds, rails, ducks, herons, and other attractive species, vanish with them. Sometimes this cannot be helped, but in every region at least a few samples of every original type of bird habitat should be preserved. This can be effectively achieved by the establishment of public and private refuges, wild parks, and public hunting grounds.

Increasingly dangerous to bird life are the new insecticides, rodent and weed poisons, with which man can control virtually to the point of extermination all forms of wildlife that he considers undesirable. In nearly all wildlife communities the chief converters of vegetation into "meat" are insects and rodents. If they go, the whole carnivorous section of the community—songbirds as well as owls, foxes, and other animals—must of necessity go with them. If the seed- and berry-bearing "weeds" of crop fields and fence rows are eliminated, even our seed-eating winter birds must decrease in numbers.

Conservation problems are becoming more urgent. Transportation which makes even the most remote areas accessible, new inventions, increased leisure, and the short-sighted desire for quick profit all tend to increase the rate of exploitation of our remaining natural resources and the spoliation of our last remaining wildernesses. Government efforts are often thwarted by political expediency. To be effective conservation must have the support of every citizen interested in preserving his natural heritage.

BIRD CLUBS: Most of us find it pleasant and helpful to share our interests and enthusiasms with others. Audubon Societies, bird clubs, and ornithological groups exist in almost every state. Informal and open to everyone, these organizations provide contact with experts, aid in solving identification problems, and act as guides to the more interesting local bird habitats. Specialists like bird banders have their own societies. Many of these groups are engaged in co-operative projects, like censuses of local birds, in which everyone can participate. A number of them publish small magazines or occasional reports on special studies. If you have any difficulty in getting in touch with those in your area, write to the National Audubon Society in New York, where a complete and up-to-date record of all local bird groups is kept.

There are four large national groups that welcome anyone interested in birds: the American Ornithologists Union, with headquarters at Lancaster, Pennsylvania; the Cooper Ornithological Club, Berkeley, California; the Wilson Ornithological Club, Ann Arbor, Michigan; and the National Audubon Society, 1130 Fifth Avenue, New York 28, New York. Each publishes a magazine which you will find listed under periodicals in the bibliography at the end of this book. A letter to the editor will bring you full details about membership.

Acknowledgments

IN PREPARING THIS BOOK I have drawn freely upon the literature on North American birds which has been accumulating for more than two hundred years. I myself have had the privilege of studying birds in every state of the union, but I have made full use of the recorded observations of others. Only in this way would it be possible for anyone to present a well-rounded picture of each species throughout its range.

I owe an especial debt to Arthur C. Bent, whose *Life Histories of North American Birds*, published in many volumes by the United States National Museum, provide a thorough abstract of the extensive and widely scattered literature on birds. I have also found extremely useful the monumental works of Thomas S. Roberts and Edward H. Forbush, authors, respectively, of *Birds of Minnesota* and *Birds of Massachusetts*. In addition I wish to express my appreciation of Roger T. Peterson's *A Field Guide to the Birds* and Aretas A. Saunders's *A Guide to Bird Songs*. Since publication they have been my constant companions in the field, and I know they have improved the quality of my field work. My range paragraphs are an abbreviation of the data in the fourth edition and more recent supplements of the American Ornithologists Union's *Check-list of North American Birds*.

Don Eckelberry, in my opinion, has made an outstanding contribution to ornithology in his illustrations for this book. On his behalf and my own I wish to thank the American

Museum of Natural History for its patience in making available typical skins for use in preparing both the paintings and the identification text.

To the National Audubon Society and its directors, who have made it possible for me to undertake this book and have honored me by sponsoring it, I owe an especial debt of gratitude.

For helpful suggestions and other courtesies I am also indebted to the following: John H. Baker, James B. Chapin, L. Irby Davis, Ludlow Griscom, Nella Braddy Henney, Joseph J. Hickey, Eleanor King, Ernst Mayr, Robert C. Murphy, Charles E. O'Brien, Charles H. Rogers, Robert Seibert, Victor E. Shelford, W. E. Clyde Todd, Josselyn Van Tyne, Alexander Wetmore, Edward M. Weyer, John T. Zimmer, to my wife Moira, who doubled as my secretary throughout the preparation of the manuscript, and to the many members of the staff of Doubleday and Company who have been so helpful, especially Clara Claasen and Sabra Mallett.

RICHARD H. POUGH

April 1946
Pelham, New York

Many people ask what they can do to assist in the cause of conservation of birds and other wildlife. One of the best suggestions is that they support the work of the National Audubon Society, 1130 Fifth Avenue, New York 28, N.Y., and local Audubon societies. These and other conservation organizations deserve your aid.

Combined Color and Size Key to Small Land Birds

Birds are adult males unless otherwise specified. Dimensions are over-all lengths in inches. As standards of comparison use these common birds—Golden-crowned Kinglet 4", Yellow Warbler 5", English Sparrow 6", Wood Thrush 8", Robin 10", and Blue Jay 12".

1. CONSPICUOUS AMOUNTS OF RED, PINK, OR PURPLE

Body all or partly bright red—Painted Bunting 5¼"; Vermilion Flycatcher 6"; Scarlet 7¼" and Summer 7½" Tanagers; Cardinal 8¼".

Body extensively suffused with red or pink—House Finch 5½"; White-winged 6" and Red 6" Crossbills; Purple Finch 6¼"; Gray-crowned Rosy-finch 6¼"; Pine Grosbeak 9".

Extensive areas of red or pinkish on head—Hoary 5" and Common 5¼" Redpolls; European Goldfinch 5½"; Pyrrhuloxia 8"; Common Sapsucker 8½"; Golden-fronted 9½", Red-bellied 9½", Red-headed 9¾", Pileated 17", and Ivory-billed 20" Woodpeckers.

Red confined to small area on back of head—Varied Bunting 5"; Downy 6", Mexican 7¼", Red-cockaded 8¼", and Hairy 9" Woodpeckers; Yellow-shafted Flicker 13".

Throat only pink, purple, or red—Black-chinned 3¼", Ruby-throated 3½" and Rufous 3½" Hummingbirds; Rose-throated Becard 6½"; Rose-breasted Grosbeak 8".

Red or pinkish chiefly on or under wings—Redstart 5½"; Red-winged Blackbird 9½"; Red-shafted Flicker 13"; Scissor-tailed Flycatcher 14".

2. CONSPICUOUS AMOUNTS OF ORANGE

Body extensively orange—Baltimore $7\frac{1}{2}''$, Bullock's $8''$, Hooded $8''$, and Lichtenstein's $9''$ Orioles.

Orange areas on head—Blackburnian $5\frac{1}{4}''$ and Prothonotary $5\frac{1}{2}''$ Warblers; Western Tanager $6\frac{3}{4}''$; Carolina Parakeet $12\frac{1}{2}''$.

Orange on sides of breast—im. Redstart $5\frac{1}{2}''$.

3. CONSPICUOUS AMOUNTS OF BRIGHT OR PURE YELLOW

Body largely yellow—Common Goldfinch $5''$; Yellow Warbler $5''$; Black-headed Oriole $9''$.

Yellow confined chiefly to head regions—Verdin $4\frac{1}{4}''$; Golden-cheeked $5''$, Black-throated Green $5''$, Chestnut-sided $5''$, Golden-winged $5''$, and Brewster's $5''$ Warblers; Three-toed $8\frac{3}{4}''$ and Black-backed $9\frac{1}{2}''$ Woodpeckers; Yellow-headed Blackbird $10''$.

Under parts almost wholly pure yellow—Dark-backed Goldfinch $4''$; Blue-winged $4\frac{3}{4}''$, Nashville $4\frac{3}{4}''$, and Wilson's $5''$ Warblers; Yellow-throat $5\frac{1}{4}''$; Mexican Ground-chat $5\frac{1}{2}''$; Kentucky Warbler $5\frac{1}{2}''$; Chat $7\frac{1}{2}''$; Olive-backed Kingbird $8\frac{1}{2}''$; Kiskadee Flycatcher $10\frac{1}{2}''$.

Yellow under parts with dark markings—Prairie $4\frac{3}{4}''$, Cape May $5''$, Magnolia $5''$, Palm $5\frac{1}{4}''$, Canada $5\frac{1}{2}''$, and Kirtland's $5\frac{3}{4}''$ Warblers; Dickcissel $6\frac{1}{4}''$; Western $9\frac{1}{2}''$ and Eastern $10\frac{3}{4}''$ Meadowlarks.

Yellow chiefly on throat and/or breast—Pitiayumi $4\frac{1}{2}''$, Parula $4\frac{1}{2}''$, Yellow-throated $5\frac{1}{4}''$, Sutton's $5\frac{1}{4}''$, and ♀ Prothonotary $5\frac{1}{2}''$ Warblers; Yellow-throated Vireo $6''$.

Yellow chiefly or wholly on rear under parts—Bachman's $4\frac{1}{4}''$, Lawrence's $4\frac{3}{4}''$, Hooded $5\frac{1}{2}''$, Mourning $5\frac{1}{2}''$, Connecticut $5\frac{1}{2}''$, and Macgillivray's $5\frac{1}{2}''$ Warblers; Cedar Waxwing $7\frac{1}{4}''$; Western Kingbird $9''$; Ash-throated $8\frac{1}{4}''$, Crested $9''$, and Mexican $9\frac{1}{2}''$ Flycatchers.

Birds with patches of yellow—Bahama Bananaquit $5''$; Audubon's $5''$ and Myrtle $5\frac{1}{2}''$ Warblers; ♀ Redstart $5\frac{1}{2}''$; Evening Grosbeak $8''$.

4. CONSPICUOUS AMOUNTS OF BLUE OR BLUE-GRAY

Wholly blue—Indigo Bunting 5½″.

Blue associated only with white or gray—Cerulean Warbler 4½″; im. Indigo Bunting 5½″; Mountain Bluebird 7¼″; Scrub 11½″ and Blue 12″ Jays; Belted Kingfisher 13″.

Blue or blue-gray with some other color or black—Brown-headed Nuthatch 4¼″; Blue-gray Gnatcatcher 4½″; Red-breasted Nuthatch 4½″; Blue-throated Blue Warbler 5¼″; White-breasted Nuthatch 6″; Eastern Bluebird 7″; ♀ Belted Kingfisher 13″.

Dark blue often appearing black in poor light—Blue Grosbeak 7″; Barn Swallow 7″; Purple Martin 8″.

5. BLACKISH OR CONSPICUOUSLY BLACK AND WHITE

Uniformly dark often with iridescence—Brown-headed 8″ and Red-eyed 8½″ Cowbirds; Starling 8½″; Rusty 9½″ and Brewer's 9½″ Blackbirds; Common Grackle 12″; Groove-billed 12″ and Smooth-billed 13½″ Anis; Boat-tailed Grackle 16½″; Fish 17″ and Common 19″ Crows; White-necked 20″ and Common 25″ Ravens.

Large black and white areas on body producing a bold pattern—Morellet Seedeater 4″; Snow Bunting 7″; Spotted 7½″ and Eastern 8″ Towhees; ♀ Three-toed Woodpecker 8¾″; Loggerhead Shrike 9″; ♀ Black-backed Woodpecker 9½″; Northern Shrike 10¼″; ♀ Ivory-billed Woodpecker 20″; Black-billed Magpie 20″.

Black and white markings largely or wholly on head—Black-capped Vireo 4½″; Red-breasted Nuthatch 4½″; Carolina 4½″ and Black-capped 5¼″ Chickadees; Black-throated Sparrow 5½″; Black-crested Titmouse 5½″; Chestnut-collared 5¾″ and McCown's 6″ Longspurs; White-breasted Nuthatch 6″; Lapland 6¼″ and Smith's 6½″ Longspurs; White-throated 6¾″, White-crowned 7″, and Harris's 7½″ Sparrows; Horned Lark 7¾″; Canada Jay 11½″.

Black and white markings confined to wing or tail area
—Northern Wheatear 6¼″; im. Common Sapsucker 8½″; Lark Bunting 7″; im. Red-headed Woodpecker 9¾″.

Fine broken or speckled over-all black and white pattern
—Black-throated Gray 4¾″, Black and White 5¼″, and Blackpoll 5½″ Warblers; ♀ Downy 6″, ♀ Red-cockaded 8¼″, and ♀ Hairy 9″ Woodpeckers.

6. PREDOMINANTLY GREENISH, DULL YELLOWISH, OR SOME TONE OF OLIVE-GREEN

Body extensively greenish or dull yellow both above and below— ♀ Dark-backed Goldfinch 4″; Buff-bellied Hummingbird 4½″; Philadelphia 4¾″ and Bell's 4¾″ Vireos; im. Blue-winged 4¾″ and Orange-crowned 5″ Warblers; Common Goldfinch 5″; White-eyed Vireo 5″; ♀ Painted Bunting 5¼″; im. Yellowthroat 5¼″; im. Blackburnian Warbler 5¼″; Pine 5½″, fall Bay-breasted 5½″, and Blackpoll 5½″ Warblers; Yellow-bellied Flycatcher 5½″; ♀ Red 6″ and White-winged 6″ Crossbills; Yellow-green Vireo 6½″; ♀ Tanagers (3 species) 6¾″–7½″; ♀ Evening Grosbeaks 8″; ♀ Orioles (6 species) 7¼″–9″; ♀ Pine Grosbeak 9″; Green Jay 11½″.

Greenish tone confined largely to upper parts— ♀ Ruby-throated 3½″, ♀ Rufous 3½″, and ♀ Black-chinned 3¼″ Hummingbirds; Golden-crowned 4″ and Ruby-crowned 4¼″ Kinglets; Tennessee 5″, im. Golden-winged 5″, ♀ Black-throated Blue 5¼″, and Worm-eating 5½″ Warblers; Warbling Vireo 5¾″; Acadian Flycatcher 5¾″; Olive Sparrow 5¾″; Ovenbird 6″; Tree 6″ and Bahama 6″ Swallows; Northern Water-thrush 6″; Blue-headed 6″ and Red-eyed 6¼″ Vireo; Louisiana Water-thrush 6¼″; Black-whiskered Vireo 6½″; Green-tailed Towhee 6¾″; Green Kingfisher 7½″.

7. LARGELY OR EXTENSIVELY GRAY

Almost wholly uniform grays although often paler below than above—Beardless Flycatcher 4½″; Chimney Swift 5½″; Rough-winged Swallow 5¾″; Wood 6½″ and Western 6½″ Pewees; Olive-sided Flycatcher 7½″; ♀ Brown-headed

Cowbird 8"; juv. Starling 8½"; Townsend's Solitaire 8¾"; Catbird 9"; ♀ Rusty 9½" and ♀ Brewer's 9½" Blackbirds; im. Canada Jay 11½".

Uniform gray above, white or very pale below— ♀ Verdin 4¼"; Bank Swallow 5¼"; Least 5¼", ♀ Vermilion 6", and Alder 6" Flycatchers; Slate-colored 6¼" and White-winged 6½" Juncos; Eastern Phoebe 7"; Eastern 8½" and Gray 9" Kingbirds; Mockingbird 10½".

Gray with some areas of color—Tufted Titmouse 6"; Pink-sided Junco 6¼"; Gray-breasted Martin 7"; Say's Phoebe 7½"; ♀ Purple Martin 8"; Catbird 9".

Fine or broken gray pattern—juv. Cedar Waxwing 7¼"; Screech 10", Snowy 25", and Great Gray 27" Owls.

8. EXTENSIVE AREAS OF UNIFORM BROWN

Bold pattern involving large areas of brown—Brown-capped Chickadee 4¾"; Bay-breasted Warbler 5½"; Cave 5½" and Cliff 6" Swallows; Tufted Titmouse 6"; Pink-sided Junco 6¼"; Barn Swallow 7"; Orchard Oriole 7¼"; ♀ Towhees 7½"–8"; Robin 10".

Almost wholly brown although often paler below than above— ♀ Morellet Seedeater 4"; winter Northern Wheatear 6¼"; im. Gray-crowned Rosy-finch 6½"; ♀ Rose-throated Becard 6½"; Cedar 7¼" and Bohemian 8" Waxwings; im. Saw-whet Owl 8"; Gray's Thrush 10"; im. Common Grackle 10"; ♀ Boat-tailed Grackle 12½"; Black-eared Cuckoo 12½".

Uniformly brownish above, white or very pale below—Swainson's Warbler 5"; ♀ Varied Bunting 5"; ♀ Indigo Bunting 5½"; Olive Sparrow 5¾"; juv. Scissor-tailed Flycatcher 7"; Black-billed 11¾" and Yellow-billed 12¼" Cuckoos.

Uniformly brown above, more or less speckled below—Veery 7", Hermit 7", Olive-backed 7", Gray-cheeked 7¾", and Wood 8" Thrushes; Sage Thrasher 8¾"; juv. Robin 10"; Curve-billed 11", Long-billed 11½", and Brown 11½" Thrashers.

9. FINE BROKEN PATTERNS COMPOSED LARGELY OF SMALL BROWN, BLACK, AND WHITE MARKINGS

Birds with an over-all broken brownish pattern—Cañon Wren 5½″; Ferruginous Pygmy Owl 6¾″; Poorwill 7½″; Saw-whet Owl 8″; Trilling Nighthawk 9″; Burrowing Owl 9″; fall Rusty Blackbird 9½″; Whip-poor-will 9¾″; Common Nighthawk 10″; Screech 10″ and Boreal 10″ Owls; Chuck-will's-widow 12″; Pauraque 12″; Hawk 12″, Long-eared 15″, Short-eared 15½″, Great Horned 18″, and Barred 20″ Owls.

Birds with light unstreaked under parts—Short-billed Marsh 4″, Winter 4″, House 4¾″, and Long-billed Marsh 5″ Wrens; juv. Henslow's 5″, Grasshopper 5⅛″, and Chipping 5¼″ Sparrows; Bewick's Wren 5¼″; Clay-colored 5½″, Field 5½″, and Rufous-crowned 5½″ Sparrows; Brown Creeper 5½″; Swamp 5¾″, Botteri's 5¾″, and Cassin's 5¾″ Sparrows; Carolina Wren 5¾″; ♀ McCown's Longspur 6″; European Tree 6″, Pinewoods 6″, Tree 6¼″, Lark 6¼″, and English 6¼″ Sparrows.

Birds with light under parts, speckled or streaked in whole or in part—Leconte's 5″ and Henslow's 5″ Sparrows; Pine Siskin 5″; juv. Grasshopper Sparrow 5⅛″; Baird's 5½″; and im. Rufous-crowned 5½″ Sparrows; im. Cañon Wren 5½″; ♀ House Finch 5½″; Rock Wren 5¾″; ♀ Chestnut-collared Longspur 5¾″; Lincoln's 5¾″, Savannah 5¾″, and Sharp-tailed 5¾″ Sparrows; Seaside 6″, Merritt Island 6″, Cape Sable 6″, and Vester 6″ Sparrows; ♀ Lapland Longspur 6¼″; ♀ Purple Finch 6¼″; im. Dickcissel 6¼″; Sprague's Pipit 6¼″; Song 6¼″, Ipswich 6¼″, and im. Lark 6¼″ Sparrows; ♀ Smith's Longspur 6½″; Water Pipit 6½″; ♀ Lark Bunting 7″; ♀ Blue Grosbeak 7″; Fox Sparrow 7¼″; ♀ Bobolink 7¼″; im. Harris's Sparrow 7½″; ♀ Rose-breasted Grosbeak 8″; Cactus Wren 8″; ♀ Red-winged Blackbird 9½″; Barn Owl 18″; Road-runner 23″.

Parrots and Allies
Order PSITTACIFORMES

<u>PARROTS</u>   Family PSITTACIDAE

Carolina Parakeet*   *Conuropsis carolinensis*—✻10

IDENTIFICATION: L. 12½, T. 6½. The long pointed tail and yellow head, becoming rich orange around the bill, are unlike those of any other North American bird. Immature birds are green except for the orange forehead and lores.

HABITS: This gorgeous, hardy parrot was once abundant along river bottoms, where it fed on a variety of wild fruits and seeds in the forest and along the open riverbanks and bars. It was especially fond of the seeds of cocklebur, bur grass, and thistle as well as of pecans and beechnuts. In winter it ate the seeds of cypress, sycamore, and pine. It was gregarious throughout the year and, though non-migratory, flocks often wandered long distances in search of food.

The bird was ill adapted for survival under the conditions which followed the coming of the white man. It was edible, its plumage could be sold for millinery, it was in demand as a cage bird here and in Europe, and it was destructive to a variety of cultivated crops, including corn and other grains, apples, pears, and oranges. It needed hollows in great river-bottom trees for nesting and roosting and it was so attached to its companions that when part of a flock was shot the remainder came back again and again until all were killed. By 1860 it was gone from much of its range and by the '80s it could be found only in sparsely settled areas. A few may survive in some remote southern swamp, but it is doubtful.

VOICE: A series of loud, discordant screams given continuously in flight.

NEST: They nested in hollow trees and laid 2 or 3 white eggs (1.35 x 1.10).

RANGE: (R.) Formerly from s. Virginia on the Atlantic coast and Ohio, Indiana, Illinois, Missouri, Arkansas, and e. Texas in the interior south to s. Florida and the Gulf Coast.

Cuckoo-like Birds
Order CUCULIFORMES

CUCKOOS, ROADRUNNERS, and ANIS
Family CUCULIDAE

Black-eared Cuckoo*   *Coccyzus minor*—❊1

IDENTIFICATION: L. 12½, T. 6. Even immature birds, without
the black "ears" and gray crown of adults, have the characteristic buff under parts that distinguish this from our
other cuckoos.

HABITS: It is a bird of low, dense thickets near the coast. In
Florida, where it is a breeder and summer resident from
March to September, the "mangrove cuckoo" is found
chiefly in the tangles of red and black mangrove that
border the west coast and extend into the shallow salt
water. Like most cuckoos, it is an insect eater, feeding on
hairy caterpillars, grasshoppers, and moths.

    The occurrence of the bird in Florida represents the ex-
treme northward range of an otherwise non-migratory
tropical species. The individuals that visit Florida to breed
are considered a distinct race or subspecies to which the
name Maynard's cuckoo has been given. Possibly this
race represents the first step in the evolution of a new migratory species.

VOICE: A slow, deliberate series of deep, guttural calls somewhat like the bark of a squirrel.

NEST: A flat mass of twigs in dense mangrove with 2 pale
greenish-blue eggs (1.22 x .92).

RANGE: (P.M.) The Florida Keys and west coast north to
Anclote Keys, West Indies, Trinidad, n.e. South America,
and Central America north to c. Mexico. Absent from
Florida in winter.

Yellow-billed Cuckoo*   *Coccyzus americanus*—☀1

IDENTIFICATION: L. 12¼, T. 6¼. This and the black-billed
cuckoo closely resemble each other. They are slim, long-
tailed birds that stay well hidden in foliage. They move
deliberately when feeding, and when they fly it is with a
fast, direct movement straight from the center of one tree
to the center of another. Look for the rufous coloring in
the wings which shows well in flight. The large white spots
on the ends of the black tail feathers are also conspicuous. Less easily observed is the yellow lower mandible and
the yellow eyelids.

HABITS: The yellow-billed is the more southern of the two
cuckoos, but their ranges overlap. Both seem to have benefited from man, as they prefer dense tangles of second
growth in rural areas and are seldom found in really deep
woodlands. They find moist areas attractive and are usually
common in streamside willow thickets. Brush-grown country roads and run-down orchards are also favored habitats.
Cuckoos' chief food is caterpillars, and they are among
the few birds that eat the very hairy species.

VOICE: A series of clucking notes with a hollow wooden quality. The most characteristic is a long series of clucks, fairly
fast until the end, when they abruptly become slower and
longer as they run down the scale.

NEST: A flimsy, almost flat platform of short twigs, usually
rather thinly lined with soft material and placed 4 to 8
feet aboveground in a dense shrub or tree which is often
thorny or evergreen. The 3 or 4 eggs (1.22 x .92) are dull
greenish-blue.

RANGE: (M.) Breeds from New Brunswick, s. Ontario, North Dakota and British Columbia south to the Florida Keys, the Gulf Coast, Tamaulipas, and s. Lower California. Winters from Venezuela and Colombia to Uruguay and n. Argentina.

Black-billed Cuckoo* *Coccyzus erythropthalmus*—※1

IDENTIFICATION: L. 11¾. Both mandibles are black. The eyelids form a red ring around the eye. Better characteristics are the slimmer build, the lack of rufous in the wings, and the narrow white tips of the gray-brown tail feathers.

HABITS: The feeding habits of the two cuckoos appear identical, but the black-billed seems fonder of extensive woodlands and more active at night.

Unlike the European cuckoo, American cuckoos only occasionally lay their eggs in the nests of other birds. When they do the young cuckoo usually succeeds in throwing out the other young and usurping the attention of its foster parents. The species imposed upon include chipping sparrows, yellow warblers, catbirds, wood thrushes, and even other cuckoos. A young cuckoo is naked and coal black, but within six days it bristles with quill-like feather tubes. These it removes with its bill, exposing the fluffy juvenile feathers. By its seventh to ninth day it is an active little bird, climbing about the branches. If it drops to the ground it is able to mount quickly into the shrubbery.

VOICE: A long series (sometimes up to several hundred) of evenly spaced soft notes, of uniform pitch, single or in groups, with almost the quality of a low whistle. Frequently they are preceded by a few harsh notes, but there is never an ending like that of the yellow-billed.

NEST: A rather more substantially built nest than that of the yellow-billed and more amply lined with soft material; placed 2 to 4 feet off the ground in a dense clump of woody growth. The 2 or 3 eggs (1.09 x .82) are of a blue-green color averaging darker than those of the preceding species.

RANGE: (M.) Breeds from Prince Edward Island, s. Quebec, and s.e. Alberta south to North Carolina, Georgia (mts.), Arkansas, and Kansas. Winters in n.w. South America south to e. Peru.

Roadrunner* *Geococcyx californianus*—⋇1

IDENTIFICATION: L. 23, T. 12. The most striking feature is the long tail. The wings are short and rounded with a curved white line running through them. Both wings and tail are more used for steering and quick turns than flight. The long powerful legs are another distinctive feature. The tracks are unmistakable, as two toes point forward and two backward.

HABITS: In many areas this bird goes by the name of "chaparral cock." Since it is shy and spends most of its time on the ground, where it can run as fast as man, it is hard to see. Only with difficulty can it be flushed into a short flight which generally ends in the nearest thicket.

Open country with scattered cover is its chosen habitat. Insects are its staple food, especially grasshoppers and crickets, although it will eat any insectlike animal large enough to be worthy of notice, even poisonous scorpions, centipedes, and tarantulas. It also catches small snakes, lizards, mice and other rodents, and occasionally birds. Because sportsmen have accused it of destroying quail eggs and young, careful studies have been made of its food habits. These indicate that such depredations, if they occur, are so infrequent as to have no appreciable effect on the quail population. This is fortunate, as it would be a tragedy to exterminate this amusing bird. All in all he is one of our most delightful bird characters, with his comical way of swinging his great tail and raising his rough crest as he peers from side to side.

VOICE: The roadrunner makes a variety of noises variously described as clucking, crowing, cooing, and a whining like a puppy. His spring song is a series of *coo* or *ook* sounds, loud and rather hoarse, which run down the scale, the whole performance being repeated over and over again.

NEST: A compact flat mass of sticks lined with soft material, usually well hidden in shrubbery or low trees from a few feet aboveground to about 15 feet. The 3 to 5 eggs (1.55 x 1.20) are chalky-white or slightly ivory.

RANGE: (R.) From s.w. Kansas, s. Utah, and n. California south to Mexico City, and east to c. Texas and the Gulf Coast of s. Texas.

Smooth-billed Ani*   *Crotophaga ani*—¥1

IDENTIFICATION: L. 13½, T. 7½. The ani can hardly be confused with any other bird except possibly a male boat-tailed grackle. The huge curved horny ridge on the upper mandible gives it a unique and grotesque appearance. The two anis, however, are hard to tell apart except by note, the whining notes of this species being in sharp contrast to the soft double note of the groove-billed. Only in good light can the presence or absence of grooves in the ridge on the upper mandibles be noted, but in the smooth-billed this horny growth is much higher and more sharply curved. The only great difference in plumage is in the tips of the nape feathers, which in this species are bronze, in the next grayish. Young birds are sooty-brown, somewhat darker above than below.

HABITS: As this ani is abundant in the Bahamas, Cuba, and Jamaica, it is not surprising that it turns up occasionally in Florida. Normally the birds occur in loosely knit flocks of from one half to two dozen individuals. They like open, cultivated country and are most apt to be found near cattle, feeding like cowbirds or even sitting on the animal's back picking off ticks. The larger, less active insects on or near the ground or stirred out of the soil by cattle are their chief food, but they also eat wild seeds and fruits.

VOICE: A slurred double note with a metallic quality and a rising inflection. Sometimes referred to as a whining whistle and likened to the call of a wood duck.

NEST: A large, bulky, rather flat structure 6 to 30 feet above the ground in dense vegetation. Where the bird is abundant a number of females generally use the same nest, depositing the eggs in layers separated by dead leaves. The females share the responsibility for their incubation, several often sitting at the same time. As the eggs in each layer hatch, the leaves are removed and the next layer is incubated. The eggs (1.40 x 1.05) are a glaucous blue or blue-green, covered with a thin chalky-white deposit that rubs off easily. As many as 20 eggs have been found in one nest separated into 4 or 5 layers, but it is not known how many eggs each female lays.

RANGE: (R.) South America from Paraguay north to Panama and through most of the West Indies to the Bahamas. It may occasionally turn up almost anywhere in Florida or along the Gulf Coast as far west as Louisiana.

Groove-billed Ani*   *Crotophaga sulcirostris*—❋1

IDENTIFICATION: L. 12, T. 6¾. Stray anis encountered in any of the Gulf States might be this bird of the Rio Grande Valley or the smooth-billed of the Bahamas and West Indies. The smaller size of the groove-billed is no help in the field. Note differences under the preceding species. The bill distinguishes them from the boat-tailed grackle, the common long-tailed blackbird of the area, and their appearance in the air is distinctive, as their wings and tails seem to be loosely attached and coming askew.

HABITS: This ani occurs in both humid and arid areas if the country is open and has some brushy cover. Feeding habits appear to be the same as the smooth-billed's.

VOICE: Many varied, rather liquid soft notes. Alarmed, a double call with the first part short and high and the second lower, harsher, and prolonged, the whole repeated over and over.

NEST: A mass of dead twigs with a lining of fresh green leaves, usually 6 to 12 feet high in a shrub or tree which is often thorny. Nests are the work of from 1 to 3 pairs of anis. Each female contributes from 3 to 4 eggs (1.24 x .96), pale blue with a chalky-white coating.

RANGE: (R.) Texas (Rio Grande Valley), s. Sonora, and Lower California south to Peru, Trinidad, and British Guiana.

Owls
Order STRIGIFORMES

BARN OWLS   Family TYTONIDAE

Barn Owl*   *Tyto alba*—✳2

IDENTIFICATION: L. 18. The barn owl is relatively slim and notably long-legged. In flight it appears to have an enormous head, and the bird looks snow-white from below. It has the typical loose, deep wingbeat of an owl. The tone of the golden-brown upper parts varies but is generally slightly darker in the female.

HABITS: Open country, where it can locate small mammals as it flies overhead on silent wings, is its normal habitat. The bulk of its food is the most abundant rodent of the locality, varying from gophers, ground squirrels, and jack rabbits in the West to meadow mice and cotten rats in the East. As it frequents towns more than most owls, it takes numbers of house mice and Norway rats. It appears to have excellent hearing as well as eyesight. A series of squeaks will often draw it out of the night sky to hover over one's head for a few seconds.

In the fall most of these owls go south, although some remain north all winter. During the southward flight and in winter they become gregarious, with flocks of a dozen or more at favored roosts. When no suitable cavity or building is available for a roost they use dense evergreens.

VOICE: The commonest note in flight is a harsh hissing sound at widely spaced intervals. Around the nest it utters a variety of weird notes. One is an unpleasant scream, another is like the cry of a nighthawk, another is an insect-like, rapid snapping noise made with the bill.

NEST: These owls will use almost any dark and sheltered place —cavities and hollows in trees, bird boxes, caves, barns, abandoned buildings and belfries, tunnels in banks, and burrows in the ground. Very rarely one nests in the open on the abandoned nest of some other large bird. No nest is built, but sites are often used year after year, and the ground becomes well carpeted with the broken pellets of fur and bone which an owl regurgitates after a meal. A clutch consists of from 5 to 11 pure white eggs (1.73 x 1.32). They are laid at all seasons of the year, but March to September are the usual dates. Now and then a pair will breed almost continuously the year round.

RANGE: (P.M.) The world. In North America south from Massachusetts, s. Ontario, Minnesota, and s. British Columbia.

TYPICAL OWLS   Family STRIGIDAE

Screech Owl*   *Otus asio*—✳3

IDENTIFICATION: L. 10. In many areas this owl occurs in 2-color phases, one a rich rufous, the other almost solid gray. This difference bears no relation to age or sex, and an individual never changes. Rarely an intermediate brownish bird is encountered. The screech is our smallest "horned" or "eared" owl, a name which refers to the tufts of feathers on its head. It is also either the reddest or the grayest owl.

HABITS: The screech owl is a common bird of open woodlands and clearings, orchards and suburbs. It roosts during the day in the same type of cavity in which it nests, and comes out after dark. Its note is easily imitated, and the bird will usually call back in answer to such an imitation even in broad daylight.

The downy young owls are snow-white, and adults are bold in defending them. In towns they have been known to knock the hats off passers-by on the sidewalk under the nest.

The screech owl eats almost any animal food. It catches night-flying beetles and moths and takes birds, frogs, cray-fish, snails, reptiles, fish, bats and other small mammals, and even earthworms. Its diet depends largely upon what is most readily obtained.

VOICE: A low, tremulous whistle often rising at first, then fall-ing. It has a plaintive, mournful quality and is sometimes described as a whinny.

NEST: The commonest site is an old woodpecker hole, but natural cavities are used and birdhouses are often accepted when the bottom is covered with sawdust. Sites vary from a few feet to 80 feet above the ground. Both birds often sleep in the nest during the day. The usual clutch is 4 or 5 white eggs (1.42 x 1.20).

RANGE: (R.) From New Brunswick, Ontario, s. Manitoba, s. British Columbia, and s.e. Alaska south to the Florida Keys, the Gulf Coast, and c. Mexico.

Great Horned Owl*   *Bubo virginianus*—❊2

IDENTIFICATION: L. 18 to 25. This is our largest "eared" owl. The sexes are alike except that the female is much larger than the male. In flight their wings seem long and broad, but the "ears" are held flat against the head. The dark under parts accentuate the white throat. In some regions these owls may be much lighter and in others much darker than the bird shown in the color plate. The Arctic race is sometimes as white as many snowy owls.

HABITS: The great horned owl is a truly magnificent wild creature, occurring almost everywhere from the deepest forests to city parks where rats are abundant. On dark days it often hunts from midafternoon on. It eats every kind of animal life large enough to be worthy of its notice and small enough to handle, from beetles and scorpions to fish and snakes. Rabbits are its chief food, supplemented by other rodents. It takes birds of all sorts, including ducks, chickens, and grouse. It frequently eats skunks and has been known to take mink, opossums, domestic cats, red-tailed hawks, and barred owls.

One should be cautious in visiting an occupied nest. The birds do not hesitate to strike an intruder on the head or back, and the flight is so silent that one seldom has warning of the owl's approach.

VOICE: The calls vary, but the commonest and most characteristic one is a series of soft, deep *hoo* notes with considerable carrying power. In the distance it sounds like the baying of a dog, nearer like the *coo* of a dove. A distinctive series is *hoo hoo hoooo, hoo hoo,* lower and more uniform in pitch than the call of the barred owl with which it might be confused. Its scream, a loud, terrifying sound, is seldom heard.

NEST: They appear never to build a nest but to take over the nest of some other large bird. Those of red-tailed hawks, bald eagles, and herons are frequently used, but the owls also nest on protected ledges, in caves, and in hollow trees. In most areas they are the earliest nesters, the 2 or 3 white eggs (2.25 x 1.88) being laid in February even in New England.

RANGE: (R.) The Western Hemisphere from the northern limit of trees in the Arctic south to the Strait of Magellan.

Snowy Owl*   *Nyctea scandiaca*—❋2

IDENTIFICATION: L. 25. Snowy owls vary in the amount of dark barring on their feathers, young being more heavily marked than adults, females than males. In flight their heavy build, round head, and broad white wings are distinctive. The flight is jerky, as the upbeat of the wings is faster than the downstroke and is frequently interrupted by a short sail.

HABITS: This owl is fairly active all day and is distinctly a bird of open country. In the North it prefers rolling to flat tundra and spends much of its time on such lookouts as banks, boulders, or knolls. When it visits the United States in winter it is found in marshes, in dune areas, and on open farmland, where it perches on haystacks and buildings, seldom on trees. In the North lemmings, ptarmigan, fish, and hares are staple foods. The periodic epidemics that decimate the lemmings undoubtedly account for the great southward flights which occur on the average every fourth year. The snowy's abundance on its breeding grounds also varies from year to year with the rise and fall of the lemming population.

VOICE: A deep, vibrant, hoarse croaking suggestive of a raven's croak; also a shrill whistle.

NEST: On the ground thinly lined with moss and feathers; located on the higher, drier spots in rolling tundra. It lays 5 to 8 white eggs (2.25 x 1.79), which are incubated as soon as laid. The young bird from the first egg is often almost ready to fly before the last egg hatches.

RANGE: (P.M.) Arctic tundra of the world, south in winter to c. Asia, c. Europe, and n. United States. Heavy flights in certain winters have carried birds as far south as South Carolina, Georgia, Louisiana, Texas, and California.

Hawk Owl*   *Surnia ulula*—※3

IDENTIFICATION: L. 15, T. 7¼. Although a true owl, this bird looks more like a hawk and is fully active in the daytime. Its short, pointed wings and long wedge-shaped tail are distinctive.

HABITS: The hawk owl frequents the brushy openings and muskegs of the northern forests. Its food includes insects, rodents, and birds. It can handle weasels, hares, ptarmigan, and grouse. It is unusually fearless and has occasionally been caught by hand.

It spends much of its time perched on the top of a dead tree, where it may sit upright like an owl or with body inclined like a hawk, frequently lifting its long tail at an angle. When it flies it skims close to the ground, stopping now and then to perch for a few seconds on the top of a low bush. Its fast and graceful flight alternates with short glides. Close-to-the-ground hunting requires great maneuverability, and the hawk owl has a long rudderlike tail like the Accipiters that hunt the same way.

VOICE: A rather melodious whistle given as a rapid trill.

NEST: In cavities in the ends of broken tree stubs, old woodpecker or other natural holes in dead trees, rarely on a cliff or in the open stick nest of some other large bird. It lays 3 to 7 white eggs (1.60 x 1.27).

RANGE: (R.) The circumpolar coniferous forest of the Northern Hemisphere: in North America from Labrador, n. Quebec, Mackenzie, and Alaska south to s. Quebec, Ontario, n. Michigan, and c. British Columbia. Occasional great winter flights have carried it to New Jersey, w. New York, s. Ontario, s. Michigan, Montana, and Washington.

Ferruginous Pygmy Owl*   *Glaucidium brasilianum*—✳3

IDENTIFICATION: L. 6¾. This owl varies from ferruginous brown to olive brown. Its head is thickly marked with fine white streaks instead of dots as in the common pygmy owl of the western mountains. The tail is usually finely barred in two shades of reddish-brown. A distinct partly dark, partly light line separates the feathers of the neck from those of the upper back.

HABITS: Only in river-bottom forests have these birds been reported north of Mexico. This little owl is often active during the day, when it selects a conspicuous lookout in the top of a tree. It has a habit of cocking its tail at an angle, and when it gives its call it throws its head back. It feeds on mammals and birds and tackles prey of remarkable size.

VOICE: Variously described as a long series of rather deliberate *chu* or *cuck* notes.

NEST: In an old woodpecker hole or a natural tree cavity. The 3 or 4 eggs (1.14 x .93) are white.

RANGE: (R.) Extreme s. Texas and Arizona south to Chile, Argentina, and Uruguay.

Burrowing Owl*   *Speotyto cunicularia*—♯3

IDENTIFICATION: L. 9. This little owl is always on or close to the ground. Its long legs and short tail are distinctive.

HABITS: During daylight it spends much of its time sitting near the entrance to its burrow, where it keeps turning its head through a full circle, scanning the sky and bowing frequently almost to the ground. This is a bird of open, treeless, short-grass country, usually occurring in loose colonies of 10 or 12 pairs in a 2- or 3-acre section. The owls seem to prefer abandoned animal burrows but are perfectly capable of digging their own. Their most active period is early evening and morning. Night-flying beetles and other insects are their most important food, but they take small rodents and an occasional bird, fish, frog, snake, or crayfish.

VOICE: The alarm note is a sharp, liquid *cack-cack-cack* . . . frequently uttered on the wing. The evening song is a long series of *cuckoo*-like notes, the second syllable drawn out to a hollow sound that carries well.

NEST: At the end of a 5- to 10-foot burrow, 1 to 3 feet underground. One or 2 sharp changes in direction are usually encountered before the nest cavity is reached at the far end. It is lined with broken pieces of horse or cow manure, grass, and roots. A normal clutch is 5 to 7 eggs (1.24 x 1.00). At the burrow entrance, which measures 5 x 3½ inches across, there is usually a mound of earth, and if the nest is active the opening is surrounded with bits of manure.

RANGE: (P.M.) C. Florida south through the West Indies and w. North America south from Manitoba and British Columbia and west from Minnesota, Iowa, Oklahoma, and rarely Louisiana. Also most of South America.

Barred Owl*   *Strix varia*—✳2

IDENTIFICATION: L. 20. This big gray-brown owl with its short tail looks chunky. Its face has the curious appearance of being almost submerged in the collar formed by the barring of the feathers of the head, neck, and upper breast. In flight its wings seem short and rounded but broad. Its wingbeats are slow, but the flight is buoyant and graceful. The bird moves with surprising skill through dense forest. It is frequently active in the later part of the afternoon and may call almost any time of day.

HABITS: The barred owl is a bird of swamps and deep woodlands but hunts over adjacent open country. It is an abundant species through most of its range. It is notably curious. A few mouselike squeaks on the back of one's hand often causes it to materialize out of nowhere to perch over one's head and peer down with its dark brown eyes that are so unlike those of other owls.

This owl is mild by comparison with the great horned. Its feet are small and weak and it seldom tackles large prey. Mice form the bulk of its food, but it eats other small mammals, frogs, crayfish, fish, insects, and birds. It

apparently takes a good many smaller owls and undoubtedly takes any small bird it is lucky enough to catch.

VOICE: A series of 8 hoots on an even pitch in 2 groups of 4,
the last part of the second group prolonged at a lower
pitch. *Who cooks for you, who cooks for you-all?* approxi-
mates the cadence. The call is easy to imitate. If a barred
owl is within hearing range an answer is usually forth-
coming, and often the bird can be drawn to one. It makes
other chuckling, grunting, and laughing sounds too varied
to be described here.

NEST: This owl prefers hollows in trees and has been known
to accept a "bird box." When a suitable tree cavity is not
available it takes over the open stick nest of a large bird
like a hawk or crow, or makes use of an old squirrel's
nest, preferably in an evergreen tree. Telltale bits of long
gray down fluttering from a shrub or branch often reveal
the location of a nest. It lays 2 or 3 white eggs (1.93 x
1.65).

RANGE: (P.M.) East of the Rockies from Newfoundland, s.
Quebec, n. Ontario, and n. Alberta south to Florida and
the Gulf Coast through Mexico to Honduras.

Great Gray Owl*   *Strix nebulosa*—❋2

IDENTIFICATION: L. 27. Although its body is about the size of
that of a barred owl, this bird has such long loose plumage
that it looks even bigger and heavier than a snowy or a
great horned owl. Its tail is long and it has a wingspread
of 5 feet or more. Its facial disks are large and sharply defined, and the head looks disproportionately massive. Its
yellow eyes, gray color, and the vertical streaks up the
breast to the throat distinguish it from the barred owl. It
often allows a close approach, and when it moves off its
flight seems heavy and labored.

HABITS: The great gray owl is seldom found far from dense
timber. There it often hunts by daylight, although it seems

to prefer late afternoon and early evening. When winter flights bring it into the United States it may occur almost anywhere. The presence of the visitor is usually well publicized by crows. Crows have a knack for locating roosting owls and hawks, and one does well to investigate a mob of crows badgering something. Not much is known of the feeding habits of this species, but it appears to levy toll on all small mammals and probably on all small birds of the woodlands.

VOICE: Hooting sounds and tremulous whistled notes like a screech owl have been attributed to this owl.

NEST: It uses large bulky tree nests, but whether it builds them or takes over the nests of other birds is not known. It lays 2 to 5 white eggs (2.14 x 1.71).

RANGE: (R.) The circumpolar coniferous forest of the Northern Hemisphere from the northern limit of trees south; in North America to Quebec, n. Minnesota, n. Idaho, and c. California (mts.). Occasional winter flights occur (probably because of a failure of their normal food supply) which take them east and south to Massachusetts, Ohio, Nebraska, and Wyoming.

Long-eared Owl*   *Asio otus*—✳2

IDENTIFICATION: L. 15. Long-eareds are our slimmest owls. They can compress their feathers and elongate themselves to look more like a broken tree branch than a bird. The long tail and the long "horns" add to the effect. The flight is buoyant but unsteady and mothlike.

HABITS: Timber in which to nest and roost seems to be the one requirement. In winter they are gregarious, and flocks of 5 or 6 to 25 occupy communal roosts. These are usually in a grove of dense evergreens.

In most areas these birds are more abundant than people realize. They are strictly nocturnal, seldom flush, and are too quiet to attract much attention. Few birds are

harder to find or study. Usually the best way to find this
and other owls is to look under a stand of conifers for owl
pellets. These cylindrical wads of tightly packed grayish
fur and whitened bones are often conspicuous against the
brown needles. They are the indigestible parts of an owl's
meal, coughed up after the digestible material has been
extracted. They are an infallible index to its food habits.

Only when a nest with young is located can one see
long-eareds to advantage. Then the adults snap their bills,
flutter on the ground in a broken-wing act, squeal, and
even strike at the intruder. Most owls eat a good many
mice, but this species eats little else. It hunts over both
wooded and open country.

VOICE: This owl seldom makes a sound except during the
breeding season. The commonest call is a soft cooing or
series of mellow, low-pitched notes. When disturbed near
the nest it utters a great variety of weird shrieks, whines,
and mews.

NEST: An old nest, usually of a crow, squirrel, or magpie,
preferably in an evergreen tree. The sitting bird usually
does not flush, even when one goes directly under the nest,
and is often invisible from the ground. Four or 5 white eggs
(1.57 x 1.28) are laid.

RANGE: (P.M.) Temperate Zone of the Northern Hemisphere:
in North America it breeds from Newfoundland, s. Quebec, n. Ontario, s. Mackenzie, and c. British Columbia
south to Virginia, Arkansas, and n.w. Lower California;
wintering from Massachusetts, c. Ontario, s. Michigan, s.
South Dakota, and s. British Columbia south to Florida, the
Gulf Coast, and c. Mexico.

Short-eared Owl*   *Asio flammeus*—✳2

IDENTIFICATION: L. 15½. The short-eared is a fairly light-colored buffy owl with pale under parts more distinctly
streaked and somewhat darker than those of the barn

owl. The "ears" are seldom visible. In flight the big round neckless head is easily noted. The wings show a dark patch on the underside and a pale one on the upper surface.

HABITS: This bird of open grasslands, marshes, and dunes hunts by day as well as by night. It rests and sleeps on the ground in a clump of vegetation, protected by its coloration. It is generally a good idea when walking across a marsh to clap one's hands as loudly as possible now and then to flush owls one would otherwise miss. In hunting this owl "hawks" back and forth with a loose deep wing-beat a few feet off the ground, dropping suddenly with feet forward when prey is sighted. At other times it sits on a post or similar vantage point waiting for some prey to reveal itself. It appears better able to catch mice than birds, and they constitute its chief food. Insects and birds are of secondary importance. These owls generally concentrate in greater abundance than any other avian predator in regions where a cyclic high in the mouse population has produced a "mouse plague."

In spring the male indulges in a spectacular aerial courtship in broad daylight. It ascends to a considerable height, uttering a repeated series of low-pitched *toots*. Finally it draws its wings together beneath its body and dives, clapping or rubbing them together to produce a fluttering sound.

VOICE: The short-eared is silent except during the breeding season, when it utters a variety of barking, squealing, and rasplike hissing notes.

NEST: On the ground, usually in a slight depression more or less lined grasses and placed, as a rule, in the shelter of a tall clump of grass or weeds. There are normally 5 to 7 white eggs (1.53 x 1.22).

RANGE: (P.M.) North and South America, Europe, and Asia. In North America it breeds from Baffin Island and Alaska south to New Jersey, Ohio, Kansas, Utah, and c. California, and winters from Massachusetts, s. Ontario, Montana, and s. British Columbia south to Florida, the Gulf Coast, and Guatemala.

Boreal Owl*   *Cryptoglaux funerea*—✳3

IDENTIFICATION: L. 10. This owl is about the size of a screech owl but lacks "horns." Its larger size, yellow bill, and the black outer part of its facial disks distinguish it from the saw-whet owl. Also, its head is spotted with white, not streaked, and it has a number of large round white spots on its back. The American race is known as Richardson's owl.

HABITS: Its home is in the conifer forests of the North, and little is known about it. It apparently eats mice, birds, and insects. When these owls periodically invade the United States they appear quite tame and have a tendency to seek shelter in buildings.

VOICE: Several calls have been described, but the commonest, which may be a courtship call, is like the sound of a soft high-pitched bell or of falling water.

NEST: In natural tree hollows or, most commonly, in the old nest of a flicker or pileated woodpecker. Farther north they often use open stick nests of other birds. The female lays 4 to 6 white eggs (1.27 x 1.06).

RANGE: (P.M.) Europe, Asia, and North America. It breeds from the northern limit of trees south to n. New England, s. Manitoba, and n. British Columbia. In winter they come south in numbers that vary from year to year, occasionally reaching n. New Jersey, Illinois, Colorado, and Oregon.

Saw-whet Owl*   *Cryptoglaux acadica*—✳3

IDENTIFICATION: L. 8. This is much the smallest of Northern owls and is more likely to be encountered in the United States than the boreal owl. The young wear the distinctive rich brown juvenile plumage most of the summer—longer than most birds.

HABITS: Saw-whets frequent dense woodlands, apparently preferring evergreen to deciduous trees and low, wet areas to dry woods. They hunt and roost close to the ground but are so completely nocturnal that they are not often seen. Even where they are common their presence is often unsuspected unless one listens for them during their early-spring courtship. They can be decoyed by a whistled imitation of their notes, and fully grown adults often allow themselves to be caught by hand.

VOICE: Silent except in late winter and early spring, when they become quite noisy. The calls are extremely varied. The best known, uttered in groups of three, sounds like the filing of a saw. Commoner is a monotonous and interminable series of whistled notes, closely spaced and rapidly uttered.

NEST: Old woodpeckers' holes, usually the flickers'. This owl is hard to flush from its nest, but pounding at the base of the tree will cause it to look out. Five to 6 white eggs (1.18 x 1.00) are a normal clutch.

RANGE: (P.M.) Breeds from Nova Scotia, Ontario, c. Alberta, and s.e. Alaska south to Connecticut, the mountains of Maryland, n. Indiana, Missouri, c. Arizona, and in the mountains of Guatemala. In winter, casually south to Virginia, Louisiana, and s. California.

Goatsuckers and Allies
Order CAPRIMULGIFORMES

GOATSUCKERS   Family CAPRIMULGIDAE

Chuck-will's-widow   *Caprimulgus carolinensis*—※6

IDENTIFICATION: L. 12. This, our largest goatsucker, seems chunkier than the whip-poor-will. The male differs from the female in having white on the ends of the outer tail feathers and in having a narrow, ill-defined white band across the lower throat. The smaller male whip-poor-will has the whole end of the outer tail feathers white and a much more prominent white throat band.

HABITS: This bird is abundant in southern rural districts where farming country is interspersed with patches of woodland. It is active only after dark. The day is spent crouching on or near a log, or on a horizontal limb or on the leaf litter of the forest floor. Its protective coloration makes it hard to see, as does its habit of always sitting parallel with the axis of a limb. Its food is chiefly beetles and moths, and an occasional small bird. A mouth with a gape of 2 inches plus the funnel made by a fringe of stiff bristles enables it to scoop prey out of the air. Most feeding is done on the wing close to the ground. The flight is silent and mothlike.

VOICE: The bird says *chuck, will's wid-ow* in 4 parts. The *chuck* is deep and low, the rest whistled loud and clear with the accent on *wid*. While hunting on the wing it utters a strange growl or croak. When calling steadily it pauses longer between sequences than the whip-poor-will-

NEST: No nest. The 2 eggs (1.40 x 1.00), cream-colored and blotched with different shades of brown underlaid with pale purple-gray markings, are placed on dead leaves or bare ground. Usually they are laid in a woods, frequently in such an open place that they are plainly visible unless covered by the female. If the eggs are molested the birds often move them in their bills to a new location.

RANGE: (M.) Breeds from s. Maryland, s. Illinois, and Kansas south to Florida, the Gulf Coast, and c. Texas. Winters from Cuba, the Bahamas, and Guatemala south to n. Colombia.

Whip-poor-will   *Caprimulgus vociferus*—※6

IDENTIFICATION: L. 9¾. The female lacks the broad white ends of the outer tail feathers which are so conspicuous in the male, and its throat band is buff instead of white. This species and the chuck-will's-widow differ from the night-hawk in having barred primaries, a fringe of bristles around the bill, and a rounded tail extending beyond the wing tips when the bird is perched. In flight the whip-poor-will's wings appear rounded and broad like an owl's. When the bird sails they are held out straight. To change direction a sailing bird tilts so sharply that its wings are sometimes almost vertical.

HABITS: Although common in rural country where ungrazed wood lots suitable for nesting are found, this bird is so nocturnal that it is known chiefly by its call. Its food is flying insects, and it goes through amazing gyrations in pursuing them.

VOICE: The 3-syllabled whistled call *whip-poor-will* differs from that of the preceding species in having the middle note weak, the first and especially the last accented. The preliminary *tuck* is seldom heard. The bird does not call on its wintering grounds.

NEST: Eggs are laid on the ground among dead leaves in partly open spots near the borders of predominately deciduous woodlands. The 2 white eggs (1.14 x .84) are scattered with gray blotches and often with brown specks.

RANGE: (M.) Breeds from Nova Scotia, s. Quebec, n. Michigan, s. Manitoba, and c. Saskatchewan south to e. Virginia, n.w. South Carolina, n. Alabama, n. Louisiana, and n.e. Texas; also in the mountains of s. Arizona and New Mexico to Honduras. Winters from lowlands of e.c. South Carolina and the Gulf States south to Costa Rica.

Poorwill* *Phalaenoptilus nuttalli*—⚥6

IDENTIFICATION: L. 7½. When perched, the poorwill's small size, pale gray-brown upper parts with sharp crossed black lines in the feathers, clear white throat, and tail feathers narrowly tipped with white are distinctive. In the air its shorter, more rounded wings lack the nighthawk's white spot, and its short tail shows only a little white at the end. In the female the white tail tips are narrower. Young have all markings less sharply defined and the throat buffy instead of white.

HABITS: Poorwills are typically birds of dry open country, where they spend the day on the ground under a clump of brush. In some areas they are found roosting on trees in the open forests of the lower mountains. The poorwill's flight is mothlike and erratic, and it generally hunts close to the ground. It eats flying insects, which it often watches for from an open spot on the ground and captures in a short sally into the air.

VOICE: A harsh and melancholy 3-note *poor-will'-ee*. At a distance the last note is lost and the call becomes soft and pleasant. In flight they have a clucking note.

NEST: The 2 faintly pinkish eggs (1.07 x .78) are laid on bare ground, rocks, or gravel near a tuft of grass or a low bush.

RANGE: (P.M.) Breeds from n.w. North Dakota and s.e. British Columbia south to c. Mexico and from w. Iowa, e. Kansas, and c. Texas west to the Pacific, w. Oregon, and e. Washington. Winters from s. Texas and s. California south to c. Mexico.

Pauraque   *Nyctidromus albicollis*—❄6

IDENTIFICATION: L. 12. This bird has a broad white band across the base of the wing tips like a nighthawk, but its wings are heavier and shorter. Its long rounded tail with a narrow white streak down each side is also quite different. These white markings are much reduced in area and often heavily tinged with buff on the smaller female.

HABITS: Although permanent residents, the birds seem to disappear after the nesting season when they stop calling, and leave the more open nesting country for daytime roosts on the ground in river-bottom thickets.

VOICE: A soft, mellow, whistled *ko, whe-e-e-e-w*, which carries well. The first note is low, the second loud at the beginning and drawn out, with a rise in pitch at the end.

NEST: On bare level ground in fairly open places with a scattering of woody vegetation. The 2 eggs (1.17 x .88) are placed near the foot of a shrub. They are pinkish buff with small brown blotches.

RANGE: (R.) Southern half of the Texas coast and n. Mexico south to n. Argentina.

Common Nighthawk   *Chordeiles minor*—❄6

IDENTIFICATION: L. 10. The sexes are much alike. Both have the distinctive white patch toward the ends of the long pointed wings. The female lacks the white band near the end of the tail, and its throat is buff instead of white. When perched, the tips of the closed wings reach beyond the tail. This and the pale barred sides distinguish it from other eastern goatsuckers.

HABITS: During the day fence posts are good places to look for them, especially in the South. They may be active at any hour of the day or night, although their greatest activity is just before sunrise and after sunset. Thus, unlike the other more nocturnal goatsuckers, it is often seen in migration, when it travels in flocks, and during the long summer evenings. Since the advent of tarred and graveled roofs, this nighthawk has become common in towns and cities as these roofs seem to make ideal nest sites. During courtship immediately after arrival in the spring, the birds are noisy and conspicuous.

Their food is flying insects. Stomachs have been examined containing 50 different kinds; one contained 2,175 flying ants, another more than 500 mosquitoes. The birds do all their feeding on the wing, both high in the air and close to the ground.

VOICE: As it hunts in the sky it utters at intervals a loud, buzzy note with an insectlike quality which sounds like *pee-yah* or *spe-eak*. During courtship the male makes a loud, hollow, booming sound with its wings as it pulls out of a long fast dive.

NEST: The eggs are laid on open ground and a strong preference is shown for outcrops or barren gravel. The 2 eggs (1.17 x .86) are creamy-white to olive, speckled with slaty markings.

RANGE: (M.) Breeds from Newfoundland, Quebec, n. Ontario, n. Manitoba, and s. Yukon south to n. Mexico, the Gulf Coast, Florida, the Bahama Islands, and the Greater Antilles. Winters from Colombia to Argentina.

Trilling Nighthawk *Chordeiles acutipennis*—✳6

IDENTIFICATION: L. 9. The female differs from the male in having less white on the tail and a buffy instead of a white wing spot. The spot is nearer the tip of the wing on this bird which is smaller and browner than the common nighthawk.

HABITS: This bird is found in open country, where it feeds on the wing close to the ground, thus differing from the high-flying common nighthawk. It is a very graceful and silent flier. In cloudy weather it may hunt during the day but is most often seen at dusk or dawn. After dark it is reported to feed from the ground, and many kinds of beetles are included in the almost wholly insectivorous diet.

VOICE: The most distinctive call is a sustained rapid trill like that of a tree toad. It has several other calls—a soft cluck, a louder twanglike note, and a more varied and musical trill.

NEST: Under a small bush or on open bare ground. The 2 creamy-white eggs (1.07 x .77) are peppered with fine grayish dots. They are paler and smaller than those of the common nighthawk and blend so well with the color of the ground that they are hard to find.

RANGE: (P.M.) Breeds from s. Texas, s. Utah, and c. California south to s.e. Brazil and s. Peru. In winter it is seldom found north of c. Mexico.

Swifts and Hummingbirds

Order MICROPODIFORMES

SWIFTS   Family MICROPODIDAE

Chimney Swift*   *Chaetura pelagica*—※12

IDENTIFICATION: L. 5½. The swift's narrow, slightly curved wings and apparent lack of tail give it a distinctive appearance.

HABITS: It is a fast flier, but its extremely erratic course lacks the smooth gracefulness of swallow flight. It seldom perches outside its nesting or roosting chimney but flies and sails alternately, moving in circles, even when migrating. Photography has proved false the idea that the wings do not move in unison like those of other birds.

During migration the birds roost in large chimneys, to which they return year after year. Often thousands use a single chimney. A gathering flock as it swirls in circles over the chimney is a remarkable sight. Toward dark they begin dropping in, and the whole flock may disappear in a few minutes.

The bird's food consists of small flying insects which fill the air all summer in far greater abundance than we generally realize except on those rare occasions when a beam of sunlight against a shadowy background reveals their presence.

VOICE: A rapid and often almost continuous series of sharp chattering or twittering notes.

NEST: A shallow bracketlike cup of twigs cemented to the inside of a hollow tree or chimney. The nest twigs are broken off with the feet while the bird is in flight. These are cemented together and the whole fastened to a vertical surface by a glutinous saliva from the bird's mouth. The 4 or 5 eggs (.79 x .52) are pure white.

RANGE: (M.) Breeds from Nova Scotia, s. Quebec, s. Manitoba, and e. Alberta south to Florida and the Gulf Coast and west to e. Texas and c. Montana. Winters in the Amazon basin of Brazil.

HUMMINGBIRDS   Family TROCHILIDAE

Ruby-throated Hummingbird
Archilochus colubris—✳17

IDENTIFICATION: L. 3½. This hummingbird should present no identification problem but must not be confused with the large hawk moths which also feed from flowers while in flight. Unless the sun catches the feathers of the male's throat at the right angle they appear black instead of red. The female lacks the bright throat but has white tips to its outer tail feathers which the male lacks.

HABITS: The ruby-throat is common wherever flowers occur. Its rapid wingbeat—55 to at least 75 times a second— together with its ability to turn its wing over and lead with the forewing on both the forward and backward strokes make it an avian helicopter—hovering, backing away, or moving forward at will. Its protein food consists of small insects. It also eats nectar, sap, and sugar water from artificial feeders.

VOICE: A jabber of forceful little high-pitched squeaks and squeals uttered in a nervous, excited fashion. In flight it makes a low buzzing noise with its wings.

NEST: A lichen-covered cup 1½ inches in diameter, saddled on a small downward-sloping branch 10 to 20 feet aboveground, near or over running water in an open woodland.

It is made of bud scales and plant downs held together with spider silk. The 2 eggs (.51 x .33) are white.

RANGE: (M.) Breeds from Nova Scotia, s. Ontario, and s. Alberta south to Florida and the Gulf Coast and west to e. Texas, e. Kansas, and North Dakota. Winters from c. Florida and s. Louisiana south through Mexico to Panama.

Black-chinned Hummingbird
Archilochus alexandri—❋17

IDENTIFICATION: L. 3¾. This close relative of the ruby-throat gets far enough east in migration for the two to occur in the same area in southeast Texas. In poor light, which makes the iridescent throat feathers of both species look black, the black-chinned's darker under parts and narrow white collar are diagnostic. Differences in the females are so slight as to make it impractical to try to separate them in the field.

HABITS: Areas with an abundance of bloom are often frequented by large numbers of these hummers. From lowlands, where maximum flowering comes early, they gradually work higher into mountains, where the blooming season is later. The black-chinneds' feeding habits are like the ruby-throats', but they also watch for small flying insects from a conspicuous perch and take them after the manner of a flycatcher.

VOICE: A soft, high-pitched, melodious warble and a louder, less musical chipping call.

NEST: A globular cup of plant downs bound together with spider web. Usually there are no lichens on the outside. It is saddled on a drooping branch over or near water some 4 to 10 feet above the ground. Two white eggs (.49 x .33) are usual, and 2 or 3 broods are raised.

RANGE: (M.) Breeds from w. Montana and s. British Columbia south to c. Texas, n. Mexico, and n. Lower California. Winters from n. Mexico south to Mexico City.

Rufous Hummingbird
Selasphorus rufus—✳17

IDENTIFICATION: L. 3½. The rufous-brown male is unmistakable. Females and immatures can be distinguished from ruby-throats by the rufous color on the sides and in the rump area.

HABITS: This most northern of hummingbirds is abundant throughout its range. It seems able to adapt itself to any area where flowers capable of providing nectar and insects occur. It is especially attracted by red flowers. In recent years it has become known that a small eastward movement of this species occurs along the Gulf Coast in late fall and early winter.

VOICE: On the wing the male makes a characteristic rattling or vibrating sound, and both sexes have a low-toned double chirping note.

NEST: A 1½-inch-diameter cup made of vegetable downs bonded together with spider webs and decorated with bits of moss and lichen. A favorite site is the drooping lower limb of a conifer, but it may be high or low in a variety of places. Often a dozen or more pairs nest close together. A clutch is 2 white eggs (.52 x .35).

RANGE: (M.) Breeds from Alaska (to lat. 61°) east to s. Alberta and w. Montana, and south to e.c. California. In migration, east to e. Colorado, and occasionally the Gulf Coast to n. Florida. Winters chiefly in s. Mexico.

Buff-bellied Hummingbird*
Amazilia yucatanensis—✳17

IDENTIFICATION: L. 4½. There is no other bird in the United States with which this beautiful little red-billed hummer can be confused. Sexes are alike, and the brown tail, buff-brown under parts, and bright green throat make them unlike the ruby-throats which pass through their range in migration.

HABITS: In the Rio Grande Valley this bird's home is the open woodlands and thicket edges, and it may become rare, as these are destroyed to make way for farms and orchards.

VOICE: Shrill twittering squeaks. It is quite noisy.

NEST: A cup 1⅜ inches in diameter made of vegetable fibers bound together with spider webs and decorated outside with bits of dried bark, leaves, and lichen. Three to 8 feet off the ground in a shrub or small tree; saddled on a branch or placed in a fork. The 2 eggs (.52 x .34) are white.

RANGE: (P.M.) Breeds from the lower Rio Grande Valley of Texas through e. Mexico to Yucatan. In winter Rio Grande birds migrate south.

Kingfishers and Allies

Order CORACIIFORMES

| KINGFISHERS | Family ALCEDINIDAE |

Belted Kingfisher

Megaceryle alcyon—❋11

IDENTIFICATION: L. 13. This is one of the few cases among birds where the female is more colorful than the male. She has the brown flanks and breastband. The kingfisher's blue-gray is unlike the intense blue of the blue jay, the only bird with which it could be confused. In flight it usually alternates a series of five or six wingbeats with a long glide. Except when traveling overland, it flies low, close to the water.

HABITS: Kingfishers are found wherever there is water, whether brook, pond, river, lake, or seacoast. They are solitary and seem unwilling to tolerate other kingfishers (except a mate in breeding season) on their waters. Within their territory they have regular perches, overlooking the water, between which they regularly patrol their domain. Their food is chiefly fish, but they seem able to obtain a variety of other items such as crayfish, shellfish, insects, and mice. They even eat wild fruit. The birds hunt by night as well as day. Their tendency to concentrate their feeding where heavy populations of small fish occur brings about a reduction which is usually desirable. Ordinarily more small fish are born than can be raised to maturity, so thinning is very necessary if any are to achieve a satisfactory rate of growth.

VOICE: A rapid series of loud, harsh notes often referred to as a rattle. The sound is like that of a heavy fishing reel. It carries remarkably well and has a vigorous, wild quality.

NEST: An enlarged chamber at the end of a burrow excavated by the birds in a bank steep enough to be relatively free of vegetation. The entrance is 3 to 4 inches in diameter, the upward-sloping burrow usually 4 or 5 feet long, the nest chamber about 4 inches in diameter. A bank near water is preferred but not essential. From 5 to 8 white eggs (1.33 x 1.05) are laid.

RANGE: (P.M.) Breeds from c. Labrador, Mackenzie, and n. Alaska south to c. Florida; the Gulf Coast to c. Texas, s. New Mexico, and s. California. Winters from s. New Jersey, Ohio, c. Missouri, Wyoming, and s.e. Alaska south through the West Indies and Mexico to British Guiana and Colombia.

Green Kingfisher   *Chloroceryle americana*—✳10

IDENTIFICATION: L. 7½. This small white-spotted, dark glossy-green kingfisher is unmistakable. The male has a wide brown breastband. In its place the female has two lines of green spots.

HABITS: These birds usually watch for prey from a mid-stream boulder or a sand bar, where they sit jerking their tails up and down. They prefer quiet pools and backwaters of small clear-flowing streams. Many members of this family do no fishing at all, and often the green kingfisher is found miles from water, feeding on grasshoppers, butterflies, and lizards. These are caught in flycatcher-like sallies from a lookout perch.

VOICE: On the wing it utters a sharp insectlike rattle. Perched, it gives a low clicking note accompanied by a twitch of the tail.

NEST: In a cavity at the end of a burrow about 2 inches in diameter, extending back 2 or 3 feet in a sandy bank. The entrance is often near the top and hidden by vegetation or roots. The 4 to 6 eggs (.96 x .76) are white.

RANGE: (R.) S. Texas and s. Arizona south to c. Argentina.

Woodpeckers and Allies

Order PICIFORMES

<u>WOODPECKERS</u>   Family PICIDAE

Yellow-shafted Flicker   *Colaptes auratus*—❆4

IDENTIFICATION: L. 13. Flickers are our only brownish woodpeckers and the only ones that commonly feed on the
ground. They have the typical undulating flight of most
woodpeckers. The white rump and the bright yellow under tail and wing surfaces show up when the bird is
in the air. The male differs from the female in retaining
the black patches on the sides of the throat, which both
sexes have in juvenile plumage.

HABITS: This bird of fairly open country is common in rural
areas that are well supplied with old orchards or wood
lots and in suburbs. It is migratory in the northern part
of its range, and the loose flocks of traveling birds are
quite conspicuous, especially when concentrated near wide
water barriers which they seem afraid to cross.

    Ants are their most important food, and a single flicker
stomach was once found to contain more than 5,000. It
eats a variety of other insects and wild fruit. Sour-gum,
dogwood, and poison-ivy berries are favorites.

VOICE: The flicker has many loud, distinctive calls. The commonest is a series of identical notes—*wicker, wicker,
wicker*. It also makes a loud staccato drumming with its
bill on a suitably resonant hollow limb, tin roof, or other
object.

NEST: A cavity with an entrance hole 2¾ to 3 inches in diameter, excavated by both birds in a dead tree or branch a few feet to 90 feet above the ground. Old cavities, bird-houses, or hollow trees are often used. Locally certain trees are favored; e.g., apple, sycamore, or maple, and where trees are scarce telegraph poles or fence posts are used. Six to 8 white eggs (1.06 x .81) are usual.

RANGE: (P.M.) Breeds east of the Rocky Mountains from the northern limit of trees in e. Alaska to Labrador and south to Florida and the Gulf Coast, west to Oklahoma, e. Wyoming, and British Columbia. Winters from Maine, s. Ontario, s. Michigan, and s.e. South Dakota south and west along the Gulf Coast to s.e. Texas.

Red-shafted Flicker   *Colaptes cafer*—#6

IDENTIFICATION: L. 13. This species can be separated from the yellow-shafted by the salmon-red instead of golden-yellow under wing and tail surfaces and the absence of red on the nape. Only the male has mustache marks in the adult plumage, and in this species they are red instead of black.

HABITS: The red-shafted and the yellow-shafted are so nearly identical in habits and interbreed so freely that it is questionable whether they should be regarded as distinct species. Formerly the Great Plains served as a geographical barrier to mixing, but extensive planting of trees and setting out of fence posts and public-utility poles have destroyed its effectiveness. Every possible blending of the distinctive characters of the two are known, and hybrids occur east to Pennsylvania.

Traces of red in the black throat stripes or a reddish tinge in the wings reveal red-shafted blood; black in the red stripes or traces of red on the back of the head reveal eastern flicker influence. Occasionally a curious bird is produced in which the right half of the body is differently marked from the left.

VOICE: Same as yellow-shafted flicker.

NEST: Same as yellow-shafted flicker.

RANGE: (P.M.) Breeds from c. North Dakota, c. British Columbia, and s.e. Alaska east to w. Kansas, w. Texas, west to the Pacific, and south to s. Mexico. In winter, depending upon the severity of the weather, it withdraws from the most northern parts of its range and the higher mountains. It also commonly moves eastward in winter, often as far as Iowa, Arkansas, and e. Texas.

Pileated Woodpecker   *Ceophloeus pileatus—*✳4

IDENTIFICATION: L. 17. Unmistakable. Both sexes have a red crest, but in the female it does not include the forehead and she lacks the red streaks along the sides of the throat. Young have the red crest even in the juvenile plumage.

HABITS: The pileated is a bird of extensive woodlands, although it will feed on the ground on stumps and down timber in woodland openings. It is so silent and so careful to keep out of sight that one seldom sees it. However, its feeding signs—holes 4, 5, or even 8 inches deep, roughly rectangular in shape—reveal its presence. Often these are only a few feet from the ground.

The birds know ant trees, even when they appear sound from the outside, and invariably cut directly into the center of the colony. These carpenter ants are their favorite food, but they take boring beetles in all stages from grubs to adults. Wild fruits and acorns seem to be their only vegetable foods.

VOICE: This is a very silent bird except in spring, when it calls and drums. It has a long call consisting of the same note repeated first with a rising, then with a falling inflection, a good deal like that of a flicker but louder, deeper, and more full-throated. Other short and varied calls are exchanged continually by members of a breeding pair. Its resonant rolling drum which speeds up and fades away at the end is very distinctive.

NEST: A cavity with an entrance hole about 3¼ x 3½ inches cut in a dead tree or stub 15 to 70 feet aboveground in dense shade below the main canopy of the forest. The nest tree, which is generally 15 to 20 inches in diameter at the nest, is usually in a dense stand of trees in an extensive woodland. Four white eggs (1.30 x 1.00) are the normal clutch.

RANGE: (R.) From Nova Scotia, s.e. Quebec, s. Mackenzie, and British Columbia south to Florida, the Gulf Coast, and west to s.e. Texas. Absent from the s. Rocky Mountains and Great Basin but found from c. California north.

Red-bellied Woodpecker   *Centurus carolinus*—\#4

IDENTIFICATION: L. 9½. The finely striped "zebra" back and scarlet head make identification easy. Sexes are alike except that the red of the female's head is broken by gray on the crown into two patches, one on the nape and a smaller one at the nostrils. Even the young have scarlet heads. The reddish tinge on the belly is almost impossible to see in the field.

HABITS: Throughout the South this woodpecker is abundant in swamp- and bottom-land woods and frequent in most other woodlands. It comes into the outskirts of towns and around farms if a wood lot remains. Because of its racket one is seldom in doubt as to its presence. Its food is ants, beetles, and vegetable matter, including beech and acorn mast and corn as well as wild fruits.

VOICE: The red-bellied is a noisy bird. Its varied calls are of a soft, scolding character, somewhat lower in pitch than the flicker's. The commonest consists of a single *cherr* repeated in rapid succession from 2 to 12 or more times.

NEST: A cavity cut in a dead tree on the edge of a woodland opening. The entrance hole measures about 1¾ x 2 inches and is usually not more than 40 feet high. Soft-wooded trees are preferred, and both birds help with the cutting. Often they use the same hole more than one year. Occasionally they adopt the abandoned nest of some other species of woodpecker. A normal clutch is 4 or 5 dull white eggs (1.00 x .75).

RANGE: (R.) From Delaware, w. New York, s. Michigan, and s.e. Nebraska south to Florida and the Gulf Coast and west to e. Texas and e. Kansas.

Golden-fronted Woodpecker   *Centurus aurifrons*—※4

IDENTIFICATION: L. 9½. Three colors on the head where the red-bellied has one distinguish the male of this species. The female shows only two, as it lacks the red. The best field mark is the white rump, which shows up well in flight, along with the white patch in the wing. The golden front, like the red belly of the preceding species, is hard to see in the field.

HABITS: This bird has a special fondness for mesquite trees, but it is found in upland woods and river bottoms if there are large trees for nesting. Its food differs little from that of the red-bellied woodpecker.

VOICE: This noisy bird has a variety of harsh, scolding calls. They are distinctive but must be learned in the field, as some of them resemble notes of the flicker, red-bellied, and red-headed woodpeckers.

NEST: A hole from 6 to 25 feet high in living or dead trees, also in telegraph poles and fence posts. The bird lays 4 or 5 pure-white eggs (1.02 x .77).

RANGE: (R.) North and east in Texas to Dallas and Corpus Christi and west to Eagle Pass, south through Mexico to about Mexico City.

Red-headed Woodpecker*
Melanerpes erythrocephalus—#4

IDENTIFICATION: L. 9¾. An adult red-head is unmistakable, but the ashy-brown-headed juveniles are puzzling except in flight, when they show the white inner wing feathers characteristic of this species in all plumages. The juvenile plumage is worn into the fall.

HABITS: In summer they prefer open country and are often common in one area and inexplicably absent from similar habitats near by. When present they are conspicuous around farms, rural roads, and residential areas.

While the red-head does orthodox woodpecker feeding on grubs and other insects in dead wood, it obtains many flying insects. Watching from a conspicuous perch, it catches them in the air in sallies like a flycatcher's. When wild fruits begin to ripen it becomes vegetarian to a considerable degree. In winter it is more of a forest bird, and smaller acorns and beechnuts are staple foods.

VOICE: This noisy bird has a variety of indescribable scolding sounds, some harsh, some not unpleasant. One is like the crested flycatcher's scold; others are like the syllables *tchur-tchur* or *queer, queer, queer.*

NEST: A cavity from a few inches to 2 feet deep with a 1¾-inch-diameter entrance hole cut in dead wood, most frequently in a tree but in some areas in a telephone pole or fence post. A normal clutch is 5 pure-white eggs (1.00 x .75), and 2 broods are common.

RANGE: (P.M.) Breeds from s. New Brunswick, s. Quebec, s. Ontario, s. Manitoba, and s.e. Alberta south to Florida and the Gulf Coast and west to c. New Mexico, c. Colorado, and e. Wyoming. In winter it leaves that part of its range north of s.e. Pennsylvania, West Virginia, Tennessee, and Oklahoma.

Common Sapsucker
Sphyrapicus varius—#5

IDENTIFICATION: L. 8½. Adults of the eastern race are distinctive. The female is like the male except for her white throat. The dull-colored juveniles are best distinguished by the long white patch along the closed wing, a characteristic marking in all plumages. There are several western races with more red on the head. One, the red-breasted, has as much red as a red-headed woodpecker.

HABITS: In summer this is a forest or wood-lot bird which likes to be near water and small open spaces. It eats the nutritious inner bark of trees, making an extensive series of small, evenly spaced pits in doing so, and returning later to feed on the bleeding sap and the insects attracted by it. It does some fly-catching and enjoys fruit. Its brushlike tongue is not adapted to the normal type of woodpecker feeding.

VOICE: Many different, rather plaintive squeaks, mews, and whines, some of which sound cat- or squirrel-like. A common one is a downward-slurred *keeyew*. It is a loud drummer, hammering on resonant limbs, tin roofs, or wires with irregularly timed raps.

NEST: A cavity about a foot deep which the birds cut in a dead or dying tree, frequently a poplar or birch, near water. The normal 1¼-inch opening is barely large enough to admit the parents. Five or 6 white eggs (.89 x .67) are the normal clutch.

RANGE: (M.) Breeds from Newfoundland, the south end of James Bay, n. Manitoba, s. Mackenzie, and s.e. Alaska south to New Hampshire, the Virginia mountains, n. Ohio, c. Missouri, New Mexico, and s. California. Winters from s. New Jersey, s. Ohio, Kansas, and s. British Columbia south to the West Indies and Central America.

Hairy Woodpecker   *Dryobates villosus*—※5

IDENTIFICATION: L. 9. Females lack the bright red spot on the nape. Young males are often pale reddish on top of the head but not on the nape. Neither the larger size nor the unbarred outer tail feathers are good field marks, but the proportionately much longer, heavier bill always serves to separate this woodpecker from the downy.

HABITS: The hairy is essentially a forest dweller, but in fall and winter many birds move into more open country and even come into towns and villages. Its most important food is the larvae of boring beetles, which it extracts from the tunnels in the wood with its extraordinarily extensible barb-tipped tongue.

VOICE: A loud, sharp, high-pitched, and emphatic single *peek* or group of separate notes. Also a rapid series of notes slurred into a rattle which drops in pitch as it progresses. Its "song" is a drumming made by striking a resonant dead tree with its bill. It is louder than a downy's but not so prolonged, although the intervals between raps are longer.

NEST: In holes cut by the birds in living or dead trees. The entrance is 2 inches in diameter and the cavity about a foot deep. The site is often in or near a swampy opening in the forest. They will occasionally use a bird box. Four white eggs (.94 x .72) are a normal clutch. One brood is raised.

RANGE: (R.) Newfoundland, Ontario, n. Manitoba, and s. Alaska south to the Bahamas and Panama.

Downy Woodpecker   *Dryobates pubescens*—※5

IDENTIFICATION: L. 6. The downy is in many ways a small edition of the hairy woodpecker. Except for the barred outer tail feathers, the plumage is similar and sex and age differences are the same. The tiny conical bill is the only reliable field character.

HABITS: Downys are commonest in farm country with scattered trees and small wood lots. It is often a resident of towns and becomes very tame. The birds are fond of suet and will accept a loglike box with a handful of sawdust in the bottom both for nesting and for night roosting in winter.

The downy does much of its feeding in the bark of trees and in small dead branches. Its most important food is wood-boring ants, but it likes weevils and caterpillars. Much fall and winter feeding is in the dead canes of large non-woody plants, where it finds borers and gall insects.

VOICE: As it feeds it frequently utters a very abrupt *pik*. This carries well, although it is sharper and not as loud as the hairy's similar note. The downy utters the same sound as a staccato roll of a dozen or more notes, each distinct, but those at the end dropping in pitch.

NEST: A cavity 8 to 12 inches in a dead stub or branch which is often a part of an otherwise live tree. The entrance is about 1¼ inches in diameter, and the nest may be from a few feet to 60 or more feet above the ground. A normal clutch is 4 or 5 white eggs (.76 x .59).

RANGE: (R.) Newfoundland, Ontario, s. Manitoba, s.w. Mackenzie, and n.w. Alaska south to s. Florida, the Gulf Coast, s.c. Texas, s. New Mexico, and s. California.

Mexican Woodpecker *Dryobates scalaris*—⚥6

IDENTIFICATION: L. 7¼. This little bird is the only woodpecker in its range with the back regularly barred with black and white. The female is like the male except for the top of the head, which is black where the male is red. Young birds are similar, but in juvenile plumage both sexes have some red in the crown.

HABITS: Throughout its range it is the common woodpecker of woodlands, mesquite thickets, and urban shade trees. In more arid areas it feeds in agave, yucca, cactus, and other desert vegetation. It feeds low, often on the ground. Besides the usual woodpecker diet of insects, it eats fruits of cactus and other wild plants.

VOICE: A shrill single or double note and a rapid series of ringing notes on a somewhat lower pitch.

NEST: A cavity in a decayed tree branch about 12 feet aboveground near water. When the branch slopes, as is often the case, the 1½-inch-diameter entrance is on the underside. The bird also nests in fence posts, telephone poles, agave, yucca, and cactus. A normal clutch is 4 or 5 white eggs (.81 x .62).

RANGE: (R.) The s.e. coast of Texas north to w. Oklahoma, s. Utah, and s. California and south to British Honduras.

Red-cockaded Woodpecker   *Dryobates borealis*—※5

IDENTIFICATION: L. 8¼. Adults are black-capped, ladder-backed birds, but males have a small tuft of red feathers on either side of the black crown. Young birds are like adults, but their under parts are buffy instead of white, and the dark markings are sepia rather than black. The birds have more brightly colored heads in juvenile than in adult plumage, the center of the crown being crimson.

HABITS: This is the common woodpecker of open piny woods in the South. During the non-breeding season the birds travel in bands of six to ten and constantly call back and forth to one another. Several nesting pairs are generally found in fairly close proximity. When feeding, the birds fly restlessly from one tree to another, chasing each other and working the topmost pine branches, often upside down like nuthatches. Their food is chiefly wood-boring insects, but they occasionally visit cornfields and extract worms from ripening ears.

VOICE: This is a noisy bird with 2 rather different calls. One is short and nuthatch-like. The other, which is longer, is somewhat like the noise young songbirds make when the parent arrives with food.

NEST: A cavity 20 to 100 feet aboveground in a live pine with a rotten heart; used year after year as long as the bird can get resin to run from the nicks it makes in the bark around the nest hole. Where pine is not available it will use other trees. A clutch is normally 4 white eggs (.96 x .70).

RANGE: (R.) S.e. Virginia, Tennessee, s. Missouri, and n.e. Oklahoma south to s.e. Texas, the Gulf Coast, and Florida Keys.

Black-backed Woodpecker   *Picoides arcticus*—#5

IDENTIFICATION: L. 9½. The solid black back and the strongly barred flanks of this bird make it distinctive in any plumage. The female lacks the yellow fore crown of the male and has a black cap. Young birds are duller. Like the following species, this woodpecker has only three toes and is often called the Arctic three-toed woodpecker.

HABITS: Black-backed and three-toed woodpeckers live in the pine, spruce, fir, and larch forests of the North and are unsuspicious and fearless. They are found in greatest abundance where fire or lumbering has left dead or weakened trees or where beaver dams have flooded and killed extensive timber stands. Regular "colonies" often build up where the spruce budworm or the larch sawfly have opened stands to the inroads of flat-headed, bark-boring beetles—the bird's chief food. Most of their feeding is done by flaking off the bark rather than by working into old snags like most woodpeckers. Extensive trunk areas newly barked and still "bright" are typical feeding signs.

As dead trees soon lose their bark, such areas afford ideal feeding grounds for only a few years, and there are always likely to be many individuals seeking new feeding grounds. These may wander considerable distances and become common in areas outside their normal range. This species as a rule comes farther south than the less abundant three-toed.

VOICE: The black-backed is much the noisier of the two yellow-headed woodpeckers. It has a sharp, short *clucking* note, a rattling call, and in flight a loud, shrill cry. In winter it is usually silent.

NEST: A cavity normally at no great height aboveground (2 to 15 feet) in a living or dead tree, usually near an opening in the forest. The entrance is 1¼ to 2 inches in diameter, the lower side often beveled in to form a "doorstep" for the birds. A single brood is raised, and a clutch is ordinarily 4 white eggs (.84 x .75).

RANGE: (R.) Newfoundland, n. Quebec, n. Manitoba, n. Mackenzie, and c. Alaska south to New Hampshire, n. New York, n. Michigan, n. Minnesota, n.w. Wyoming, and c. California.

Three-toed Woodpecker   *Picoides tridactylus*—#5

IDENTIFICATION: L. 8¾. The most conspicuous difference between the three-toed and its larger relative, the blackbacked, is its cross-barred black-and-white back. Young are similar to adults but duller. Both sexes show yellow on the head in juvenile plumage, the amount increasing in the male and disappearing in the female as adult plumage is acquired.

HABITS: This circumpolar species breeds farther north and, in our western mountains, farther south than its relative. It is rarely as common as the black-backed where the two occur together, nor is it as uniformly distributed through the coniferous forests which form the habitat of both species. It is seldom seen outside its normal breeding range or far from the deep woods.

Voice: Like the black-backed's, but weaker and less sharp. It is a rather silent bird, less noisy even in drilling.

Nest: The 4 white eggs (.92 x .71) are deposited in a tree nest similar to that of the black-backed but with an entrance hole averaging about ¼ inch smaller.

Range: (R.) North to the limit of trees in North America, Europe, and Asia, south to n. New Hampshire, n. Michigan, n. Minnesota, and s.w. Oregon, and in the mountains to Arizona.

Ivory-billed Woodpecker   *Campephilus principalis*—⋇4

Identification: L. 20. Sexes are similar except that the female lacks red in her crest. Since the abundant and widely distributed pileated woodpecker is frequently mistaken for this rare bird, great care should be used in verifying its identity. The big, conspicuous, creamy-white bill and the white lower halves of the folded wings are its most notable characters. In flight the rear half of the long inner wing is pure white.

Habits: The ivory-bill's most important food is the larvae of wood-boring beetles, especially the flat-headed kind that work between the bark and wood of dying and newly dead trees. Their feeding sign is similar to that of the black-backed and three-toed woodpeckers—extensive trunk and branch areas from which the bark has been chipped to reveal bright wood beneath. As an ivory-bill will strip extensive areas of bark in a few feedings, it is most abundant where there has been an abnormal tree mortality because of fire, drought, wind, or insects. A normal healthy forest has a low carrying capacity for ivory-bills. It is likely that most nesting has always been in "die-off" areas, since only these seem capable of providing enough flat-headed borers to feed a pair of adults and their brood.

Destruction of the vast forests of the South, especially the luxuriant hardwood forests of the river bottoms, has apparently doomed this splendid bird—largest of our wood-peckers. It is so rare that any record of one is noteworthy and should be passed on at once to the National Audubon Society, which is trying to save the bird from extinction.

Voice: A high-pitched, nuthatch-like note, clear and musical but plaintive. The call note sounds like *kent*, by which name the bird is sometimes known. The birds are not es-pecially noisy, and their calls do not carry far. They have a characteristic fast double rap, given at well-spaced in-tervals, which sounds like a single loud knock on a very hollow tree trunk.

Nest: A cavity well up in a large living or dead tree. The en-trance hole is usually oval, averaging 6 or 7 inches high by 3 or 4 wide. The birds normally lay 3 white eggs (1.37 x .99).

Range: (R.) Formerly the South Atlantic and Gulf States from s.e. North Carolina to e. Texas and up the Mississippi Valley to s. Illinois and Ohio. Also Cuba.

Perching Birds
Order PASSERIFORMES

COTINGAS   Family COTINGIDAE

Rose-throated Becard   *Platypsaris aglaiae—*✳10

IDENTIFICATION: L. 6½. Juveniles look much like females. In immature plumage, in which they often breed, the throat of the male shows only a trace of pink, the full color taking two years to develop. The dark, bushy, erectile crown gives the bird a "big-headed" look, which is accented by the short tail. A light buffy collar is the female's most distinctive character.

HABITS: This bird prefers deep woods that are comparatively open below the tree crowns. Here it feeds in typical fly-catcher fashion, sitting quietly between forays on a look-out perch which is often inconspicuously located on a leafy branch. Its food is flying insects and wild fruits.

VOICE: A soft, plaintive whistle preceded by softer chattering notes. The whistle starts high and drops as the volume fades away.

NEST: A globular mass of fibrous material about a foot long and 9 inches in diameter, suspended from the drooping end of a branch 20 to 50 feet aboveground. The entrance is in the side, and a clutch is 5 brown-spotted white eggs (.91 x .67).

RANGE: (P.M.) From s. United States adjacent to Mexico south to Costa Riça. In winter there is some withdrawal southward from areas near the northern limit of the range.

TYRANT FLYCATCHERS   Family TYRANNIDAE

Eastern Kingbird*   *Tyrannus tyrannus*—#8

IDENTIFICATION: L. 8½. The eastern kingbird's black tail with its white terminal band is its best field mark.

HABITS: Open country with perches from which it can watch for insects is this kingbird's habitat. It is sometimes found 'n wooded areas if an occasional tree rises high enough to furnish a lookout above the trees. Kingbirds are capable of rapid flight and a variety of aerial maneuvers, many of which are performed with such short, quick wingbeats that the bird's wings appear to quiver. It is always conspicuous and noisy and very aggressive toward any large bird invading its breeding territory. Flying insects caught on the wing are its staple food, supplemented by wild fruits.

VOICE: A single high-pitched strident note sometimes prolonged into a squeaky chatter. A common call is *tzi, tzee*. The true song, a rolling series of sharp notes followed by a phoebe-like ending, is seldom heard except in the half-darkness of predawn.

NEST: A rather loose mass of sticks, straws, and other material lined with a well-constructed inner cup of fine grass, roots, and hair. Outside diameter about 5½ inches. Normally placed 20 to 25 feet up on the horizontal limb of a tree growing in the open. The bird favors the vicinity of water and will nest on low shrubs, stumps, and fence posts. It lays 3 or 4 creamy-white eggs (.95 x .70) irregularly speckled and spotted with brown and underlying blotches of gray.

RANGE: (M.) Breeds from New Brunswick, s. Ontario, c. Manitoba, and s.w. British Columbia south to s. Florida, the Gulf Coast, Texas, n. New Mexico, n. Utah, and w. Oregon. Winters from Costa Rica east to British Guiana and south through w. Brazil to s. Bolivia and Peru.

Gray Kingbird* *Tyrannus dominicensis*—✳8

IDENTIFICATION: L. 9. This large pale gray kingbird with its oversize bill, solid gray square tail, and dark ear coverts is unmistakable.

HABITS: The vicinity of the seacoast is the normal home, and it matters little whether the area is a wild stretch of mangrove or a busy town. Most of the time the bird stays on a conspicuous perch, watching for insects or intruders. Telephone wires seem to be preferred. Territorial defense, which in most birds is enforced only against intruding males of their own kind, is extended in this pugnacious species to all manner of larger birds and mammals, including man. Insects and wild fruits are its only known foods.

VOICE: This bird is seldom quiet. It constantly utters a loud, shrill, 3-note chatter—*pe-cheer-y*—with the accent on the middle note. A loud snapping noise made with the bill is common.

NEST: A flimsy structure of coarse twigs lined with grasses, placed in a thicket, preferably of red mangrove, 3 to 20 feet high and often over salt water. The 3 pinkish eggs (.99 x .72) are well blotched with brown.

RANGE: (P.M.) Breeds from s.e. South Carolina and w. Florida south along the coast through the West Indies, and the coast of Central America to Venezuela and Colombia. In winter absent from that part of its range lying northwest of Hispaniola, the birds apparently migrating to n. South America.

Olive-backed Kingbird* *Tyrannus melancholicus*—✳8

IDENTIFICATION: L. 8½. There are a number of gray-headed kingbirds with yellow under parts. The distinguishing characters of this species are its slightly forked brown tail without white and its brilliant yellow under parts. The olive-green back is variable, as the green feathers bleach out and become gray by spring.

HABITS: This wide-ranging bird seems able to adapt itself to any open or semiopen country. Agricultural areas with scattered trees are well suited to it. Occasionally it is found around forest openings and river and lake borders.

VOICE: Rapid, metallic, staccato notes in an ascending high-pitched series.

NEST: A Texas nest was described as 6 inches in diameter, made of Spanish moss and twigs and lined with fine rootlets and hairlike material. It was 20 feet aboveground on a small lateral tree branch. A normal clutch is 3 or 4 creamy-pink eggs (.98 x .73) with small brown spots.

RANGE: (P.M.) Breeds from s. Texas and s. Arizona south to Argentina. Withdraws in winter from the extreme northern part of its range.

Western Kingbird* *Tyrannus verticalis*—※8

IDENTIFICATION: L. 9. Its white outer tail feathers are the best field mark. In young birds colors are duller, and sometimes white is lacking in the tail. Absence of wing bars and brown on the wings and tail separates it from the crested flycatchers.

HABITS: This is a bird of open country. It is common around ranch buildings and comes into towns. It avoids woodlands but wanders over treeless country if fences or telephone wires are available. The opening up of the once heavily forested East is making it possible for this and other western birds to extend their breeding range eastward.

The western has most of the typical kingbird characteristics but is more tolerant of its own kind than the eastern bird. Often a tree has more than one nest and several pairs may occupy a small grove. Grasshoppers form an important part of the food supply, which is almost wholly insect.

VOICE: A variety of high-pitched squeaks, chatters, and twitters a little less shrill than those of the eastern kingbird.

NEST: All sorts of fibrous and soft materials are intermixed to build a nest about 6 inches in diameter with a 3-inch inner cup well padded with wool and downs; located almost anywhere if trees are not available. In trees it is usually 15 to 30 feet up on a horizontal limb. The 4 eggs (.93 x .70) are like those of the eastern kingbird.

RANGE: (M.) Breeds from s. British Columbia and s. Manitoba east to Michigan, Missouri, and Oklahoma and south to n. Texas and n. Mexico. Winters from n.w. Mexico south along the Pacific side to El Salvador. During fall migration occurs regularly in small numbers on the Atlantic coast.

Scissor-tailed Flycatcher   *Muscivora forficata*—✳10

IDENTIFICATION: L. 14, T. 9. Sexes are similar, but the female can usually be distinguished by her smaller size, shorter tail, and somewhat less vivid and extensive underwing color. The even duller brownish-backed young birds lack the patch of orange-red where the underwing joins the body.

HABITS: Scissor-tails are birds of open country, where scattered trees provide lookout perches. They often sit on roadside fence wires, oblivious of passing cars. They are kingbird-like in habits and are great harriers of larger birds. Their long tail gives them a maneuverability in the air which they seem to enjoy showing off. During courtship in the spring the male engages in wonderful sky dances. Even at other seasons it frequently executes a series of vertical zigzags while rapidly opening and closing its deeply forked tail, chattering all the while. Although they catch most of their food on the wing, the birds eat few flies. Grasshoppers, crickets, and beetles are their chief food, and they occasionally go to the ground for them. Little non-insect food is taken.

VOICE: Kingbird-like twittering notes; also a harsh double-noted call repeated in rapid succession.

NEST: Placed about 15 feet high in an isolated tree or man-made structure; bulky and roughly built out of soft and fibrous material. The 5 creamy eggs (.89 x .67) are spotted with brown.

RANGE: (M.) Breeds from s. Nebraska, w. Arkansas, and e. Texas south to s. Texas and west to s.e. New Mexico and w. Oklahoma. Winters from s. Texas south to Panama.

Kiskadee Flycatcher*   *Pitangus sulphuratus*—※10

IDENTIFICATION: L. 10½. This large heavy flycatcher with intense yellow under parts and rufous wings and tail is unmistakable. Young birds are slightly duller and lack the yellow crown patch.

HABITS: This wide-ranging species is usually common along water courses lined with dense vegetation, but it also frequents agricultural country and is often abundant in towns. It uses conspicuous perches when hunting food, much of which consists of large flying insects. Fruit is relished at certain seasons. Its most interesting habit is its fishing. Perched over water like a kingfisher, it dives after fish near the surface, but the dive is not as deep and clean-cut as the kingfisher's. After about 3 sorties its plumage requires drying in the sun before diving can be continued.

VOICE: A variety of loud 2- or 3-note calls given rather slowly and deliberately. When the bird is excited they are speeded up to a shrill chatter.

NEST: A bulky 14-x-10-inch structure of mixed fibrous and soft material with the entrance in the side; about 20 feet high, preferably in a thorny tree. The 4 creamy-white eggs

(1.15 x .82) are sparingly spotted with brown around the large end.

RANGE: (R.) From the lower Rio Grande Valley south to Argentina.

Crested Flycatcher*   *Myiarchus crinitus*—⚹8

IDENTIFICATION: L. 9. The cinnamon wings and tail are the best field marks. Young differ from adults only in duller coloring. These noisy birds are more often heard than seen.

HABITS: This is essentially a woodland bird. It prefers open mature forests but is found around openings in denser second growth. Adaptable to some degree, it frequently lives in old orchards and around buildings and shade trees in farm country. During the breeding season each pair defends a large territory against other crested flycatchers, and the nest tree is usually a dangerous place for any larger bird. Leafy tops of taller trees provide concealed lookout perches, and the bird does much of its feeding in the forest canopy. Insects of many kinds furnish the bulk of its food, augmented in fall by wild fruits.

VOICE: A loud, clear, whistled *wheeeep*, often followed by a few raucous scold notes. The calls are varied, and some are much like those of a red-headed woodpecker.

NEST: In a cavity, preferably natural, not more than 6 to 15 feet high, in an old tree or branch; also in woodpecker holes and bird boxes. If too deep the cavity is filled with trash to within 12 to 18 inches of the opening. The nest is of any convenient material—feathers, rags, string, hair, grass, roots, and fibers. Recently shed snakeskins, wax paper, cellophane, and onionskins are often included. The 5 or 6 eggs (.89 x .68) are creamy-white with brown spots and erratic wavy lines.

RANGE: (M.) Breeds from New Brunswick, s. Ontario, and s.e. Manitoba south to s. Florida, the Gulf Coast, and e.

Texas and west to c. Kansas and e. South Dakota. Winters
from s. Texas and s. Florida to Colombia.

Mexican Flycatcher*   *Myiarchus tyrannulus—*✳8

IDENTIFICATION: L. 9½. The crested flycatcher has some 16
close relatives in Mexico and Central America. This
grayer-backed bird is a slightly larger and much paler
edition of the crested, with a wholly dark bill and browner
head.

HABITS: This bird frequents heavy timber, but where giant
cacti full of woodpecker holes are present for nest sites
it occurs in treeless country.

VOICE: Loud and harsh, the commonest sound being a short
double call accented on the second note. It also has a loud,
clear, whistled call that is not unmusical.

NEST: In natural cavities or woodpecker holes in trees, fence
posts, and giant cacti, placed 5 to 30 feet aboveground; a
mass of vegetable fibers, feathers, and hair. The 3 to 5
eggs (.95 x .72) are creamy-buff, like those of the crested
flycatcher, but less heavily marked.

RANGE: (R.) From s. Texas, c. Arizona, and s. California
south to El Salvador.

Ash-throated Flycatcher*   *Myiarchus cinerascens—*✳9

IDENTIFICATION: L. 8¼. This bird is noticeably smaller than
the two preceding species, and its back is clear gray-brown
with a little trace of olive. Its black bill is similar to that
of the Mexican but much smaller, and its throat is nearly
white.

HABITS: This is a bird of dry bush or cactus country. It does
most of its foraging in low vegetation, seldom fly-catching
from a fixed perch but ranging over a large territory. Some

insects are caught in the air; others, like caterpillars, are picked from leaves.

VOICE: Like that of the crested flycatcher; a clear, whistled note, a harsher *che-hoo*, and some soft, mellow whistles.

NEST: In natural cavities seldom over 20 feet aboveground. When such sites are absent the birds use the abandoned ovenlike nests of cactus wrens and all sorts of cavities in man-made structures. The 4 or 5 creamy-white eggs (.88 x .65) are more lightly marked than those of the Mexican flycatcher.

RANGE: (P.M.) Breeds from c. Washington, n. Utah, and w.c. Texas south and west through n. Mexico to the Pacific. Found in winter from s. Arizona south to Costa Rica.

Eastern Phoebe*   *Sayornis phoebe*—#9

IDENTIFICATION: L. 7. The black bill and the lack of an eye ring or distinct wing bars (except in juvenile plumage) separate this from other flycatchers. Its best field character is its habit of constantly waving its tail with a sideways as well as an up-and-down motion.

HABITS: This, our hardiest flycatcher, comes north early and stays late. An occasional bird stays north of the normal wintering ground all winter. In wild areas the phoebe usually stays near running water, probably because natural nest sites are plentiful along steep-sided streams. It has responded favorably to civilization and is common in the country near buildings of all sorts. Flying insects are the chief food, and their abundance around barnyards make these especially favorable nesting places.

VOICE: The phoebe says its name over and over in a low, forceful voice. The delivery is emphatic and the tone has a rough aspirate quality. The bird also has a few shorter and longer calls.

NEST: Originally phoebes nested on rock shelves or in cavities on the walls of steep-sided ravines, but now they nest extensively on man-made structures. All they require is overhead shelter and a reasonably flat projecting surface to which the nest can be attached. Bridge girders, rafters in open buildings, window sills, and shutter tops near the eaves are popular. The nest is a 4½-inch cup of mud and moss with a lining of grass and hair. The 5 eggs (.75 x .55) are pure white. Two broods are normal, 3 rare.

RANGE: (M.) Breeds from Nova Scotia, s. Ontario, c. Manitoba, and c.w. Mackenzie south to s.e. Virginia, n. Georgia, Arkansas, and e.c. New Mexico. In Kansas and the Dakotas seldom ranges west of the one hundredth meridian. Winters from about the southern limit of its breeding range south to s. Florida, the Gulf Coast, and s. Mexico.

Say's Phoebe*   *Sayornis saya*—#9

IDENTIFICATION: L. 7½. Even juveniles have the rusty-brown under parts that make this species unmistakable.

HABITS: This phoebe frequents dry country with stunted vegetation and is seldom found in forested areas or on rich land. When feeding it flits over low growths with a strong, somewhat erratic flight. From low perches it watches for insects in the air or on the ground. It is a hardy species and an early migrant. When its insect supply fails it turns to wild fruits.

VOICE: A soft, plaintive 2-note call like *phee-eur*. Also a more rapid 3-note call and occasionally a trill.

NEST: Site preferences are virtually the same as those of its eastern relative; a flat soft nest of plant fibers, grasses, wool, and hair. Four to 5 white eggs (.77 x .60) are a normal clutch, and it raises 2, rarely 3, broods a season.

RANGE: (M.) Breeds from s. Manitoba, n. Alberta, and c. Alaska south to n. Mexico and from s.w. Yukon, e. Washington, and e. California east to c. North Dakota, w. Iowa, and w. Oklahoma. Winters from c. Texas and c. California south to s. Mexico.

Yellow-bellied Flycatcher* *Empidonax flaviventris*—✳9

IDENTIFICATION: L. 5½. During migration it is generally impossible to identify any of the *Empidonax* flycatchers in the field unless the bird gives its distinctive call. Of the four species, this one, because of its coloring, might constitute an exception. At all seasons it is much yellower below than the others and is the only one with a really yellow throat.

HABITS: In summer these flycatchers live in damp, sphagnum-carpeted northern forests of spruce, tamarack, paper birch, and fir. Dense alder swamps are the best place to look for them in migration, but their habit of perching and feeding close to the ground makes them hard to see. Often only their soft, plaintive *peas* reveal their presence.

Small insects that can be caught on the wing are the standard food of all little flycatchers. When unseasonable cold weather keeps insects from flying they can survive for a few days on berries.

VOICE: Its common call is a soft, mournful 2-note whistle, the second note rising and slightly prolonged, the whole like an abbreviated wood pewee song. The bird also utters an abrupt song that sounds like a sneeze.

NEST: On or near the ground in the side of a mossy mound or in the roots of a fallen tree. A rather bulky cup of moss and rootlets lined with hairlike roots and grass. The 3 or 4 dull white eggs (.68 x .53) are sparingly dotted with brown.

RANGE: (M.) Breeds from Newfoundland, c. Quebec, c. Manitoba, and s. Mackenzie south to s. New Hampshire, n. Pennsylvania, s. Wisconsin, and c. Alberta. Winters from n. Mexico to Panama. Migrates east of the Plains.

Acadian Flycatcher*   *Empidonax virescens*—✳9

IDENTIFICATION: L. 5¾. Their small size, conspicuous eye ring, and double wing bars set the *Empidonaxes* apart from other flycatchers. The head and back of the Acadian are greener and often lighter than those of any other *Empidonax* but the yellow-bellied, but in the absence of direct comparison this is not of much use for field identification.

HABITS: The summer home is in the deep shade of dense and fairly mature woodlands. Beech stands are favorites. It feeds in the open area beneath the foliage canopy, watching for flying insects from a dead twig, where it sits motionless except for a quick tail jerk every time it utters its distinctive note.

VOICE: Its call is a short *peet*, its so-called song an abrupt *ka-reep*, with the accent on the higher-pitched and longer second note, which has a rough quality. In flight it sometimes utters musical twittering notes.

NEST: A woven basket of plant stems and other fibrous material suspended between horizontal twigs at a fork near the end of a tree branch. The birds are reported to use spider and insect silk in construction, and though fragile-looking the nests are durable. Ten feet aboveground is an average height, and they are often over a stream. The 3 white to buffy eggs (.72 x .54) are sparingly dotted with brown chiefly at the large end.

RANGE: (M.) Breeds from s. Vermont, n. New York, s. Ontario, s. Michigan, and e. Nebraska south to c. Florida, the Gulf Coast, and s. Texas. Winters in e. Colombia and e. Ecuador.

Alder Flycatcher*   *Empidonax traillii*—✳9

IDENTIFICATION: L. 6. Although it is larger and much browner than the Acadian and has the whitest throat of the whole group, one cannot surely separate this species from the Acadian except by habitat and voice.

HABITS: This is ordinarily a bird of shrubby thickets in swampy areas where alder, willow, and swamp rose thrive. Alders of the Midwest nest differently and have a different song (a sneezy 2-note *fitz-bew*) and are found in dry upland pastures thickly overgrown with hawthorn and other shrubs as well as in orchards, suburbs, and roadside growths. If the separation of birds into species were not so exclusively based upon differences in the appearance of their skins, the alder flycatchers of the Mississippi drainage might be regarded as a separate species.

Alder flycatchers sing and fly-catch from conspicuous perches on tall shrubs.

VOICE: The alarm note is an abrupt *wit*. A common song is composed of 3 forceful syllables, the first short, the second accented and slurred off to the third, which is in a lower pitch—like an emphatic *way-be-o*. Other similar but shorter or longer calls are easily recognizable.

NEST: Usually about 2 to 4 feet from the ground in the upright fork of a swamp shrub, occasionally in a fern clump. It is suspended above the crotch and not set down in it like that of a least flycatcher. The $3\frac{1}{2}$- to 4-inch nest is loosely woven, with many hanging ends. It is generally of grasses, weed stems, and bark, lined with a well-constructed cup of fine grass and fiber. The birds in the Midwest that nest away from swamps saddle their nests on horizontal limbs as high as 20 feet from the ground. The 3 or 4 creamy-white eggs (.70 x .52) usually have a few fine brown dots.

RANGE: (M.) Breeds from e.c. Labrador, n. Ontario, Mackenzie, and c. Alaska south to n. New Jersey, West Virginia, s. Illinois, c. Texas, and n. Mexico. Winters from s. Mexico to Venezuela and Ecuador.

Least Flycatcher*

Empidonax minimus—❄9

IDENTIFICATION: L. 5¼. This bird is grayer on the back, whiter below, and smaller than other *Empidonaxes* and is the only one with a fairly dark lower mandible. These are poor field marks and superfluous in spring, when it repeatedly calls its common name—*chebec*.

HABITS: This flycatcher is less specific in habitat requirements than other members of the genus and as a result is widely distributed. Open country well scattered with trees is ideal, and it is usually abundant around orchards, gardens, towns, parks, and rural country. It becomes scarce in really deep woods.

VOICE: The least's song is an emphatic *chebec* strongly accented on the higher second note. The bird is the noisiest of its group, since it utters this sound almost constantly during spring and early summer. Each repetition is accompanied by a toss of the head and flick of the tail. Its call is a single short *whit*.

NEST: A rather deep thin-walled cup about 2¾ inches across, made of bark fibers, weed stems, and a variety of soft substances, lined with fine grasses, hair, down, and feathers. About 6 to 15 feet aboveground is a normal height. The nest is always firmly wedged in a crotch. The 4 creamy-white eggs (.63 x .51) are unmarked.

RANGE: (M.) Breeds from Nova Scotia, Ontario, n. Alberta, and w.c. Mackenzie south to n. New Jersey, s.w. North Carolina, Indiana, and s.w. Missouri west to s.e. Wyoming and e. British Columbia. Winters from n.e. Mexico to Panama.

Eastern Pewee*

Myiochanes virens—❄9

IDENTIFICATION: L. 6½. Indistinct wing bars, a yellowish lower mandible, long wings, and a short tail which it does not wag separate the pewee from the phoebe. Its large size, the absence of an eye ring, and the pale line down the center of the breast separate it from the *Empidonax* fly-catchers.

HABITS: The pewee inhabits the mid-level in tree growths and readily accepts any area that is reasonably supplied with large trees, from deep woods to old orchards and town plantings. A lookout perch well up in a tree is used in feeding, and the bird commonly returns to it following each sally after a passing insect.

VOICE: The pewee's song is given for about ¾ of an hour after the first sign of daybreak and again in the late evening. It is composed of slurred 2- and 3-note phrases—*pee-wee, pe-ah-whee*, and an unslurred *hi-de-dee*—continuously delivered in a regular pattern. The tone is a clear, sweet, plaintive whistle. During the day the slurred phrases and a chip note are uttered at intervals while the bird feeds.

NEST: A thick-walled shallow cup saddled on a horizontal limb about 20 feet high, generally so well covered with lichens as to be almost invisible from below. Weed stems, bark shreds, and other fibers are used, and the nest is lined with plant downs, wool, etc. Three creamy-white eggs (.72 x .54) wreathed at the larger end with blotches and specks of brown.

RANGE: (M.) Breeds from Nova Scotia, s. Ontario, and s. Manitoba south to Florida, the Gulf Coast, and s. Texas and west to c. Oklahoma, e. Kansas, and e. North Dakota. Winters from Costa Rica to Colombia and Peru.

Western Pewee*   *Myiochanes richardsoni*—✳9

IDENTIFICATION: L. 6½. The grayer upper parts, the more extensive and more deeply olive-gray under parts, the darker throat, and darker lower mandible of this species are of doubtful value in separating the two pewees in the field. On the other hand, their notes are quite distinct. The western's harsh, rasping slur, not unlike the call of a nighthawk, is in sharp contrast to the clear sweet whistles of the eastern.

HABITS: The 2 pewees are much alike in habits. This bird, however, accepts more open areas than the eastern and frequently avoids the denser woodlands.

VOICE: The song is a rising 3-note phrase delivered in a clear whistle and accented on the first note, alternating with a harsh, buzzy downward slur unlike any note of the eastern pewee. The bird is often quiet by day but may sing into the night.

NEST: Differs from that of the eastern in lacking the outer covering of lichens. Also, it is larger and deeper and often has feathers in the lining. The location is generally the same, and the eggs of the 2 species are undistinguishable.

RANGE: (M.) Breeds from s. Manitoba, s. Mackenzie, and c. Alaska south through Mexico and east to e. Manitoba, w. Nebraska, and w. Texas. Winters from s. Mexico to Bolivia. In migration reaches the s. Texas coast.

Olive-sided Flycatcher*   *Nuttallornis borealis*—※8

IDENTIFICATION: L. 7½. A large-billed, heavy-headed, dark flycatcher sitting upright on the topmost twig of a dead tree is likely to be this bird. The dark flanks contrast strongly with the otherwise white under parts, and often a tuft of long silky white feathers can be observed on either side of the lower back just above the tail.

HABITS: The edge of an opening in a coniferous forest is the best place to look for this species. It likes small ponds, bogs, and burns with a few dead trees for lookouts. As it is aggressive in defense of its territory, breeding pairs are well separated. The olive-sided feeds heavily on the ant-wasp-bee group of insects.

VOICE: The calls of this noisy bird carry a long way (some say up to a mile) and are uttered frequently all day. *Quick three beers* is an interpretation of one, the *quick* shorter and weaker than the other 2 notes, the *beers* long and slurred downward. Its 1- and 2-note calls are delivered in the same loud, emphatic scream.

NEST: At varying heights but generally well up in a conifer near the end of a horizontal limb where twigs or cones offer support. The foundation is loosely woven of coarse twigs, and the top and cup are finished off with usnea lichen, moss, rootlets, and grasses. The 3 pale cream to buffy-pink eggs (.85 x .63) have a ring of scattered brown spots around the larger end.

RANGE: (M.) Breeds from Newfoundland, Ontario, n. Saskatchewan, and c. Alaska south to w. North Carolina, n. Wisconsin, c. Arizona, and n. Lower California. Winters from Colombia to Peru.

Vermilion Flycatcher *Pyrocephalus rubinus*—※10

IDENTIFICATION: L. 6. The adult male, except in one of its 2 rare color phases in which the under parts are yellow-orange or deep wine-purple, is unmistakable. The female is salmon-pink or at least yellow in the belly region but, unlike the similar Say's phoebe, has streaked under parts, light gray lores, and a whitish forehead. Young birds have scaled backs, round spots below, and only a trace of yellow on the belly.

HABITS: Stream- and river-bottom willows, cottonwoods, and shrubs are its usual habitat. Roadside plantings, shade trees, and isolated tree clumps some distance from water are occasionally occupied. It feeds in the typical flycatcher manner, but at no great height aboveground. Its lookout perch is usually a weed stalk or shrub, and it often takes insects from the ground.

Voice: Its common calls are 2- or 3-note phrases given in a loud, energetic whistle, accompanied by an upward jerk of the head. It also has a beautiful soft twittering or tinkling flight song which is part of the courtship performance. This is delivered at intervals while the bird hovers in the air on rapidly fluttering wings.

Nest: Set into a horizontal fork well out from the trunk and ordinarily about 10 to 20 feet from ground near running water. The flat nest is made of fine and fibrous materials, including feathers, bound together with spider webs. Frequently the outside is decorated with lichens. The 3 creamy-white eggs (.69 x .51) are heavily marked with brown at the larger end.

Range: (P.M.) Breeds from s. Texas, s. Utah, and s. California south to c. Argentina. In early fall most individuals breeding in the United States migrate into Mexico, but a few move northwest to the Pacific Coast and northeast along the Gulf Coast as far as n. Florida.

Beardless Flycatcher*   *Camptostoma imberbe*—⚹9

Identification: L. 4½. This nondescript little bird may behave like the flycatcher it is, but often it feeds like a warbler or vireo. It is no bird for the beginner to try to identify unless it is heard as well as seen. Sometimes old birds have a decided crest of sooty feathers. Young birds are brown above with cinnamon wing bars.

Habits: The beardless flycatcher inhabits large trees and forest growths, dense second growth, and in south Texas seems partial to the low bushes of the chaparral and the mesquite thickets. Although an insect eater, there are times when it feeds heavily on small wild fruits.

Voice: The loud song of the male, delivered from the top of the tallest tree, consists of 3 long slow notes followed by a trill. The call is a shrill but not unmusical series of 4 or 5 short notes on a descending scale, loudest in the middle.

NEST: A globular mass of plant fibers with a downward-sloping entrance on the side; center cavity padded with plant downs or fur. The nest may be at any height in a tree or shrub where the bird can find supporting material such as a clump of mistletoe or Spanish moss. The 3 white eggs (.65 x .48) are finely speckled with brown.

RANGE: (P.M.) Breeds from s. Texas and s. Arizona south to Costa Rica. Withdraws from the United States in winter.

LARKS   Family ALAUDIDAE

Horned Lark   *Otocoris alpestris*—✻ 17

IDENTIFICATION: L. 7¾. Head and chest markings of female and young are less vividly black than the male's, and they lack the male's black forehead. Horned larks from different areas vary in the color of the throat, forehead, and eyeline. In the common race of the eastern Arctic these are bright primrose-yellow, while in the race that breeds in eastern United States they are practically white. The best field characters are the habit of walking rather than hopping (see water pipit) and the black tail that contrasts so sharply with the white under parts when the bird is seen from below in flight.

HABITS: The more barren and unattractive an area, the better it seems to suit the horned lark. As soon as cover develops, even weeds and tall grass, the birds desert it. Every breeding pair seems to require some bare exposed earth within its territory. Lumbering, plowing, soil impoverishment, and overgrazing have enabled this species to expand its range and increase its numbers. In winter the birds gather in flocks that may number thousands, but their habitat preference seems the same. In summer they feed on insects, but throughout the year seeds of grasses and weeds form their staple foods.

VOICE: In winter as the birds flush and fly off they utter 1- to 3-note calls. These are high-pitched, sibilant, and more prolonged than a pipit's, the most distinctive being a double note, one part higher in pitch than the other. The song which the bird starts very early in spring is a rapid series of high 1- and 2-note phrases varying in pitch to produce a weak, wiry twittering.

NEST: In the open on bare ground in a slight depression or near a stone or clod, the outer cup of grasses, the inner of plant downs or hair and feathers. Four eggs (.85 x .62) are normal, their gray or greenish background color often obscured by a thick sprinkling of fine brown specks. In some areas the birds habitually nest so early that the first eggs are destroyed by snowstorms one year in every three.

RANGE: (P.M.) Breeds from the coasts of the Arctic Ocean south to n. South America, n. Africa, and s. Asia. In winter retires from its northerly range, wintering from New Brunswick, s. Ontario, n. Minnesota, and s. British Columbia south. In eastern North America rarely gets south to the Gulf States.

SWALLOWS   Family HIRUNDINIDAE

Bahama Swallow   *Callichelidon cyaneoviridis*—✳13

IDENTIFICATION: L. 6. This bird's outstanding character is its deeply forked (about 1 inch) long tail and dull velvety green head and back. Females are smaller and duller with a sooty wash behind the eye and on the sides of the breast and center of chest. Young birds are brownish above with a green luster and have a touch of sooty on the sides of the breast.

HABITS: Not much is known about these swallows, but they seem to be either somewhat migratory or great wanderers. There would probably be more Florida records if observers on the southeast coast and keys kept watch for them.

VOICE: A low, musical, chirping note.

NEST: In old woodpecker holes or natural cavities or under the eaves of buildings.

RANGE: (R.) Occurs throughout the Bahamas from Grand Bahama to Great Inagua and on the northern coast of Cuba.

Tree Swallow*   *Iridoprocne bicolor*—✳13

IDENTIFICATION: L. 6. Adults are unmistakable. Young can be confused with the browner-backed bank and rough-winged swallows but are whiter below, and the grayish chest band is fainter and narrower than that of the bank swallow in any plumage.

HABITS: A small body of water, a marsh, or a wet meadow are an essential part of their habitat as the birds do most of their feeding as they skim low over such areas. Their rapid wingbeat and slightly flickering flight are distinctive. When they sail, as they frequently do, it is with shoulders forward and wing tips down. Aggregations in late summer and fall may number thousands. The birds make quite a spectacle as they sit shoulder to shoulder on wires or festoon bushes and trees and overflow to the ground. This hardy swallow is an early spring migrant, turning to berries (especially bayberries) and seeds when cold weather makes flying insects scarce.

VOICE: Varied twitterings of a sweet, liquid quality, often run together into a rippling chatter.

NEST: Their wild nest site is a natural cavity in a tree or one cut by woodpeckers, but they readily accept man-made structures. A nest site in open sunlight near water or a wet meadow is preferred. Loose colonies often occur where a beaver dam has created a body of water filled with dead tree trunks. Colonies of more than 100 pairs have been established artificially in many areas by putting up individual nest boxes on scattered poles. Such colonies have proved effective in reducing crop-eating insects, which the birds catch during the adult flying stage before they have laid eggs. This easy, cheap, and virtually automatic form of insect control continues year after year once the easily constructed nest boxes are up. Four to 6 white eggs (.74 x .52) are normal, and 2 broods are raised. The nest cavity is lined with grasses and the inner cup is made of feathers.

RANGE: (M.) Breeds from Newfoundland, n. Manitoba, Mackenzie, and n. Alaska south to Maryland, c. Missouri, Colorado, and s.w. California. Winters from North Carolina and the Gulf Coast, n. Mexico, and s. California south through Cuba to Guatemala.

Bank Swallow* _Riparia riparia—_ #13

IDENTIFICATION: L. 5¼. This bird with its brownish head and back and darker wings and tail is not easily confused with any other species except the larger rough-winged. When perched, the bank's dark chest band settles the matter, but as this is not easily seen in flight, the clear white throat is the better field mark. Young birds are like adults except that much of their plumage is washed with light reddish-brown.

HABITS: The highly specialized nest-site requirements of this cosmopolitan bird appear to control its distribution and abundance. Natural sandy banks seldom remain sufficiently steep unless the base is being constantly cut away by wave action or water currents. Since man started digging gravel pits and railroad and highway cuts the birds have made increasing use of them.

When feeding, these swallows generally fly low, with a fluttery and erratic motion as they twist and turn at full speed. When sailing, they tend to hold their wings close to the body. Their food is wholly insectivorous.

Voice: Irregularly alternating clear high-pitched and lower notes with a slight vibrating quality, run together into a chatter or twitter.

Nest: A loose cup of grasses lined with feathers in a cavity at the end of a 2- or 3-foot burrow which the birds dig near the top of a steep-faced sand or gravel bank. The birds nest in colonies from a dozen to more than 100 pairs. The burrow entrances measure about 1 inch high by 2 inches wide and are often only a few inches apart. Usually more burrows are started than finished, and many birds eventually nest in burrows of previous years. Four or 5 white eggs (.70 x .50) are a normal clutch, and 2 broods are common.

Range: (M.) Breeds in the whole Northern Hemisphere. In North America from n. Labrador, Mackenzie, and n. Alaska south to s. Virginia, c. Alabama, s. Texas, and s. California. American birds winter chiefly in Brazil.

Rough-winged Swallow*   *Stelgidopteryx ruficollis*—⚹13

Identification: L. 5¾. Adult rough-wings are larger and browner than bank swallows, with back, wings, and tail the same color and throat and forward under parts uniformly gray. Young are similar but lighter, with light brown edgings on their feathers, and should not be confused with young tree swallows.

Habits: Nest sites seem to be the sole factor controlling the bird's distribution, and it has benefited even more than the bank swallow from human activities. It is not averse either to wet or arid country, so long as a sandy bank is available. All feeding is done coursing low over ground or water. A powerful flier, this swallow's wingbeats are deeper but slower than a bank's, and its motion is more in a straight line, with fewer twists and turns and more gliding and sailing.

VOICE: A rasping, short single or double note, harsher and lower than the bank swallow's.

NEST: These solitary nesters use a variety of locations—ends of burrows in steep-faced sandy banks or cuts, crevices in rock ledges, drainpipes, and crevices about bridges or buildings. The 6 or 7 eggs (.72 x .52) are laid in a loose mass of grass and other plant debris.

RANGE: (P.M.) Breeds from New Hampshire, n. Michigan, North Dakota, and c. British Columbia south to s. Brazil. In winter it is not found north of n. Mexico.

Barn Swallow   *Hirundo rustica*—✳12

IDENTIFICATION: L. 7. Unmistakable. Females and young are like males but somewhat duller.

HABITS: The barn swallow is a powerful flier and ends each wingbeat with the primaries pointing almost straight back. Unlike most land birds, it migrates by day. It follows coast lines and rivers and, like many eastern birds, reaches South America by way of the West Indian island chain to Trinidad. The shooting of the migrants as they course low over the water off beaches is unfortunately still considered great sport on such islands as Barbados.

VOICE: A series of energetic, bubbling, twittery notes at different pitches; liquid, distinctive, and not unmelodious.

NEST: The nest of mud bonded with grass is lined with soft grasses and feathers and plastered against a vertical or horizontal surface. Against the former it is the shape of a truncated half cone; against the latter it is a circular cup. Originally these birds nested in caves or in crevices and niches under overhanging rocky cliffs, and some still do. But, having discovered better protection from the weather in man-made structures, they have adopted them so widely as to become a much more abundant species. Since they greatly reduce flying insects around barnyards, every farm building should have one or two small openings to let them in to nest. Nesting birds may be solitary or in colonies of 50 to 60 pairs in a building. The 4 or 5 white eggs (.74 x .53) are variably marked with reddish-brown spots or dots; 2 broods are raised.

RANGE: (M.) Breeds throughout the Northern Hemisphere and winters mainly in the Southern. In the Western Hemisphere breeds from s. Labrador, Ontario, s. Manitoba, n. Mackenzie, and n.w. Alaska south to North Carolina, n.w. Alabama, Arkansas, and c. Mexico. Winters from Colombia and British Guiana south to c. Argentina.

Cliff Swallow* *Petrochelidon pyrrhonota*—✳13

IDENTIFICATION: L. 6. The pale reddish rump and almost square tail set the adults apart from other swallows. The forehead varies from creamy-white to pale brown or even darker in the cliff swallows of the Southwest and Mexico. Young birds are similar to adults but duller and less strongly marked.

HABITS: Like all swallows, the cliff wants open country over which to feed. Its distribution is puzzling, as it is abundant in some areas while in other apparently similar areas only a few scattered colonies are present. This bird has the longest migration route of any American land bird. Its return north in the spring follows a fairly rigid schedule, not to the day and hour, as is absurdly claimed for the San Juan Capistrano birds, but generally within two or three days of a given date. Occasionally they are decimated by late cold spells during which they starve to death because insects are not flying. Their food is wholly insect, including numbers of such crop destroyers as weevils and chinch bugs.

VOICE: An incessant chatter of husky creaking notes.

NEST: Generally a retort-shaped vessel of mud with a narrow protruding neck on the side as an entrance. Sometimes an open cup like the barn swallow's. Cliff swallows are gregarious, some colonies numbering thousands. Originally and to some extent still cliff dwellers, they have increased and spread into cliffless areas by nesting on buildings, under the eaves. They can easily be encouraged by nailing a narrow strip of wood just below the eaves to provide support for the nests, which the birds find hard to cement to painted wood. In some cases a mud supply must also be provided. The 4 or 5 eggs (.80 x .55) are creamy to pinkish-white, variously spotted with brown.

RANGE: (M.) Breeds from Nova Scotia, n. Ontario, n. Mackenzie, and n. Alaska south to c. Virginia, n. Alabama, Missouri, and Guatemala. Winters from s. Brazil south to c. Argentina.

Cave Swallow*   *Petrochelidon fulva*—⚹13

IDENTIFICATION: L. 5½. The pale reddish-brown throat without a black patch, the dark brown forehead, darker rump, and broad white streaking on the back readily separate this species from the cliff swallow.

HABITS: Still apparently dependent upon natural nest sites, this swallow is uncommon in south Texas, although possibly no more so than the barn and cliff swallows were before they began to nest on man-made structures. Its accidental occurrence on one of the Florida Keys with migrating swallows in early spring suggests that it may be to some extent migratory.

NEST: In caves or under overhanging cliffs; a bracketlike mud cup attached to the wall or built into a crevice. The nest, unlike the cliff swallow's, is well lined with grass, roots, and feathers. Occasionally nests are found in abandoned buildings. The 4 eggs (.77 x .55) are like the cliff swallow's.

RANGE: (M.) Breeds from s.c. Texas south to s. Mexico and on all the Greater Antilles. Range at other seasons unknown.

Purple Martin

Progne subis—※12

IDENTIFICATION: L. 8. Females and young differ from males in their duller blue backs with patches of dark gray and their gray under parts, which become lighter toward the belly. In flight these martins continuously alternate between flapping and sailing. Their broad-based triangular wings are distinctive.

HABITS: Martins may nest in any good agricultural country if boxes are provided, but there are puzzling gaps in their distribution, and many seemingly ideally situated boxes stay unoccupied year after year. In many sections they have become the most domestic of wild birds. Through community interest in putting up boxes some towns have become famous for their martin population. In some cases thriving colonies have been established on the busiest street in town. In fall the birds form enormous temporary roosts before leaving for South America; when these are in village shade trees the martins become less popular for a few weeks. Flying insects and a few from the ground are the martin's food. Some observers have noted a great appetite for eggshells.

VOICE: A rich low-pitched chirruping composed of liquid gurgling notes of varying pitch. This is often given in flight and serves to identify birds passing overhead.

NEST: Originally in holes and cavities in trees, cliffs, and among loose rocks. The early settlers found the Indians putting gourds on a tall pole for the martins and copied them. Today most nesting is in artificial sites, the birds occupying anything from the simplest single-room box to elaborate 200-compartment houses, provided they are in the open and up on a 15- or 20-foot pole. The nest is a loose heap of grass and other debris piled into the cavity. A normal clutch is 4 or 5 dead-white eggs (.96 x .69).

RANGE: (M.) Breeds from Prince Edward Island, Quebec, Ontario, s. Manitoba, c. Alberta, and s. British Columbia south through the West Indies to Tobago and c. Mexico. Winters in the Amazon Valley of Brazil.

Gray-breasted Martin   *Progne chalybea*—✳12

IDENTIFICATION: L. 7. Both sexes look much like a female purple martin. An old male has upper parts of a dark steel blue which occasionally extends to the sides of the breast, but most young males and all females are dark sooty-gray above, faintly washed with blue. The best field marks for this species are the dark forehead and the clear white unstreaked belly, which is in sharp contrast to the gray breast. In the female purple martin the forehead is heavily speckled with pale gray and the under parts are well streaked with narrow dark gray lines that run through the centers of the gray breast feathers. Also the feathers of the lower breast lighten gradually and merge imperceptibly with the pale gray or dirty white of the belly instead of contrasting sharply.

HABITS: Human settlements seem to provide ideal habitats. During the breeding season the birds are found in towns and cities and near isolated rural dwellings. Later they appear to wander through more or less open country.

VOICE: A rather pleasant low twittering or warbling.

NEST: In the wild they probably nest like purple martins, but now that they are abundant in cities and towns most nesting is in rafters of open buildings, under eaves, and in bird boxes. The 3 to 5 eggs (.87 x .60) are white.

RANGE: (R.) Occurs from n. Mexico (probably s. Texas) south all over Central and South America to n. Argentina.

JAYS and CROWS   Family CORVIDAE

Canada Jay*   *Perisoreus canadensis*—✳7

IDENTIFICATION: L. 11½. This soft gray fluffy jay with its small bill looks very much like an oversized chickadee. Although the head pattern is variable, adults are unmistakable. Juveniles are a uniform sooty color, darkest above, becoming almost black about the head.

HABITS: Throughout its range the Canada jay is found almost exclusively in coniferous forests. As a scavenger it is much attracted by human activities, and from woodland camps it takes off and caches not only food but any small items that take its eye. This "camp robber" eats almost everything from baked beans (a special delicacy) to insects, seeds, fruits, and buds.

VOICE: The calls are varied. Most are pleasant and unjaylike, but a frequent one is a weak complaining or querulous cry. Another is a single clear whistle. The rallying cry is a loud *ka-whee* or *ka-we-ah*.

NEST: A bulky compact structure of twigs, bark strips, and much soft material, placed near the trunk and rather low (4 to 30 feet) in a dense conifer, occasionally in a willow. The center cup is thickly lined with fur, feathers, and similar material to help keep the eggs warm. This species often lays in February, when temperatures may be below zero. The usual clutch is 4 grayish eggs (1.12 x .80) evenly marked with dots and spots of olive-brown.

RANGE: (R.) Occurs from the northern limit of trees in Labrador, c. Quebec, n. Mackenzie, and n. Alaska south to Nova Scotia, New Hampshire, n. New York, c. Michigan, s.w. South Dakota, n. New Mexico, and n. California. In winter sometimes wanders as far south as Pennsylvania and Nebraska.

Blue Jay* *Cyanocitta cristata*—※7

IDENTIFICATION: L. 11¾. Young do not differ appreciablv from their parents.

HABITS: The big, noisy blue jay is one of the most colorful of the wild birds that have responded favorably to civilization and become common in the shade trees of eastern towns, but it is essentially a woodland creature and is still most abundant in open oak and beech forests. After breeding, jays gather in flocks that do much to enliven the fall woods with their calls and flashes of blue.

The blue jay is about three quarters vegetarian—acorns, beechnuts, and corn being its staple foods. During summer its diet becomes preponderantly insectivorous. Jays bury more acorns and beechnuts than they can eat and are therefore important agents in planting oak and beech forests.

VOICE: Extremely varied: harsh calls, a trumpeting whistle, a scream like a red-shouldered hawk, a flicker-like call, and a song of soft warbles and twitters.

NEST: In a tree crotch or on branches near the main trunk up about 10 or 15 feet; made of sticks with grass and other softer material at the center to form a cup. The 4 to 6 buff to greenish eggs (1.10 x .80) are spotted with brown, most heavily at the large end.

RANGE: (P.M.) Occurs from Newfoundland, Quebec, n. Manitoba, and s. Alberta south to Florida and the Gulf Coast, west to c. Texas and e. Colorado. There is a marked north-south movement, but some birds remain in all parts of the range throughout the year.

Scrub Jay* *Aphelocoma coerulescens*—※7

IDENTIFICATION: L. 11½. Scrub jays are long slender birds with long expressive tails. The gray back, light throat, and dark breastband are distinctive. Young birds are patterned like adults, except that blue is replaced by shades of gray and brownish-gray. The Florida race is smaller and duller with a darker throat.

HABITS: These noisy birds are often hard to see as they are never far from dense brush or scrub. In the West they occur in a variety of habitats from stream-bottom willow thickets to dry mountainside woodlands mixed with chaparral. In the piñon country they are found in juniper thickets and live largely on pine nuts. These jays do much of their feeding on the ground but disappear into brush at the first sign of danger.

The range of the Florida race, formerly regarded as a distinct species (Florida jay), is separated by more than 1,000 miles from the range of the nearest western race, a curious situation paralleled by the Florida burrowing owl, Florida sandhill crane, and Audubon's caracara, except that all the latter species also occur in Cuba, where the scrub jay is unknown.

VOICE: Their calls are varied, but most are distinctive. The commonest are emphatic and abrupt 1- or 2-note calls uttered in a loud, harsh voice. Some are much like those of a boat-tailed grackle. Their song of soft, musical notes and trills is seldom heard.

NEST: A fairly bulky structure composed of sticks and lined with rootlets; placed in a dense bush or small tree from 2 to 12 feet from the ground. The normal clutch is 4 buffy to greenish eggs (1.05 x .80) with dark brown or greenish-brown spots.

RANGE: (R.) Occurs in the Florida peninsula and from s. Wyoming and s. Washington south to s. Mexico and from w. Nebraska and c. Texas west to the Pacific.

Green Jay*

Xanthoura yncas—❋7

IDENTIFICATION: L. 11½. Both sexes wear the same plumage, and young birds are similar but paler.

HABITS: This is a bird of dry thickets and forests with dense undergrowth. Like most jays, these are found in small flocks outside the breeding season, when they often wander into more open country around towns and ranches. Green jays have the family curiosity that prompts all jays to gather for a look when any unusual visitor invades their territory. A lone jay is often furtive, but backed by companions, it becomes bold and fearless. Green jays feed on insects, seeds, and fruits, and are very fond of corn.

VOICE: Their calls vary from harsh screams to more musical whistles. They are noisy birds and make their presence known by their calls.

NEST: Five to 15 feet from the ground in a bush or small tree in a thicket; a typical jay nest loosely made of thorny twigs and lined with fine rootlets. Four grayish eggs (1.05 x .80) thickly spotted with brown are the normal clutch.

RANGE: (R.) Occurs from the lower Rio Grande Valley of Texas and Jalisco south to Peru and Venezuela.

Black-billed Magpie*

Pica pica—❋7

IDENTIFICATION: L. 20, T. 10. This striking black-and-white-backed bird with its enormous tail and partly white wings is unique. Young birds have white spots on the black throat and upper breast, and their white markings are washed with sooty.

HABITS: Thickets lining the banks of watercourses through open western country are the home of this magpie, but it ranges over croplands, pastures, and sagebrush. The birds are seldom seen except in flocks. If not molested they are

frequent visitors around farm and ranch buildings. Their
food is chiefly animal, large insects being the most important single item, but they take mice, snakes, young
birds and eggs, carrion, fruit, and waste grain.

VOICE: The magpies' calls range from harsh *cacks* to mellow
whistles. In captivity they imitate human speech. They are
always noisy, and a flock keeps up a steady chatter.

NEST: A huge mass of coarse sticks with an opening in both
sides leading to a cup of fine twigs, grasses, and rootlets
cemented with mud and lined with fine grass and hair. Magpies breed in loose colonies. Streamside willow thickets
are preferred sites. Nests may be almost on the ground or
as high as 50 feet. The 5 to 9 eggs (1.25 x .90) are evenly
and heavily marked with brown.

RANGE (R.) Northern Hemisphere. In North America from s.
Manitoba, c. Alberta, c. Yukon, and s. Alaska south to n.
Arizona and n.w. Texas; from Kansas and the Dakotas
west to the Sierra and Cascade mountains. In winter
wanders casually east to Illinois.

Common Raven*   *Corvus corax*—❊7

IDENTIFICATION: L. 25. The common raven is the largest passerine bird. Its wingspread is more than 4 feet against the
3 or less of the common crow. It has a longer, heavier bill,
a more triangular head, a rough shaggy throat, and long
central tail feathers which make the tail appear rounded at
the end. In flight it seldom holds a steady course but turns
from side to side and sails at frequent intervals. When
overhead a bulge in the head near the base of the bill is
noticeable. In flight the wings break sharply at the
shoulder, the primaries tend to fan out until they separate,
and when the bird sails the wings are held flat, not up in
a V like a crow's.

HABITS: These ravens seem most at home along seacoasts and
large rivers and in rugged mountainous country. In the

North, where they are valued as scavengers and not molested, they are village birds, but farther south they retire
from settled areas. They learn the range of a gun quickly
and take no chances, but their scavenging habits make
them frequent victims of baited traps and poisoned car-
casses.

During the breeding season ravens are solitary. They
seem to pair for life and use the same nest site year after
year. Cliffs are preferred, and the birds often nest in close
association with cliff-nesting falcons. Excellent fliers, they
are prone to such aerial acrobatics as wing overs, dives,
and tumbles. They can soar and hover like a hawk and
seem to revel in mock combat with hawks and other large
birds. Crows frequently call attention to the presence of a
raven by mobbing it as they do hawks and owls. In the fall
there is a movement to better feeding grounds toward the
seacoast or southward, and ravens are occasionally seen
along the main hawk flyways. In winter they often feed
and travel in small flocks and, when abundant, spend the
night in communal roosts.

Ravens are essentially scavengers and compete with gulls
and vultures in cleaning up dead animals and picking up
refuse. When nesting near large bird colonies they prey
heavily on eggs and young. Berries are eaten in the fall and
in the spring, like gulls, ravens will follow the plow for
insects. Small mammals—mice, lemmings, rabbits, and
young seals—are caught, often through the co-operative
efforts of the pair. Again like gulls, ravens have learned to
drop shellfish from a height to break them open.

VOICE: Ravens have a wide vocabulary, varying from the well-
known deep, harsh, guttural croak to rich, almost bell-like
gurgling notes. The croak, their commonest call, distinguishes them from a crow.

NEST: A thick mass of heavy sticks 3 to 4 feet across with a
cup in the center of such soft material as fur, hair, moss,
lichens, or seaweed. The site may be a protected cliff

ledge or a tree, generally a conifer, where the nest is lodged in a main crotch as near the top as possible. The 4 or 5 greenish eggs (1.90 x 1.28) may be heavily or lightly spotted with brown. The bird is an early nester.

RANGE: (R.) Northern Hemisphere. In North America from n. Greenland, the Arctic islands, and n.w. Alaska south to coastal Maine, n. Georgia, Michigan, North Dakota, and Nicaragua.

White-necked Raven*   *Corvus cryptoleucus*—✳7

IDENTIFICATION: L. 20. This bird has all the typical raven characteristics but is not much larger than a crow. It looks black unless the neck and breast feathers are ruffed up to show their white bases. Young birds have the base of the mandible pale pink and lack the pointed feathers that give the throats of the adults such a rough appearance. The voice is the best field character.

HABITS: This raven is a bird of level short-grass country and adjacent desert scrub. Solitary nesters, they become gregarious after breeding and gather at night into large roosts in the brush. They move southward in fall and spend the winter in flocks that are sometimes enormous. They show little fear of man and visit towns and villages to feed in streets and yards.

Their food is about half animal and half vegetable—insects, especially grasshoppers and worms; carrion and wild fruits, plus cultivated crops like grain sorghum, corn, peanuts, and melons.

VOICE: Guttural croaks deeper than a crow's but less resonant and not as deep as those of its larger relative.

NEST: The birds use any bush, tree, or artificial structure that enables them to get the nest as far off the ground as possible. This may be 4 or 40 feet. Usually the nest is quite conspicuous in the open country which they inhabit. Nests, used year after year, are loosely built of thorny twigs, with an inner cup lined with bark shreds, wool, or moss. The bird nests late. Five to 7 greenish eggs (1.75 x 1.20) with longitudinal purple streaks overlaid with brown spots are a normal clutch.

RANGE: (P.M.) Breeds from c. Texas, New Mexico, and Arizona south to c. Mexico. Winters from s. Texas and southern border of New Mexico and Arizona south.

Common Crow*   *Corvus brachyrhynchos*—⚹7

IDENTIFICATION: L. 19 (remember this length and use it as a yardstick to measure other birds). The common crow is distinguished by its deep, steady wingbeat. The bird often looks as if it were rowing through the air.

HABITS: The changes wrought by civilization have been almost wholly favorable to the common crow. Croplands replacing forests give year-round feeding grounds, and scattered forest remnants provide ideal nesting sites, while in the former grasslands man has provided both food and nest trees.

When the breeding season is over crows begin to gather in flocks, and in fall the more northern birds move south-ward. In winter communal roosts are established where from 5,000 to 200,000 birds gather for the night. During the day they travel out as much as 50 miles to feed.

The common crow eats quantities of insects, both as adults and as larvae. Its staple winter food is waste corn, and the cornfield acreage of an area roughly determines the number of wintering crows. The birds are omnivorous: as opportunity presents they eat carrion, shellfish, mice, reptiles, wild fruit, seeds, nuts, and the eggs and young of birds. They are often persecuted because of these much-exaggerated depredations. Actually there is no proof that any species of bird is less numerous because of the crow.

VOICE: Everyone knows the adult's *ca-ah, ca-ah, ca-ah*. Young crows have a different squawk-like call and adults are capa-

ble of a variety of calls at various pitches. These should be
learned so they will not be mistaken for those of a raven or
fish crow.

NEST: Usually in woods well up in a tree but occasionally as
low as 6 feet. Sometimes in an isolated tree or bush. The
large, well-built nest is made of sticks and lined with soft
material. The 3 to 5 greenish eggs (1.65 x 1.19) are irregularly blotched with brown. Crow nests weather well
and are often used in subsequent years by other birds, like
long-eared owls and various hawks.

RANGE: (P.M.) Breeds from Newfoundland, s. Quebec, n.
Manitoba, s.w. Mackenzie, and c. British Columbia south
through Florida, the Gulf Coast, New Mexico, and n.
Lower California. Winters from extreme s. Canada south.

Fish Crow*   *Corvus ossifragus*—※7

IDENTIFICATION: L. 17. The fish crow is much slimmer, has
more pointed wings, and is smaller than a common crow.
Its note is its best field character. The longer, more squawk-
like call of a young common crow should not be confused
with the short, abrupt call of this species. Habitat, gregariousness, soaring, and hovering help identification.

HABITS: The fish crow is a bird of low coastal country, but it
also frequents rivers, swamps, and lakes for some distance
inland. It is found almost everywhere in Florida. Fish crows
are at all seasons more gregarious than the common crow.
In winter their enormous night roosts are often shared with
their larger relative. The fish crow sails almost as much as
a raven and often hovers in one place as it looks for food
on the surface of the water.

It is always in evidence around nesting colonies of
southern water birds, as it is very fond of eggs. It eats
insects, corn, and many kinds of wild fruits, but much of
its food is gleaned along the shore and in the tidal marshes,
where it obtains marine and aquatic organisms of all kinds.

VOICE: The call is a short, hoarse *kock*, closer to a black-crowned night heron's *quowk* than to a common crow's *caw*. A 2-note *ob-ob* is frequent.

NEST: Small breeding colonies are usually formed in favorable sites. Nests may be high in deciduous trees in swamp woodlands or lower in clumps of hollies, cedars, or pines near the coast. The nest is compactly built of sticks and lined with bark shreds, often pine needles, and sometimes hair. The 4 or 5 eggs (1.50 x 1.10) are like the ordinary crow's in color.

RANGE: (P.M.) Breeds along the Atlantic and Gulf coasts from s. Connecticut south to Florida and west to e. Texas. In fall there is a considerable southward movement, but some birds winter around New York City. In spring a few get as far north as Massachusetts.

TITMICE   Family PARIDAE

Black-capped Chickadee*   *Parus atricapillus*—✻15

IDENTIFICATION: L. 5¼. The black cap separates this species from the more northern brown-headed chickadee. The narrow white feather edges which give the folded wing a finely striated look and the white tipped lower throat feathers which effect a gradual transition from the black of the throat to the white of the breast are the only plumage differences between it and the Carolina chickadee. In the field the difference in voice is the best means of identification.

HABITS: In summer this is a woodland species, but it often ranges into adjacent orchards and shade trees. Later the birds roam more widely in small noisy flocks that are often joined by other birds. Their easily whistled notes, a kiss on the back of the hand, or a screech owl imitation attracts them. They come readily to window-shelf feeders baited with sunflower seeds, suet, or peanut butter. Their natural food is chiefly insects—adults and larvae in summer, eggs and pupae in winter—plus some wild berries, seeds, and fruits.

VOICE: This bird was named after its best-known call, a rapid *chick-a-dee*. The final *dee* is usually a series of 3 to 10 notes. Another call is a slower softly whistled *dee-dee*, the first note higher than the second.

NEST: Typically a cavity excavated by the birds in the center of a very rotten birch or pine stump, the entrance 1 to 10 feet aboveground. Natural cavities, old woodpecker holes, and bird boxes up to 50 feet high are also used. The cavity is filled with moss, plant downs, fur, and feathers. Six to 8 white eggs (.60 x .48) lightly speckled with brown are normal, but 10 is not unusual.

RANGE: (P.M.) The Northern Hemisphere. In North America from Newfoundland, c. Quebec, n. Ontario, c. Mackenzie, and c. Alaska south to n. New Jersey, North Carolina (mts.), Indiana, s. Missouri, n. New Mexico, and n.w. California. In winter south to Maryland and c. Texas.

Carolina Chickadee*   *Parus carolinensis*—※15

IDENTIFICATION: L. 4½. This small southern chickadee has a relatively shorter tail and larger bill, more uniformly gray wings, and a sharper line of separation between the black of the throat and the white of the breast than the black-capped. The extra notes in the *dee-dee* call are the best field character.

HABITS: The Carolina chickadee is more closely confined to woodlands and is more sedentary than the black-capped. Moths and their larvae and eggs, acorns and poison-ivy berries are the most important animal and vegetal foods. Despite the remarkable similarities between this bird and the preceding, the boundary between their ranges is sharply defined, and apparent hybrids are uncommon.

Voice: The *chick-a-dee* is more hurried and at a higher pitch than a black-capped's. Instead of giving a simple, clear, whistled *dee-dee*, the Carolina doubles each note to *tsee-dee, tsee-dee* or *dee-tsee, dee-tsee,* the *tsee* softly whispered and lower.

Nest: Nesting habits, nest, and eggs are essentially like the black-capped's, but this species is a little more likely to choose a wet woodland for nesting.

Range: (R.) Occurs from c. New Jersey, c. Ohio, c. Missouri, and n. Oklahoma south to Florida and the Gulf Coast to c. Texas.

Brown-capped Chickadee*   *Parus hudsonicus*—✳15

Identification: L. 4¾. Its brown cap, rich brown flanks, and distinctive *chick-a-dee* give all the field characteristics one needs.

Habits: The vast northern forests to the limit of trees is the year-round home of these delicate-appearing little birds. They seem equally at home in conifers, birches, and streamside willow thickets. In fall and winter they wander through the woods accompanied by black-capped chickadees, nuthatches, and woodpeckers. At times there is a southward movement, but it is erratic. Their food is chiefly tree-infesting insects, plus some fruit and the seeds of conifers and birches. It is amazing that these tiny birds can get enough food in a northern winter day of only a few hours to enable them to survive the sub-zero temperatures of the long nights when they cannot refuel themselves.

Voice: This species says *chick-a-dee* in a weak, husky voice, with each phrase drawn out and slurred downward. It has a number of distinctive *chip* notes uttered in a sharp, petulant tone. It also has a short warbled song.

Nest: In a natural cavity, woodpecker hole, or a hole dug by the birds in a rotten stump at a height of from 1 to 10 feet aboveground. The eggs are closely held in a mass of moss, bark shreds, and fur. Five to 7 white eggs (.61 x .50) sparingly speckled with reddish-brown are normal.

RANGE: (R.) Occurs from Labrador, c. Mackenzie, and n.w. Alaska south to Maine, n. New York, c. Ontario, c. Manitoba, and s. British Columbia.

Tufted Titmouse*   *Parus bicolor*—#15

IDENTIFICATION: L. 6. The crest and brown flanks are the best field marks. The Carolina wren repeats a similar series of identical phrases, but its voice is richer and the phrases always 3-noted.

HABITS: The tufted titmouse is seldom far from woodland and in the breeding season shows a preference for moist bottom lands and swamps. If shade trees are dense it may be common in residential areas. In winter it wanders over the countryside in the company of chickadees, kinglets, and other small birds. Titmice feed like chickadees, working twigs, buds, and bark for insect egg masses and pupae. Their most important food in summer is caterpillars, in winter beechnut and acorn mast.

VOICE: A series of 4 to 8 clear, whistled phrases consisting of a high followed by a lower note, rarely the reverse. The phrases vary from *peter* or *peta* to *wheedle* or *daytee,* but all in a series are the same. The titmouse is a loud, persistent singer the year round.

NEST: In any natural cavity in a tree, in an old woodpecker hole, or a bird box, the height ranging from 3 to 90 feet. The cavity is stuffed with leaves, bark shreds, and moss; the center cup padded with hair, string, or rags and, quite often, a cast-off snakeskin. The 5 to 6 white eggs (.73 x .65) are evenly speckled with fine brown dots.

RANGE: (R.) Occurs from New Jersey, Ohio, Illinois, and Nebraska south to s. Florida, the Gulf Coast, and c. Texas.

Black-crested Titmouse* *Parus atricristatus*—❋15

IDENTIFICATION: L. 5½. The color of the forehead is always distinctive although it varies from pure white to deep brown, possibly as a result of hybridization with the tufted titmouse. The black crest feathers of females and young are gray-tipped, but the crest is always darker than the tufted's.

HABITS: This bird is common wherever trees are reasonably plentiful. It behaves and feeds like the tufted titmouse and is equally noisy.

VOICE: A monotonous whistled repetition of a short 1-note call—*pete* or *hew*.

NEST: In a cavity from 3 to 20 feet up in a tree or fence post, or in a woodpecker hole or bird box, wherever there is timber. The nest is the usual titmouse collection of soft materials from a variety of sources and generally includes a snakeskin. The 4 to 7 white eggs (.67 x .51) are spotted with brown.

RANGE: (R.) Occurs from c. Texas east almost to Louisiana and south to e.c. Mexico.

Verdin* *Auriparus flaviceps*—❋16

IDENTIFICATION: L. 4¼. The female is slightly duller than the male, but both are unmistakable. Young birds lack yellow or brown and are a uniform brownish-gray above, paler below. Bush tits are similar but have longer tails and a different voice.

HABITS: The verdin seems to have no need of water either for drinking or bathing. Although commoner in dense thickets, it is found in arid country wherever scattered thorny desert shrubs and cacti occur. Its frequent associates are cactus wrens, curve-billed thrashes, and horned toads. Insects and berries, for which it forages like a chickadee, seem to be its sole foods.

VOICE: The song, which carries a long way, is a series of 3 or 4 clear, whistled notes on the same pitch. Its numerous calls are chickadee-like sequences rapidly uttered and run together. While feeding, mated birds keep together with a frequent loud "slip" note.

NEST: A large (up to 8 inches) ball-like mass of thorny twigs woven around a fork near the end of a branch. The entrance is in the side, and the center is lined first with leaves and grasses, then stuffed with feathers. The nests are from 2 to 20 feet up in low trees or shrubs. In addition, individual birds build similar but often smaller (3-inch) nests in which they spend winter nights. The 4 or 5 pale bluish-green eggs (.58 x .43) are marked with scattered brown dots.

RANGE: (R.) Occurs from s. Texas, s.e. New Mexico, s.w. Utah, and s. California south through n. Mexico.

NUTHATCHES   Family SITTIDAE

White-breasted Nuthatch*   *Sitta carolinensis*—☀14

IDENTIFICATION: L. 6. The habit of creeping down tree trunks headfirst distinguishes the nuthatches. The solid black cap (sometimes gray in females or young) and the under parts, which are clear white except for an inconspicuous rusty wash on the flanks and under tail coverts, are good field marks.

HABITS: This species frequents large trees in forests, orchards, and towns. The birds seem to stay paired for life and to maintain a winter as well as a breeding territory, though in winter they sometimes join mixed bands of chickadees and kinglets as they forage through the woods. Nuthatches obtain most of their food on the trunks and larger branches of trees. Insect eggs, pupae, and hibernating adults which they find in the crevices of bark are their winter mainstays, but they also eat seeds, acorns, fruits, and feeding-station suet.

VOICE: Throughout the year both sexes constantly utter a distinctive nasal *yank*. The rarely heard spring song is a series of about a dozen low notes whistled on the same key.

NEST: In a cavity at almost any height aboveground. Rotted-out knotholes or similar natural openings seem preferred, but old woodpecker holes are used. Occasionally the birds excavate their own hole or use a bird box. The cavity is lined first with twigs, bark shreds, grass, and leaves, the eggs being laid on an inner lining of fur and feathers. The 5 or 6 eggs (.75 x .56) are lightly speckled with red-brown and pale purple.

RANGE: (R.) Occurs from s. Quebec, c. Ontario, s. Manitoba, and s. British Columbia south to Florida, the Gulf Coast, and s. Mexico.

Red-breasted Nuthatch*   *Sitta canadensis*—✳14

IDENTIFICATION: L. 4½. The small size, the white line over the eye, and the extensively brown under parts are distinctive. Females and young have slate-gray rather than black head markings and are paler below.

HABITS: This active little bird is a resident of northern evergreen forests. The seeds of conifers seem to be its important winter food, and its periodic southward flights are presumed to be correlated with a scarcity of such seeds. In the South it also feeds on insects in the bark of deciduous trees but continues to prefer conifer seeds. The birds are commonly found among the finer twigs and branches of treetops. They like suet, nutmeats, and sunflower seeds and will carry food off and hide it in holes and bark crevices.

VOICE: The call is an *ank,* more abrupt, nasal, and high-pitched than a white-breasted's. The song is a rapid series of short musical notes with a tin-horn quality.

NEST: Usually in a hole which the birds excavate at almost any height in the soft wood of a dead stub. They may use an old woodpecker hole, natural cavity, or bird box. The 5 or 6 white eggs (.60 x .50) are rather heavily spotted with red-brown.

RANGE: (P.M.) Breeds from Newfoundland, s. Quebec, n. Manitoba, c. Yukon, and s.e. Alaska south to Massachusetts, s.w. North Carolina (mts.), Michigan, Colorado, and s. California. In winter moves south in varying numbers and occasionally reaches n. Florida, the Gulf Coast, and n. Mexico.

Brown-headed Nuthatch*　　　　*Sitta pusilla*—※14

IDENTIFICATION: L. 4¼. The brown head and white nape spot are diagnostic. Young birds are duller, the head gray-brown to gray and the sides brown.

HABITS: Although found in all types of open woodland from cypress to scrub oak, this species is most abundant in pine. Decaying snags in burns and clearings attract them, and they often feed in young seedling pines on abandoned farmland. After the breeding season they form bands of 6 to 20 individuals and roam noisily through the woods with woodpeckers, kinglets, and titmice. They commonly forage from the main stem of a tree to the topmost branch tips. Pine seeds and many kinds of insects appear to be their food.

VOICE: Nasal, but much reedier and harsher than that of the two preceding species. The various notes are too numerous to describe: some are like a chickadee's, others like a gold-finch's. The birds generally keep up a stream of chirping, twittering, and hissing. The commonest sound is a 3-note call.

NEST: At any height, but normally 4 to 10 feet up in a dead tree stump or fence post. The birds excavate the hole and line it with bark shreds, fur, feathers, and pine-seed wings. The 5 or 6 white or creamy eggs (.62 x .49) are heavily spotted with shades of red-brown.

RANGE: (R.) Occurs from s. Delaware, Kentucky, and s. Missouri south to Grand Bahama, the Gulf Coast, and e. Texas.

CREEPERS   Family CERTHIIDAE

Brown Creeper*   *Certhia familiaris*—⚹15

IDENTIFICATION: L. 5½. The creeper's habit of spiraling up a tree trunk, then dropping to the base of another to repeat the process, is distinctive. Its slim curved bill is a good point to note.

HABITS: Mature forests are the favored home, but the birds occur in most well-wooded regions either as breeders or winter visitors. The dense growth in wooded swamps, together with the greater frequency of dead trees with hanging strips of loose bark, attracts them to such areas for breeding. In migration and on its wintering grounds almost any tree will do, in or out of a forest, and at such times they are often fairly gregarious. Frequently small bands of creepers work through the winter woods with a sociable assemblage of chickadees, kinglets, and woodpeckers. They seem largely insectivorous, but they like suet.

VOICE: The year-round call notes are a faint single, short, kinglet-like lisp and a rather long, thin, high-pitched, rolling trill. The song is a variable 5- or 6-note jumble of long-and-short, somewhat musical, but high, thin notes with a hissing quality.

NEST: Generally not far aboveground against the trunk of a dead tree underneath a strip of loose bark. Occasionally in a rotted-out cavity or old woodpecker hole. The nest is made of bark shreds, moss, sticks, and feathers. The 6 or 7 white eggs (.58 x .48) are sparsely scattered with fine brown spots.

RANGE: (P.M.) Breeds throughout a large part of the Northern Hemisphere. In North America from Nova Scotia, c. Ontario, s. Manitoba, and c. Alaska south to Massachusetts, North Carolina (mts.), n. Indiana, e. Nebraska, and in the western mts. south to n. Nicaragua. Winters south to s. Florida, the Gulf Coast, and c. Texas.

WRENS   Family TROGLODYTIDAE

House Wren*   *Troglodytes aedon*—\#16

IDENTIFICATION: L. 4¾. The house wren's best characteristic is its lack of distinctive markings. It is dull gray-brown above, dull white below, with a moderately long tail and no pronounced eyeline.

HABITS: This wren does most of its feeding in low woody vegetation, preferably deciduous, and is found in brushy areas on the edges of woodland, in sunny openings within the forest, and in the East near human dwellings when suitable growths and nest-site cavities are present. Its food consists wholly of small insects.

With few exceptions, all breeding birds defend an area about the nest from intrusion by others of their kind. This area, or territory, varies from a few inches in colonial nesters to a quarter of a mile or more with hawks. Generally the presence of other species is ignored, even when they, too, are nesting, but the house wren occasionally breaks the rule and punctures the eggs or kills the young in the nests of other birds within its domain.

VOICE: Wrens are great scolders, and this species utters a deep, grating chatter. Its song is a long series of short, not very musical notes poured out in a rapid burst that suddenly rises and then falls. It is a persistent singer, but the effect is remarkable more for bubbling energy than beauty.

NEST: Under wild conditions the site is a tree hollow or old woodpecker hole. Now a bird box or almost any sort of cavity about a building seems preferred. The entrance is seldom more than 10 feet aboveground. Sticks, grass, and other debris are stuffed into the enclosed space until a small hollow, lined generally with softer material, is left for the 6 to 8 white eggs (.65 x .50), which are thickly speckled with fine brown dots.

RANGE: (M.) Breeds from New Brunswick, s. Ontario, s. Manitoba, c. Alberta, and s. British Columbia south to w. South Carolina, Kentucky, s. Missouri, c.w. Texas, s. Arizona, and n. Lower California. Winters from South Carolina, the Gulf States, Texas, and California south to s. Florida and s. Mexico.

Winter Wren*   *Troglodytes troglodytes*—⚹16

IDENTIFICATION: L. 4. The very short tail and dark barred belly of this tiny wren are distinctive, as are its continuous nervous babbling and its habit of cocking its tail over its back.

HABITS: In summer the winter wren is found in the depths of coniferous woodlands, in swamps, at streamsides, and in other cool, moist spots. It obtains its insect food among fallen logs, brush piles, and tangles of low shrubbery near the ground. In the deciduous woodlands which it visits at other seasons it is found in similar locale. When not in song it is so secretive that it is often overlooked. In marked contrast to our many wrens, Europe has only this one species.

VOICE: The alarm notes are a short single or double high-pitched *tick* or a longer *crrrrrip*. The song has great beauty and remarkable length. The high-pitched notes, uttered rapidly, rise and fall to produce a clear, melodious, and bubbling warble broken by 1 or more trills.

NEST: The most favored location is in a recess in the upturned root mass of a fallen tree. Other sites are under stream banks, among fallen logs or the roots of old trees. A bulky mass of twigs and moss with the entrance on the side; the center is lined with feathers and fur. The 5 or 6 eggs (.69 x .50) are sparingly to well speckled with brown dots.

RANGE: (M.) Much of the Northern Hemisphere. In North America it breeds from Newfoundland, n. Ontario, s. Manitoba, s. Alberta, s. Alaska, and the Pribilof Islands south to Massachusetts, n. Georgia (mts.), c. Michigan, c. Minnesota, n. Colorado, and c. California. Winters from s. New England, s. Michigan, Iowa, Colorado, and s. British Columbia south to c. Florida, the Gulf Coast, s. New Mexico, and s. California.

Bewick's Wren* *Thryomanes bewickii*—※16

IDENTIFICATION: L. 5¼. Its slim shape and long fanlike, white-tipped tail which it constantly flirts from side to side are its best field marks.

HABITS: This wren likes the varied landscape which general farming produces—brush piles, thickets, and fence rows with an abundance of good nest sites about the buildings. Sometimes it is the commonest bird of urban residential areas. In wild country it frequents open or sparsely wooded land, provided there is a dense undergrowth of scrubby trees or shrubs. It depends wholly upon insects and seldom feeds far from the ground.

In parts of the Midwest this species appears to be extending its range northward at the expense of the house wren. Neither will tolerate the other on its breeding territory. In areas that have recently become warm enough or have been otherwise altered so Bewick's can remain through the winter, the birds stake out their territorial claim long before the arrival of the migrant house wren, and this seems to give them a critical advantage in the struggle.

VOICE: Call, a single or double *plit.* Alarm notes are a series of low, buzzy sounds. The highly variable song is often loud (carries ¼ to ½ mile), clear, and melodious, suggesting those of the lark and song sparrows.

NEST: In the wild, in knothole openings, old woodpecker nests, and dense brush piles. Around buildings, in tin cans, in coats, hats, or baskets hung in sheds, in openings behind loose boards, or almost anywhere else that provides a suitable cavity. The nest, which is open on top, fills the cavity. It is made of sticks, leaves, and other debris, finished off with a deep cup of feathers and other soft material. The 5 to 7 white eggs (.66 x .50) are irregularly marked with brown dots.

RANGE: (P.M.) Breeds from c. Pennsylvania, s. Michigan, s. Nebraska, s. Utah, and s. British Columbia south to w. South Carolina, c. Alabama, c. Arkansas, and s. Mexico. In winter wanders south to c. Florida and the Gulf Coast.

Carolina Wren*   *Thryothorus ludovicianus*—✳16

IDENTIFICATION: L. 5¾. This large chunky wren is redder above than any other and buffy below, especially on the flanks.

HABITS: Woodland thickets, stream-bank tangles, fallen tree-tops, and rocky brush-grown slopes are favorite haunts. Like the Bewick's and house wrens, this species becomes common about dwellings in some regions, but in others shows little tendency to adapt itself to such environment. Insects, plus a few berries and seeds, like bayberry, poison ivy, sumac, and sweet gum, are its only known foods. The best way to see this or any other wren is to sit still and squeak on the back of one's hand. Before long the wren, bobbing up and down, waving its tail and scolding, comes to see what is going on.

Along the northern limit of its range the Carolina varies in abundance. Population pressure or a tendency to wander brings young birds north of where they were raised; if the winter is mild they survive to breed the following spring. Over a number of years this may result in a northward spread of many miles and the establishment of large colonies. Eventually, however, an especially severe winter wipes out the northern population, and the process starts all over again.

VOICE: This wren sings all year, all day, in all weather. The song consists of a highly variable 3- (occasionally 2-) note phrase like *toodlewee* or *tawee,* repeated rapidly 4 to 6 times in a loud, ringing whistle. A frequent call note is a long-drawn-out trill *chirrrrrrr.*

NEST: Although displaying the customary wren preference for cavities, this bird occasionally builds a ball-like nest of sticks with a side entrance to a center cavity lined with feathers. The nest may be in a tree or close to the ground in matted vegetation. More commonly the bird uses holes in trees, stumps, roots of fallen trees, and crannies about man-made structures. The 5 whitish eggs (.74 x .60) are variable but generally heavily spotted with browns.

RANGE: (R.) Occurs from Long Island, New York, s. Pennsylvania, and s. Iowa south to Florida, the Gulf Coast, and n. Mexico and west to e. Nebraska and c. Texas.

Cactus Wren*   *Heleodytes brunneicapillus*—⚹18

IDENTIFICATION: L. 8. This big wren looks more like a thrasher. The concentration of dark markings on the upper breast (less pronounced in young birds), the strong white eyeline, and the black-and-white barring of the outer tail feathers are diagnostic.

HABITS: These wrens are closely confined to arid areas where desert plants provide nest sites and refuge. The males sing from prominent perches and are easily seen. Although often abundant, there are not as many pairs in an area as one would assume from the nests. Generally each pair has several dummy nests besides the one currently in use for raising young or for night roosting. The cactus wren varies its insect diet with more seeds and fruits than most wrens and does most of its feeding on the ground.

VOICE: This wren sings the year round and is a persistent all-day singer. The song is an unmusical, accelerating series of uniform notes which sound something like grating stones. Its scolding calls are harsher.

NEST: A football- or retort-shaped mass of coarse to fine plant fibers lined in the center with fur or feathers and entered from the side; conspicuously placed in the tops of thorny desert shrubs or cactus. The 4 or 5 slightly buffy eggs (.95 x .65) are thickly but finely sprinkled with brown.

RANGE: (R.) Occurs from c. Texas, s. Utah, and s. California south to c. Mexico.

Long-billed Marsh-wren*
Telmatodytes palustris—✳16

IDENTIFICATION: L. 5. White-streaked backs distinguish the marsh-wrens. The solid, unstreaked crown bordered by a strong white eyeline, the larger size, the long, slender, curved bill and wetter habitat preference help to separate this from the short-billed species.

HABITS: These birds are found only where tall, coarse vegetation grows in shallow water over a fairly extensive area. Males are commonly polygamous, with 2 or more mates, the females being established in adjacent territories of about 1/3 acre each. The presence of other species within these territories is sometimes resented and their eggs punctured. Two broods are generally raised.

VOICE: When alarmed the birds give a series of grating notes run together in a chatter. The male's song is delivered from a reed or as it flutters in air on trembling wings. The song begins with a few scraping notes, then breaks into a loud, rapid, almost trill-like series of rattling notes, ending abruptly in a weak whistle. During the nesting season the birds sing endlessly in the darkness of early morning or late evening and through much of the day.

NEST: In cattails, bulrushes, tules, or other tall marsh plants growing in shallow water. The large coconut-shaped nest with its side entrance is lashed to the supporting stems and leaves at a height of from 1 to 3 feet. The outside is woven of long, coarse, water-soaked leaves. Inside, the material becomes finer and softer toward the center cavity, which is lined with feathers. While the female is building the actual nest the male may build a half dozen or so incomplete "dummy" nests. The 5 or 6 pale brownish eggs (.64 x .45) are heavily sprinkled with fine brown dots.

RANGE: (P.M.) Breeds from s. New Brunswick, s. Ontario, c. Manitoba, c. Alberta, and c. British Columbia south to c. Florida, the Gulf Coast, Texas, New Mexico, and n. Lower California. Winters from s. New Jersey, the Gulf States, c. Texas, Utah, and Washington south to s. Florida and c. Mexico.

Short-billed Marsh-wren*   *Cistothorus platensis*—⚹16

IDENTIFICATION: L. 4. Its smaller size and bill, streaked head, and more uniformly brownish appearance, without a sharply defined blackish area on the back, distinguish this species from the long-billed. However, song and habitat differences are safer field guides.

HABITS: Shallow sedge marshes and damp grassy meadows with little or no standing water but frequent scattered shrubs are the home of this, our smallest bird except for the hummingbirds. Its breeding habitat often lies between dry uplands and the cattail home of the long-billed. Favored areas are often densely colonized while others, equally appropriate, have few or no birds, and the population in any given area is apt to fluctuate from year to year. The birds can be flushed but are hard to observe, as they flutter only a short distance before dropping back into the grass.

VOICE: The call note, a short, high *tick*, is easily recognized. The weak, dry, unmusical song opens with several deliberate notes which change to a series of rapid, falling notes that accelerate to a buzzy trill at the end—*chap-chap-chap-chap-cherrrrrrr*. The song is generally delivered from a fixed series of strategically located vantage points.

NEST: The inconspicuous, well-hidden nests are placed in thick growths, preferably of grasses or sedges, close to the ground. The ball-like structure with its small side entrance is made of dead and growing grass leaves and lined with finer material, including feathers and fur. Males, like long-billeds, construct numerous, apparently useless, "dummy" nests. The 7 eggs (.69 x .50) are pure white.

RANGE: (M.) Breeds from s. Maine, s. Ontario, c. Manitoba, and s.e. Saskatchewan south to n. Delaware, c. Indiana, c. Missouri, and e. Kansas. Winters from s. New Jersey and s. Illinois south to s. Florida, the Gulf Coast, and s. Texas.

Cañon Wren*   *Catherpes mexicanus*—✳16

IDENTIFICATION: L. 5½. The rich reddish-brown belly contrasting with the pure-white throat distinguishes this species from the equally spotted but much grayer-brown rock wren.

HABITS: The cañon or canyon wren is well named, as its favorite home is the steep, rocky side of a canyon, preferably one carrying water. A singing bird is often hard to pick out among the broken rocks, even when it is flooding the valley with music. The bird lives on insects and seems to do all its feeding on rock surfaces. In some places it has adopted stone buildings and is common in business and residential areas—fearlessly entering and even nesting in occupied houses.

VOICE: The song is a startlingly loud series of 7 to 12 silvery, bell-like whistles, beginning high and running down the scale to end in a low trill. The effect as these echo from the walls of a narrow canyon is startling.

NEST: In crevices in rock walls, on rock shelves in caves and overhangs, occasionally in cavities about buildings or under eaves. The flat, open-topped, cuplike nest is made of fibrous and soft material, like moss, catkins, wool, and feathers. The 5 or 6 white eggs (.70 x .52) are sparingly marked with fine reddish-brown dots.

RANGE: (R.) Occurs from c. Texas, n. Colorado, and s. British Columbia south to s. Mexico.

Rock Wren*   *Salpinctes obsoletus*—¾16

IDENTIFICATION: L. 5¾. The pale color, the faintly and finely streaked breast, and the broad black band near the end of the tail are the best field marks.

HABITS: Rocky barrens, talus slopes, bare outcrops, eroded badlands, and rough cliff walls exposed to full sunlight, often far from water, are the home of this wren. It seldom invades the shady, well-watered canyons where the cañon wren makes its home. In summer the birds range into high mountains, but many retire to lower levels in winter. They feed on rock surfaces and in crevices between rocks, where they find spiders and insects.

VOICE: The calls and songs are too varied for full description. Common calls are a loud *purr*-like trill and a *tick'-ear*. The song, which varies from harsh to sweet and musical, is

composed of 3 or 4 couplets or double syllables. It begins
slowly and accelerates toward the end.

NEST: Under rocks, in old rodent burrows, holes, and crevices about cliffs, rocky ledges, gully banks, and stone walls.
Less commonly in hollow logs and stumps or about buildings. The birds carefully pave the nest cavity with small,
flat rock chips or similar hard material, often extending
the entrance pathway for many feet. One bird used 1,665
pieces of stone, iron, shell, and bone for this purpose. The
nest is of plant stems and roots, lined with finer material
and finished off with fur and feathers. The 5 or 6 white
eggs (.72 x .54) are sprinkled with brown dots.

RANGE: (P.M.) Occurs from w.c. Saskatchewan and s. British
Columbia south to Guatemala and east to w. North Dakota and c. Texas.

MOCKINGBIRDS   Family MIMIDAE

Mockingbird*   *Mimus polyglottos*—✳18

IDENTIFICATION: L. 10 ½. A long-tailed, pale gray bird is apt
to be a mocker. The white wing patches and outer tail
feathers are distinctive but hard to see except in flight.
The Townsend's solitaire of the West is darker below, has
a white eye ring and a quite buffy wing patch.

HABITS: Our idea of what constitutes a pleasant, attractive
setting for a rural or suburban home seems to coincide
with a mockingbird's. It asks plenty of open area with a few
trees, dense shrubbery, and a variety of edible fruits.
Today mockers are commoner about towns and gardens
than in the wild, though they still occur in suitable brushy
spots on the edge of woodlands or in clearings. Their chief
foods are berries, seeds, and fruits (wild or cultivated),
supplemented by quantities of insects at certain seasons.
    The imitative ability of the mocker extends beyond

birds and often seems to include all common sounds of their environment, from the squeak of a wheel to the bark of a dog. The courtship performances are spectacular. The birds seem to establish a year-round territory which they defend not only against other birds but snakes, cats, and other potential enemies.

VOICE: The mocker has several harsh, grating calls. Its song is a medley of rich, melodious notes interspersed with harsher notes and imitations. Commonly each note is repeated, usually 3 times, before the bird shifts to another triple-noted phrase or imitation. Often the only way to distinguish the imitation from the real thing is that it is given 3 times in rapid succession. Occasionally a group of notes is repeated over and over before shifting to a phrase which is repeated a dozen or more times. Singing is usually from a high, conspicuous perch. It continues throughout the year but is most vigorous in spring, when the birds commonly sing through bright moonlight nights.

NEST: Generally about 4 to 12 feet up in a low tree or shrub; a bulky, loosely woven cup of sticks, stems, and trash. The 3 to 5 greenish to buffy eggs (.95 x .70) are blotched and spotted with brown.

RANGE: (R.) Occurs from Maryland, Ohio, s. Iowa, s. Wyoming, and c. California south to the Greater Antilles, the Gulf Coast, and s. Mexico. Rarely but regularly found as far north as s. Maine.

Catbird*   *Dumetella carolinensis*—※18

IDENTIFICATION: L. 9. There is no other black-capped, uniformly gray bird with brown under-tail coverts.

HABITS: The catbird's favorite wild environment is dense shrubbery and vine tangles near streams, ponds, and open alder swamps, but the brushy cut- or burned-over lands, hedgerows, field borders, and ornamental shrubbery of civilization have greatly expanded its range. Small fruits seem to be the preferred food, but before these ripen the birds eat insects. Young are almost wholly reared upon insects. If catbirds are in the neighborhood they are invariably the first to arrive in response to a squeak upon one's hand to call out the bird population.

VOICE: Its common call is a catlike, mewing scold; others are a soft cluck and a series of sharp, snapping notes. Like its 2 relatives, it can be a fine singer and imitator, but it does little repeating and is more apt to sing from a concealed perch in shrubbery than from an exposed one. Its softer song consists of short phrases of 5 or 6 different notes broken by pauses and interspersed with mews and imitations. It often sings on moonlight nights and is one of the birds that has a fall "song period," during which it gives a rather formless and usually barely audible "whisper" song.

NEST: From 4 to 8 feet aboveground in dense shrubbery or vines; a bulky, ragged mass of twigs, leaves, and stems lined with a well-made cup of fine fibers. The 4 to 6 eggs (.95 x .70) are an unmarked glossy blue-green; 2 broods are usually reared.

RANGE: (M.) Breeds from Nova Scotia, s. Ontario, s. Manitoba, and c. British Columbia south to c. Florida, s.e. Texas, n.e. New Mexico, n. Utah, n.e. Oregon, and w. Washington. Winters from the Gulf Coast to Cuba and Panama.

Brown Thrasher*   *Toxostoma rufum*—✳18

IDENTIFICATION: L. 11½. The thrasher's long curved bill, long tail, and brown streaked breast separate it from the thrushes.

HABITS: Dry thickets, brushy pastures, new second growth, and woodland borders and openings are the normal home. Willingness to accept similar habitats near dwellings varies in different parts of the country. Thrashers do most of their feeding on or near the ground, where they throw the dead leaves aside with their bills and dig into the soil for insects. Two thirds of their food is insects, the rest berries, mast (chiefly acorns), and grain.

VOICE: Common call notes are a hissing sound, a clicking noise, and a 3-note whistle. The loud, rich song resembles a mocker's, but the majority of the bold, abrupt phrases are doubled rather than tripled notes. The song is less frequently interspersed with obvious imitations than the mocker's or catbird's. Singing is usually from a conspicuous treetop perch.

NEST: Commonly from 1 to 5 feet up in a dense and preferably thorny shrub. Rarely are they higher and in New England especially they are often on the ground under dense cover. The nest is large and often of 4 concentric layers, the outer of coarse twigs, the next of leaves, the third of small twigs and stems, the lining of fine rootlets. The 4 or 5 pale blue eggs (1.08 x .80) are evenly covered with fine brown dots; 2 broods are usually reared.

RANGE: (P.M.) Breeds from n. Maine, s.e. Ontario, n. Michigan, and s. Alberta south to s. Florida and the Gulf Coast to e. Louisiana. Winters from North Carolina and s.e. Missouri to s. Florida and c.s. Texas.

Long-billed Thrasher*   *Toxostoma longirostre*—✳18

IDENTIFICATION: L. 11½. This species differs from a brown thrasher in its darker, less reddish upper parts, black breast streaks, and the grayer sides to the head and neck. The bill is longer and only slightly curved.

HABITS: These birds are found in greatest numbers in dense undergrowth in rich bottom-land forests, but they also inhabit the dry mesquite and cactus tangles of the uplands. They seem to be chiefly insectivorous but take some fruits.

VOICE: The call notes are higher-pitched and sharper than a brown thrasher's, but the song does not differ significantly.

NEST: From 4 to 8 feet aboveground in the heart of a thorny plant or thicket. The nest is very like those of its near relatives. The 4 eggs (1.07 x .78) are like a brown thrasher's.

RANGE: (R.) Occurs from the c. Gulf Coast of Texas, south through e. Mexico to Puebla.

Curve-billed Thrasher*   *Toxostoma curvirostre*—✳18

IDENTIFICATION: L. 11. Of the four dull gray and brown thrashers with curved bills, this is the only one that comes east of the one hundredth meridian. The faintly spotted breast and bright reddish eyes are its most distinctive field marks. The white wing bars and tail tips are generally but not always conspicuous.

HABITS: Dry, semi-arid open country with scattered clumps of cactus and mesquite is the typical home. The bird feeds on the ground, tossing aside loose objects and digging deep for insects, its chief food. It eats some fruit.

VOICE: Its common call is a sharp 2- or 3-note whistle, but it trills and chatters like a wren. The song is a clear, melodious carol broken into short phrases with little repetition of notes.

NEST: From 3 to 10 feet aboveground in the center of a cactus clump, especially cholla, or in other thorny plants; made of twigs and lined with rootlets and other fine fibers. The 4 pale blue-green eggs (1.15 x .80) are minutely speckled with brown; 2 or 3 broods are raised.

RANGE: (R.) Occurs from s. Texas, s. New Mexico, and s. Arizona south to s. Mexico.

Sage Thrasher*   *Oreoscoptes montanus*—✳18

IDENTIFICATION: L. 8¾. Although small and short-tailed, this bird uses its wings and tail in typical thrasher fashion. The white ends of the outer tail feathers and the streaked breast separate it from a thrush.

HABITS: The dry sagebrush plains are the typical summer home. The birds range into adjacent areas where bushy plants occur and in winter may be found in any area well provided with dense thickets. They feed on the ground, where they find such insects as locusts and beetles. In migration they display fondness for small fruits.

VOICE: A blackbird-like cluck and a high-pitched rally note are its commonest calls. The song is a pure-toned warble given from a high perch or on the wing. Seldom is there a pause as the notes pour out and as the song continues it becomes increasingly varied.

NEST: Occasionally on the ground but usually in a high bush, preferably armed with thorns. The loose, bulky nest is often partly arched over. It is made of coarse twigs and lined with grass and rootlets. The 4 or 5 deep blue-green eggs (.98 x .71) are boldly marked with brown blotches.

RANGE: (M.) Breeds from s. Saskatchewan and s. British Columbia south to n. New Mexico and s. California and east to w. Nebraska. Winters from s. Texas and s. California south through n. Mexico.

THRUSHES   Family TURDIDAE

Robin*   *Turdus migratorius*—❋18

IDENTIFICATION: L. 10. (Remember this length and use it as a yardstick in estimating other medium-sized birds.) Adults are unmistakable. Females are slightly duller and paler than males, and the head is not as black. Young in juvenile plumage reveal the thrush in them by the spots on their breasts. These are lost when they molt into their immature plumage, which is much like the adult's.

HABITS: The robin is a bird of sparsely wooded barrens, cut-over areas, forest borders, and openings. With the coming of civilization it has found shade trees, orchards, lawns, and fields ideal for nesting and feeding. In many places it seems to have developed an affinity for man; often every nest in an area is near a house. In residential sections robins frequently reach greater population densities than in the wild. Those concerned over the predations of house cats would do well to ponder this fact. Wild predators are virtually absent from such areas, and nothing indicates that house cats take more than a compensatory toll. Apparently enough young robins survive out of the 2 broods each pair attempts to rear to replace the adults that die during the year.

The robin's food is varied. It is fond of fruit, eats quantities of earthworms and grubs from the ground, and many insects in their adult stages. During migration robins assemble in large flocks and on wintering grounds establish night roosts, usually in a secluded swamp. In the South such roosts are often enormous, the birds scattering during the day to feed in small flocks on the fruits of sour gum, chinaberry, and hackberry.

Every spring newspapers carry accounts of crazy robins pecking windowpanes, automobile windshields or hubcaps, or other polished surfaces. Often the birds peck until exhausted. The explanation is simple: The robin is not crazy but deluded. It takes the reflected image for a rival male trespassing on its nesting territory, and anything that stops the reflections stops the pecking.

VOICE: The robin has a variety of scolding, alarm, and call notes. Some are loud and piercing. The most unexpected is a thin, high-pitched hissing. The loud caroling song is composed of 2- and 3-note phrases broken by pauses. It has a cheerful bubbling quality, and there is a distinct change in pitch in each phrase. At daybreak, the robin's favorite song period, the carol often continues for minutes at a time. It should be carefully memorized, as many other bird songs are described in terms of similarity to, or differences from, the robin's.

NEST: Anywhere from on the ground to treetops but commonly from 5 to 15 feet aboveground. A dense bush, a fork in a main branch of a tree, or a sheltered recess in a building are among preferred sites. Generally robins seek a place where the nest is sheltered from rain and saddled on a firm support. Possibly this is why evergreens are favored for first nests, while the nest for the second brood is often in a deciduous tree. The nest is of plant stems and trash cemented with mud, smoothed on the inside to form a solid mud cap. The 3 to 5 unmarked blue-green eggs (1.15 x .80) are laid on a lining of fine grass or similar material.

RANGE: (P.M.) Breeds from Newfoundland, n. Quebec, n. Manitoba, n. Mackenzie, and n.w. Alaska south to w. South Carolina, c. Alabama, Arkansas, and through Mexico to Guatemala. Winters in varying numbers as far north as s. Maine, s. Ontario, Nebraska, Wyoming, and s. British Columbia.

Gray's Thrush*   *Turdus grayi*—❋19

IDENTIFICATION: L. 10. The robin-like appearance and behavior should make this an easy bird to identify. The dark grayish streaks on the pale throat and the slightly greenish bill with yellowish edges are unlike any thrasher's. Juveniles are thickly but inconspicuously spotted with dusky below and have pale streaks above.

HABITS: This is an abundant species throughout most of Middle America. It avoids arid areas and dense forests unless there is abundant undergrowth. Elsewhere, near clearings, forest borders, orchards and plantations, streamside and urban shade trees, it is common. In spring it sings from treetops like a robin but at other seasons is quiet. After nesting it becomes gregarious and is often considered a game bird. It feeds on insects and fruits. It is very fond of figs.

Voice: Call, a robin-like *pup, pup, pup* but higher-pitched. The song is richer than a robin's, almost like an oriole's.

Nest: Usually from 3 to 12 feet high, firmly supported without concealment in a small tree. Its construction is robin-like. The 2 or 3 pale green-blue eggs (1.13 x .84") are thickly covered with fine rusty-brown dots.

Range: (R.) Occurs from extreme n.e. Mexico south to Panama. Has occurred as far north as the Rio Grande Valley.

Wood Thrush*   *Hylocichla mustelina*—❊19

Identification: L. 8. The large round dark spots running onto the sides and flanks, and the head, which is brighter reddish-brown than the rest of the body, are distinctive. The bird is heavier-bodied than other thrushes.

Habits: This thrush is found in greatest abundance in the low-lying, moister parts of deciduous woodlands with well-developed undergrowth, especially along streams, lake borders, and swamps, but it may occur almost anywhere in or near such woodlands. In many places it has invaded residential areas. It is found in the sections that are heavily shaded by tall trees, while the robin predominates in the sunnier, more open areas. Essentially a bird of the forest floor, the wood thrush seldom rises above the lower limbs of trees, even to sing. Much of its food is insects, the balance small fruits. Most food is obtained by scratching aside dead leaves on the ground.

Voice: Alarm note, a sharp, rapid, liquid *pit, pit, pit, pit*. Calls a low *tuck, tuck* and other single notes. The clear, liquid, flutelike song is similar to a hermit thrush's, the songs of each going on and on without distinct beginning or end. The songs are nevertheless divided into short phrases (3 to 5 notes in the case of the wood thrush) broken by pauses. More variation in pitch within a phrase occurs in this species; some notes are quite low. If near the bird, one finds many of the phrases concluded with a thin, high-pitched trill running off into a sputter.

NEST: From 5 to 12 feet up in dense shrubbery, in the crotch or fork of a sapling or saddled onto the horizontal lower limb of a larger tree; made of stems and leaves cemented to an inner cup of mud or hardened leafmold lined with rootlets. The 4 unmarked greenish-blue eggs (1.02 x .72) average a little darker than a robin's.

RANGE: (M.) Breeds from c. New Hampshire, s.e. Ontario, c. Wisconsin, and s. South Dakota south to n. Florida, Louisiana, and e. Texas. Winters from s. Mexico south to w. Panama.

Hermit Thrush*   *Hylocichla guttata*—✳19

IDENTIFICATION: L. 7. The reddish-brown tail contrasting strongly with the rest of the upper parts is distinctive in any plumage, but the bird should not be confused with the reddish-tailed fox sparrow. Note that when disturbed the hermit thrush has a habit of slowly raising its tail.

HABITS: The hermit thrush inhabits areas ranging from low wooded swamps to dry hillsides and uplands, from dense, cool woodlands to rocky brush-grown pastures and recently cut- or burned-over forests. Generally the birds are associated with conifers, but in a few areas they occur in deciduous woodlands with only a sprinkling of pine or hemlock. Because of its habitat tolerance it is a common bird over a wide area. Its food is insects and berries. Most of the insects it takes on the ground among dead leaves. In fall and winter its diet becomes preponderantly vegetarian.

VOICE: Call notes, a low *chuck*, plus a mewing note and several others when on breeding grounds. The song is composed of a series of ethereal bell-like cadences of great beauty. The long, low, flutelike opening note is followed by up to a dozen shorter, thinner notes varying slightly in pitch, and run together in groups to give a tremolo effect. As the cadences continue, the openings tend to go so high as to approach the limit of audibility. The song may be delivered from a fixed treetop perch or from near, if not on, the ground. The song varies so in volume that the bird's distance is difficult to estimate.

NEST: Usually on the ground on a low knoll or hummock, occasionally in a low tree; a compact cup of moss, plant fibers, leaves, and rootlets. The 4 green-blue eggs (.85 x .65) are unmarked.

RANGE: (P.M.) Breeds from s. Labrador, n. Ontario, n.c. Saskatchewan, s.w. Mackenzie, and s.c. Alaska south to Long Island, New York, Virginia (mts.), n. Michigan, c. Minnesota, c. Saskatchewan, New Mexico, and n. Lower California. Winters from Massachusetts, Pennsylvania, s. Missouri, and Washington south to c. Florida and Guatemala.

Olive-backed Thrush* *Hylocichla ustulata*—✻19

IDENTIFICATION: L. 7. This and the gray-cheeked are similar thrushes with uniformly colored grayish-brown or olive-brown backs. In good light the olive-backed can usually be distinguished by its broader buffy eye ring and the buffier color of its cheeks, throat, and breast.

HABITS: This is a dominant bird over vast areas of spruce-fir forest. Populations are highest in low, damp areas near water and in stands of young conifers mixed with deciduous trees like birch, but it commonly ranges throughout the mature forest. Occasionally the bird may be found in low, deciduous growths with only a few scattered conifers. Like most small land birds, these thrushes migrate during the hours of darkness, and on still nights their mellow, sweet-toned whistles often fill the sky for hours. Insects are their basic food, but they are fond of wild fruits. They feed both in the foliage and on the forest floor and fly-catch as well.

VOICE: Call notes are an abrupt *whit* and a high-pitched *peep*. The throaty, gurgling song lacks the richness of the wood thrush's and the purity of the hermit's but is pleasantly musical. The bird repeats similar phrases, broken occasionally by a call note. Each phrase starts low and mounts in pitch through 12 or so paired (second note lower) but connected notes; occasionally the last few pairs are on the same pitch.

NEST: Well sheltered and firmly supported, 3 to 15 feet high in a small tree or shrub, usually evergreen. The neatly built nests are often notable for the large amount of moss or lichen worked in with the twigs, fern stems, sedges, leaf skeletons, and other fibrous materials. In some regions mud and wet leaf mold form the inner cup. The 3 or 4 pale greenish-blue eggs (.90 x .65) are evenly marked with light brown.

RANGE: (M.) Breeds from Newfoundland, c. Quebec, n. Manitoba, n.w. Mackenzie, and n.w. Alaska south to n. New England, West Virginia (mts.), n. Michigan, Colorado, and s. California. Winters in South America south to Argentina.

Gray-cheeked Thrush*   *Hylocichla minima*—✳19

IDENTIFICATION: L. 7¾. (Southern birds 6¾.) Separated from the olive-backed only by gray instead of buffy cheeks, much less buffy under parts, and the absence of a distinct eye ring. Call notes are the best way to tell the species apart.

HABITS: This, the most northerly of American thrushes, inhabits the boreal forest where tamarack and black spruce dominate and ranges through the stunted growth of the tree-line zone into the open tundra wherever dwarf willows or birches maintain a foothold. In the East it ranges south in wind-swept coastal areas and mountaintops where the spruce-fir forest is stunted by weather conditions. In migration it is found near the ground in shady woodlands or shrubbery. In fall, like all thrushes, it takes wild fruits to supplement its insect diet.

Like other essentially eastern birds, gray-cheeks, in response to suitable habitats, have extended their breeding range far to the northwest; those nesting in eastern Siberia now fly east over some 105 degrees of longitude before turning south to their winter home.

VOICE: The common call is a downward-slurred, nighthawk-like *queep* much longer than the olive-backed's abrupt *peep*. The song, occasionally heard from migrants, is a weak even-pitched series of downward slurred notes interspersed with short lower notes. It is veery-like but runs up the scale toward the end, not down.

NEST: From near or on the ground up to about 20 feet, depending upon the height of the local vegetation. The firmly lodged nest is a compact cup of woven sedges, other fibers, and decayed leaves cemented by mud. The 3 to 5 greenish-blue eggs (.92 x .67) are finely, often faintly, marked with brown dots.

RANGE: (M.) Breeds from n. Newfoundland, n. Labrador, n. Manitoba, n.w. Mackenzie, n. Alaska, and n.e. Siberia south to s.e. Quebec, mountaintops of s.e. New York, n. Ontario, n.c. Manitoba, n. Alberta, n. British Columbia, and c.s. Alaska. Winters in Hispaniola and across n. South America.

Veery*   *Hylocichla fuscescens*—✳19

IDENTIFICATION: L. 7. The uniformly tawny-brown upper parts and the faintly spotted pale buffy breast set this bird apart from other thrushes. In juvenile plumage the upper parts of all the thrushes are streaked or spotted with a lighter color. The juvenile wood thrush is spotted chiefly on the head, while in the veery all upper parts are spotted with tawny-olive. The gray-cheeked and olive-backed juveniles are finely streaked above, but the gray-cheeked has a buffier and much narrower eye ring.

HABITS: The veery prefers wooded areas open enough to encourage a fairly dense undergrowth of shrubs or ferns. Willow and alder swamps, lowland areas bordering streams and lakes, and thickets of deciduous second growth are other favored haunts, though at times the bird may be found on dry, brushy hillsides. It is characteristic of northern deciduous and southern coniferous forests where openings have stimulated deciduous shrubs and birches. Veeries obtain most of their insect food by scratching in the leaf mold of the forest floor. Nearly half their food appears to be wild fruit and seeds.

The common calls of the veery and other thrushes are easy to imitate well enough to get the birds to answer. Usually by imitation or by squeaking on the back of one's hand any thrush can be lured out of the bushes.

VOICE: The call note is an easily imitated whistled *phew* falling in pitch. The song is a rolling series of half a dozen falling or downward-slurred muffled notes, each weaker and lower than the preceding, delivered in a thin, vibrant whistle that gives it a faraway, wild, remote sound.

NEST: Commonly on the ground, often worked into the center of a fern tussock or other thick vegetation or on a log or stump; occasionally in a shrub or low tree. The bulky cup is made of leaves, moss, and fibers which become finer toward the center. The 4 greenish-blue eggs (.85 x .67) are unmarked.

RANGE: (M.) Breeds from Newfoundland, s. Quebec, s. Ontario, s. Manitoba, c. Alberta, and s. British Columbia south to New Jersey, n. Georgia (mts.), n. Indiana, c. Iowa, n. New Mexico, Utah, Nevada, and c. Oregon. Winters in South America south to Brazil.

Yellow-billed
Cuckoo
p.4

Groove-billed
Ani
p.8

Smooth-billed
Ani
p.7

p.5

Black-billed
Cuckoo

Black-eared
Cuckoo
p.3

Road-runner
p.6

Great Horned Owl
p.12

Great Gray

p.13
Snowy Owl

Barred Owl
p.17

Long-eared Owl
p.19

p.20
Short-eared Owl

Barn

PLATE 2

Saw-whet Owl
p.22

JUVENILE

Boreal
Owl
p.22

Ferruginous
Pygmy Owl
p.15

Hawk Owl
p.14

RED
PHASE

Burrowing
Owl
p.16

GRAY
PHASE

Screech Owl
p.11

PLATE 3

Ivory-billed
Woodpecker ♂
p.50

Pileat
Woodp
p.40

Yellow-shafted
Flicker p.38
♂

Red-bellied
Woodpecke

JUVENILE

Red-headed
Woodpecker
p.43

ADULT

Golden-fronted
Woodpecker ♂
p.42

PLATE 4

Black-backed Woodpecker
p.48

Hairy Woodpecker
p.45

♂

♂

Three-toed
Woodpecker
p.49

♂

Red-cockaded
Woodpecker
p.47

♂

Downy Woodpecker
p.45

JUVENILE

♂

Common
Sapsucker
p.44

PLATE 5

Red-shafted
Flicker
p.39

♂

♂

Mexican
Woodpecker
p.46

Common Nighthawk
p.27

♂ p.28 Trilling
Nighthawk

Poorwill

p.26

Whip-poor-will
p.25

♂

Chuck-will's-widow ♂

p.24

Pauraq

♂

PLATE 6

p.27

Common Raven
p.34

Black-billed
Magpie
p.83

White-necked
Raven p.86

Fish Crow
p.88

Common
Crow

p.87

p.81
Scrub Jay

Blue Jay
p.81

ENILE

Canada Jay
p.80

Green Jay
p.83

ULT

PLATE 7

Mexican Flycatcher
p.59

Crested
Flycatcher
p.58

Olive-backed
Kingbird
p.54

Olive-sided
Flycatcher
p.67

Western Kingbird
p.55

Gray
Kingbird
p.54

Eastern Kingbird
p.53

PLATE 8

Ash-throated
Flycatcher
p.59

Eastern
Phoebe
p.60

p.61
Say's
Phoebe

Eastern Pewee
p.65

Beardless
Flycatcher
p.69

Least
Flycatcher
p.65

Western Pewee
p.66

Yellow-bellied
Flycatcher
p.62

Acadian
Flycatcher
p.63

Alder Flycatcher
p.63

PLATE 9

Carolina
Parakeet
p.1

Scissor-tailed
Flycatcher
p.56

♀

Verm
Flyc

♂

p.57
Kiskadee Flycatcher

Green
Kingfisher
p.36

♂

♀

Rose-throated Becard
p.52

♂

♀

PLATE 10

Belted Kingfisher
p.35

♀

♂

ADULT

Cedar
Waxwing
p.132

Northern Shrike
p.133

ADULT

IMMATURE

JUVENILE

Loggerhead Shrike

p.134

Bohemian
Waxwing
p.131

PLATE 11

Purple Martin
p.78

♂

Gray-breasted
Martin
p.79

Chimney Swift
p.30

Barn Swallow
p.75

PLATE 12

Rough-winged
Swallow
p.74

Bank Swallow
p.73

Bahama Swallow
p.71

Cave
Swallow
p.77

Cliff Swallow
p.76

Tree Swallow
p.72

ADULT

JUVENILE

PLATE 13

Golden-crowned
Kinglet
p.126

♂ Ruby-crowned Ki
p.127

♀

♂

♀

White-breasted
Nuthatch
p.94

Brown-headed Nutho

Red-brea
Nuthe
p

PLATE 14

Black-crested
Titmouse
p.93

Tufted Titmouse
p.92

Black-capped Chickadee
p.89

Carolina
Chickadee
90

Brown-capped
Chickadee
p.91

Brown
Creeper
p.97

Blue-gray
Gnatcatcher
p.125

PLATE 15

Verdin p.

ADULT

IMMAT

Cañon Wren
p.105

Bewick's Wren p.100

Carolina
Wren
p.101

Rock Wren
p.106

House
Wren
p.98

Winter Wren
p.99

Long-billed
Marsh-Wren
p.103

Short-billed
Marsh-Wren
p.104

PLATE 16

Rufous Hummingbird
p.33
♂
♀

Buff-bellied
Hummingbird
p.33

chinned

♀

♀ ♂
p.31
Ruby-throated Hummingbird

Hummingbird

p.123
eatear

INTER ♀

Sprague's
Pipit
p.130

ater Pipit
128

p.70
Horned
Lark

PLATE 17

Brown
Thrasher
p.109

Mocking...
p.107

Curve-billed
Thrasher
p.111

Long-billed Thrasher p.110

Cactus
Wren
p.102

Sage
Thrasher
p.111

JUVENILE

Robin
p.112

C...
p.

PLATE 18

ry
19

Gray's
Thrush
p.114

Wood Thrush
p.115

mit
ush
6

Olive-backed
Thrush
p.117

Townsend's
Solitaire
p.124

Gray-cheeked
Thrush
p.118

p.121
Eastern Bluebird

♂

♀

Mountain
Bluebird

♂

♀

p.122

PLATE 19

Yellow-green Vireo p.142

Black-whiskered Vireo p.141

Red-eyed Vireo p.142

Black-capped Vireo p.137

Blue-headed Vireo p.140

Warbling Vireo p.145

Yellow-throated Vireo p.1[

Philadelphia Vireo p.144

White-eyed Vireo p.137

PLATE 20

Bell's Vireo
p.138

Bahama Bananaquit
p.146

Wilson's Warbler
p.190

♀

♂

Yellow Warbler
p.161

♂ SPRING

IMMATURE
♀

Prothonotary Warbler
p.148

♂

♀

PLATE 21

Macgillivray's
Warbler
p.186

♂

♀

♂

Bach.
War
p.155

Mourning Warbler
p.184

♀

Connecticut
Warbler
p.183

♀

♂

Nashville We

p.

IMMATURE

ADULT

PLATE 22

Mexican
Ground-Chat
p.187 ♂ ♀

Yellowthroat
p.186

♂

♀

v-breasted
p.188

♀

♂

♀

led Warbler p.189

Kentucky Warbler
p.183

PLATE 23

LAWRENCE TYPE

Hybrid Variations p.152

♂

BREWSTER TYPE

♀

Golden-winged Warbler p.150

p.151

Blue-winged   Warbler

♀

Kirtland Warbler p.177

♂

Canada   Warbler

p.191

♀

PLATE 24

Pitiayumi Warbler p.160

♂ ♀

Parula Warbler
p.159

♂ IMMATURE
♀

♂

p.171

Yellow-throated Warbler

♂

p.171

Sutton's Warbler

Cerulean Warbler
p.169

♂ ♀

PLATE 25

Blackburnian Warbler p.170

Magnolia Warbler p.16?

SPRING

SPRING ♂

♀

♀

IMMATURE

IMMATURE

IMMATURE ♂

♀

♂

Redstart p.192

PLATE 26

Audubon's
Warbler
165

♂
SPRING

Myrtle Warbler
p.164

SPRING ♂

IMMATURE

IMMATURE

♀

♀

♂

Black-throated
Blue Warbler
164

♀

PLATE 27

Cape May Warbler
p.163

SPRING ♂

SPRING ♀

SPRING ♂

IMMATURE ♀

IMMATURE

IMMATURE

p.1
Chestnut-sided Warb

SPRING ♂

IMMATURE

♀

♀

Black-throated Green
Warbler
p.167

IMMATURE
♀

Golden-cheek
Warb
p.1

PLATE 28

ackpoll Warbler
p.175

SPRING ♂

SPRING ♂

♀

♀

FALL

Bay-breasted
Warbler
p.174

ack-throated Gray
arbler
166

♀

♂

SPRING ♂

♀

Black and
White Warbler
p.147

PLATE 29

Tennessee Warbler
p.156

SPRING ♂

IMMATURE

FALL ♀

IMMATURE

IMMATURE

♂

Pine Warbler
p.176

Orange-crowned
Warbler
p.157

Swainson's Warbler
p.148

Worm-eating Warbler

PLATE 30   p.149

Palm Warbler p.179

IMMATURE

SPRING
ADULT

♂

p.178

Prairie Warbler

IMMATURE

Ovenbird
p.180

Northern Water-thrush
181

Louisiana
Water-thrush
p.182

PLATE 31

Rusty Blackbird
p.205

FALL

♂

♀

♂

Brewer's Blackbird
p.206

♀

♀

♂

Brown-head
Cowbir

♂

Red-eyed Cowbird
p.211

p.

PLATE 32

Starling
p.135

JUVENILE

FALL

SPRING

Boat-tailed
Grackle
p.207
♂

♀

♂

BRASSY-GREEN PHASE

Common Grackle
p.208

♂ BRONZE-PURPLE PHASE

PLATE 33

Yellow-headed
Blackbird
p.198

♂

FALL

Boboli

♀

♂

♀

IMMATURE ♂

Easter
Meadowlar
p.19

Red-winged
Blackbird
p.199

♀

Wester
Meadowlar
p.

PLATE 34

Baltimore Oriole
p.203

♀

♂

IMMATURE ♀

Orchard Oriole
IMMATURE ♂
p.200

♂

♀

♂

♂

Bullock's
Oriole
p.204

♀

Hooded Oriole
p.202

♀

Lichtenstein's
Oriole
p.202

Black-headed Oriole
p.201

PLATE 35

Scarlet Tanager p.212

MOLTING ♂

♂

♂ FALL

♀

Summer Tanager p.2[

MOLTING ♂

♀

♂

Western Tanager p.212

♂

♀

PLATE 36

Cardinal
p.215
♂

♀

Pyrrhuloxia
p.216
♂

♀

Spotted Towhee
p.240
♂

Eastern
Towhee
p.239
♂

♀

Green-tailed
Towhee
p.238

Olive Sparrow
p.237

PLATE 37

Rose-breasted Grosbeak
p.216

♀

♂

FALL ♂

IMMATURE ♂

IMMATURE

♀

Blue Grosbe
p.218

♂

♂

Evening Grosbeak p.223

♀

PLATE 38

Pine Grosbeak
p.227

IMMATURE ♂

♂

♀

JUVENILE

♀

Red Crossbill
p.235

♂

White-winged
Crossbill p.236

♂

♀

IMMATURE ♂

PLATE 39

Indigo Bunting
p.219

SPRING
♂

MOLTING
♂

♀

Painted Bunting
p.220

♂

♀

p.220
♂

Varied Bunting
♀

p.241
Lark Bunting

♀

SPRING
♂

PLATE 40

House Finch
p.225

♂

♀

Purple Finch
p.224

♂

♀

Hoary Redpoll
p.230

♂

Common Redpoll
p.231

♂

♀

Gray-crowned Rosy-Finch
p.228

♂

♀

PLATE 41

Common
Goldfinch
p.233

♂ SPRING

SPRING ♀

♀ FALL

IMMATURE
♂

Dark-backed
Goldfinch
p.234

♂

♂ IMMATU

♀

European
Goldfinch

p.22

Pine Siskin
p.232

Europe
Tree Sparr
p.

English Sparrow

p.193

♂

♀

PLATE 42

White-throated Sparrow
p.267

IMMATURE

IMMATURE

ADULT

IMMATURE

ADULT

White-crowned
Sparrow
p.266

ADULT

IMMATURE

Harris's Sparrow
p.265

IMMATURE

SPRING

♂

IMMATURE

IMMATURE

ADULT

♀

Dickcissel
p.221

Lark Sparrow
p.253

PLATE 43

Morellet
Seedeater
p.226
♂
♀

Cassins
Sparrow
p.256

Botteris
Sparrow
p.256

Black-throated
Sparrow
p.257

White-winged
Junco
p.258
♂

Pink-sided Junco
p.260
♂
♀

p.259
Slate-colored Junco

IMMATURE ♀
♂

PLATE 44

IMMATURE

Rufous-crowned
Sparrow
p.254

ADULT

Pinewoods
Sparrow

p.255

Chipping
Sparrow
p.262

ADULT

Tree
Sparrow
p.261

ADULT

IMMATURE

Field Sparrow
p.264

Clay-colored
Sparrow
p.263

IMMATURE

ADULT

IMMATURE

ADULT

PLATE 45

Grasshopper Sparrow
p.245
ADULT
JUVENILE

Henslow's Sparrow
p.248
ADULT
JUVENILE

Baird's Sparrow
p.246

JUVENILE

Sharp-tailed Sparrow
p.2
ADULT
JUVEN

ADULT

Leconte's Sparrow
p.247

p.251
Cape Sable Sparrow

p.251
Merritt Island Sparrow

Seaside Sparrow
p.2
JUVENIL
AD

PLATE 46

Song Sparrow
p.271

Lincoln's Sparrow
p.269

SPRING

FALL

JUVENILE

Swamp Sparrow
p.270

p.252

Vesper Sparrow

Fox Sparrow
p.268

Ipswich Sparrow
p.242

Savannah Sparrow
p.244

PLATE 47

Chestnut-collared
Longpsur
p.275

♂ SPRING

♀

McCou
Longspur

♀

s

SPRING ♂

♀

Smith's Longsp
p.

♀

SPRING

Lapland Longspur
p.273

Common Snow-bunting
p.276

FALL ♀

SPRING ♂

PLATE 48

Eastern Bluebird

Sialia sialis—#19

IDENTIFICATION: L. 7. The bright blue and reddish-brown male is unmistakable. The female is bright blue only on the wings and tail and is a duller brown below. The blue is very restricted in juveniles, and below they are white mottled with gray.

HABITS: This is a bird of open country with scattered trees. It seems especially attracted to orchards, but it occurs wherever wooded areas have been opened up by lumbering, fire, or flood. In most regions it could be more abundant if more nest sites were available. Suitable sites are scarce, and bluebirds now have to share them with two aggressive rivals from Europe, the starling and the English sparrow, as well as with the native tree swallow and house wren. It has been repeatedly demonstrated that marked increases in the bluebird population can be produced by community birdhouse campaigns. An entrance hole less than 1½ inches in diameter excludes starlings, and a location no higher than a fence post discourages English sparrows. Since the bluebird requires considerable territory, boxes should not be placed too close together.

The bluebird's diet averages about two-thirds insect to one third fruit. Grasshoppers, crickets, beetles, and caterpillars are the most important insects, many of them captured on the ground. In winter bayberry, poison-ivy, and sumac berries are important.

VOICE: The *cher-wee* call, uttered at frequent intervals even when the bird is in flight, is a sweet, liquid series of 2 or 3 notes. It carries well and is often the first indication of the presence of bluebirds. The plaintive song is a rapid series of soft, single, and slurred double *cheuery* notes with a slight variation in pitch. Often 2 variations are sung alternately.

NEST: In natural tree cavities, old woodpecker holes, and bird boxes at heights of from 2 to 25 or 30 feet; a loose cup of grasses and stems. The 4 to 6 pale blue eggs (.82 x .64) are unmarked; 2 broods are reared.

RANGE: (P.M.) Breeds from Newfoundland, s. Quebec, n. Ontario, and s. Manitoba south to s. Florida, the Gulf Coast, and Honduras; west to e. Montana, e. Colorado, w.c. Texas, s. Arizona, and Sinaloa. Winters from s. New England and s. Michigan south.

Mountain Bluebird   *Sialia currucoides*—✳19

IDENTIFICATION: L. 7¼. The pale cerulean or turquoise male is distinctive even in winter, when much of the body blue is obscured by gray-brown feather margins and tips. The buff-gray female, dark above, light below, is blue only in the tail region and on the wings. Juveniles are similar but generally blue only on tail and flight feathers.

HABITS: The mountain bluebird is widely distributed, inhabiting open areas wherever trees are available for nesting and perching. From just below the timber line in high mountains it ranges down to the foothills and pine-covered ridges of the plains and in some areas to the cottonwood groves about prairie ranch buildings. In the North it seems to be spreading eastward as a breeder, and in winter it regularly wanders east of its normal breeding range. Its food is chiefly insects, captured by pouncing from a prominent lookout perch or as the bird hovers over an open area, the prey being seized in a quick drop to the ground. In winter the birds eat many wild fruits.

VOICE: This is a remarkably silent bird, although flocks in flight sometimes give a low *terr* call. The song appears to start in darkness and stop at daybreak. It is said to be like a robin's carol given in the gentle tones of a bluebird.

NEST: In natural cavities in trees or in abandoned woodpecker holes, bird boxes, or crevices about cliffs and buildings; from close to the ground to 25 or more feet high. The nest is loosely constructed of plant debris. The 5 or 6 pale blue eggs (.86 x .65) are unmarked; 2 broods are reared.

RANGE: (P.M.) Breeds from s.c. Manitoba, c. Saskatchewan, n.w. British Columbia, and s. Yukon south to Chihuahua, and from w. Nebraska west to the Cascades and Sierra Nevadas. Winters from Colorado and Oregon south through n. Mexico and east to Kansas and e.c. Texas.

Northern Wheatear   *Oenanthe oenanthe*—✳17

IDENTIFICATION: L. 6¼. The dark wings, white rump, and distinctive tail pattern, all conspicuous in flight, are the best field marks. In summer the black-winged male becomes grayer above and whiter below. The forehead and the line over the eye are white, lores and ear coverts black. The summer female is intermediate, dark brown instead of black and buff instead of white, except in the tail area.

HABITS: The northern wheatear is a bird of bare hillsides, stony barrens, sand dunes, and other wastelands, generally observed on or flying close to the ground. At rest it is a bullheaded, short-tailed bird. It likes to perch on stones and clods, standing upright on its long legs, bobbing and waving its tail up and down. It moves rapidly on the ground by long hops. Although it eats seeds and fruits, its food is chiefly insects, many of which are caught by fluttering dashes into the air. Wheatears also search the edges of mud flats and wet places for small crustacea and mollusks.

This species has colonized the American Arctic from both the east and west: only about 1,000 miles now separate the 2 groups. Each year in migration the birds retrace the route over which their ancestors spread out from their original European and Asiatic homes. Thus some of them fly over almost as many degrees of longitude before turning south to their wintering grounds as do the gray-cheeked thrushes of Siberia. To date there is no indication that wheatears regularly migrate south in the Western Hemisphere. The ones we see are apparently wandering birds lost from regular lines of travel.

VOICE: The northern wheatear's call is a harsh double *t'chach*, *t'chach* or a *weet, chack, chack*. The song consists of a short melodious warble interspersed with harsh rattles and squeaks and imitations of other birds.

NEST: Well hidden in rabbit burrows, under rocks, in rock piles, or crevices in cliffs, walls, and buildings. The flat, loosely woven nest is made of grasses and lined with fur or feathers. The 5 to 7 pale blue-green eggs (.86 x .63) are unmarked.

RANGE: (M.) Breeds throughout Europe, Asia, and n. Africa and in North America from Greenland west to the Boothia Peninsula and south to n. Quebec; from Bering Strait east to e.c. Alaska and south to the Yukon River. Winters in tropical Africa and s. Asia, accidental in the United States.

Townsend's Solitaire*   *Myadestes townsendi*—✕19

IDENTIFICATION: L. 8¾. This is a long-tailed, short-billed, slim, dark bird with under parts slightly paler than upper parts. The light eye ring, white outer tail feathers, and buffy wing patches that show in flight identify it even in the juvenile plumage, which is spotted above and below.

HABITS: The solitaire is a bird of rough, mountainous country, where it lives in sparse growths of dwarf firs and willows above timber line on down to foothill canyons with scattered cedars. The birds reach greatest abundance in mature stands of conifers, open enough to favor their methods of obtaining food. Fly-catching from a treetop perch is common, but usually they spot their prey on the ground from a low perch, to which they return with the catch. In winter there is a partial movement to lower altitudes where cedar, mistletoe, and other berry-bearing plants are plentiful.

VOICE: The common call is a monotonously repeated short ventriloquial creaking, like a squeaky gate or wheel, which at night becomes a muffled lower-pitched chant. The song, delivered from a treetop perch or while the bird is hovering in the air, is one of the finest of bird songs, with clear, brilliant, ringing notes that rise and fall in pitch and volume as the bird warbles and trills. Birds may be heard in song almost any season of the year.

NEST: Generally secreted in a cavity under a bank or at the base of a tree or in the roots of a fallen tree; made of any convenient fibrous debris, loosely formed into a cup, with a telltale overflow outside the cavity. The 4 dull white eggs (.87 x .66) are marked with many shades of brown.

RANGE: (P.M.) Breeds from s.c. Alberta, s.w. Mackenzie, and c.e. Alaska south to n.c. Mexico and east to w. Nebraska and w. Texas. Winters from s. British Columbia and Montana south and east to e. Nebraska and e.c. Texas.

OLD WORLD WARBLERS   Family SYLVIIDAE

Blue-gray Gnatcatcher   *Polioptila caerulea*—✻15

IDENTIFICATION: L. 4½. The black-and-white tail which it waves about and frequently cocks at an angle and the white eye ring are this gnatcatcher's best field marks. Females are duller and lack the black edging to the headcap. Juveniles are a browner but paler gray. The call carries fairly well, and most individuals are located by sound.

HABITS: This is a bird of open woodlands and brushy growth interspersed with trees and isolated streamside groves. It seems to have an affinity for parklike stands of mature oaks and pines and is often found in shade trees. It is restless and active, often feeding in upper branches, where it flycatches and hovers to pluck insects off flowers or buds. Insects appear to be its sole food. In migration and in winter the birds move in small bands and may be found almost anywhere but most commonly high in forest trees.

VOICE: The distinctive call is a thin, high-pitched twanging or humming note like a plucked banjo string. The song is a soft, melodious warble, quite thin and chattery, with a wheezy or lisping quality. The bird is a great scolder, using a rapid series of buzzy squeaks.

NEST: The hummingbird-like cup of fine plant fibers and downs bound with spider webbing and decorated with lichens is saddled on a horizontal tree limb or placed in a crotch, where it looks like a knot. The height is variable, but generally it is well up in a tree. The 5 very pale blue-green eggs (.59 x .45) are speckled with brown.

RANGE: (P.M.) Breeds from s. New Jersey, w. Pennsylvania s. Ontario, s. Wisconsin, Nebraska, Colorado, s. Nevada, and n.e. California south to Great Inagua in the Bahamas, the Gulf Coast, and s. Mexico. Winters from South Carolina, the Gulf Coast, s. Texas, and s. California south through Cuba to Guatemala.

Golden-crowned Kinglet   *Regulus satrapa*—※14

IDENTIFICATION: L. 4. Kinglets are short-tailed, olive-gray birds smaller than warblers. They have the unwarbler-like habit of nervously flicking open their wings as they jump from twig to twig. They do much of their feeding at branch tips and often flutter in the air as they pick out insects. The golden-crowned has no eye ring and, except in juvenile plumage, has a conspicuous white-and-black-bordered crown patch—orange in the male, yellow in the female. The 3-note lisping call is distinctive.

HABITS: In summer this is a bird of coniferous woodlands. Spruces are necessary for nesting, but populations often seem highest in open second-growth stands mixed with birch and fir. Here the birds nest and feed lower down and are more readily observed. During migration they frequent deciduous woods and thickets and tangles of weedy growth close to the ground. Occasionally they are ensnared by the barbs of burdock burs. They seem wholly insectivorous, feeding on adults, larvae, pupae, and eggs. In winter, when they are quite gregarious, they commonly roam the woods with chickadees, brown creepers, and a downy woodpecker or two, showing a marked preference for conifers.

Voice: The call, which is heard throughout the year, consists of 1 or a series of 3 rapid, identical, high-pitched, hissing notes much like a brown creeper's single, longer call note. The song, seldom heard except on breeding grounds, opens with a series of evenly pitched or rising notes similar to the call notes, followed by a series of louder, harsh, staccato chattering notes that fall in pitch.

Nest: Occasionally low but generally 30 to 60 feet up in a sheltered spot among the thick twigs of a conifer. The nest is almost globular, with a small entrance on top. Both top and bottom are woven into the surrounding twigs. The material is chiefly moss and usnea lichen bound with spider webbing, bark shreds, and rootlets and lined with feathers and fur. The 8 or 9 creamy eggs (.56 x .44) are speckled with brown spots of varying size.

Range: (P.M.) Breeds from Cape Breton Island, s. Quebec, c. Manitoba, c. Alberta, and s.c. Alaska south to Massachusetts, North Carolina (mts.), n. Michigan, New Mexico, and s. California. Winters from Nova Scotia, New York, s. Michigan, Iowa, and British Columbia south to n. Florida, the Gulf States, and through Mexico to Guatemala.

Ruby-crowned Kinglet   *Regulus calendula*—✳14

Identification: L. 4¼. The only distinctive character of this active, plump little olive-colored bird is the white eye ring which gives its black eyes a fixed, staring look. Only the male has the ruby crown and it is seldom visible in the field. Unlike the golden-crowned, the ruby-crowned sings during spring and fall migrations.

HABITS: The summer home is in the predominantly evergreen northern forests or on their edges. This bird seems to like more open stands than the golden-crowned and often finds suitable conditions in spruce bogs and mixed woods. At other seasons it frequents any type of woody growth, although it still finds conifers attractive. Ruby-crowns are often common in streamside thickets, where they feed close to the ground. Seldom do they display marked gregariousness. Small quantities of seeds and berries are eaten in winter as a supplement to their insect diet.

VOICE: The call notes are wren-like. One is a single harsh, grating *kerr*, another a sharp, scolding chatter. The song is a beautiful one and the closing phrases amazingly loud for so small a bird. It starts with several thin, high-pitched introductory *zee, zee, zee*'s, drops to several low-pitched *kew, kew, kew*'s, and launches out into a series of loud, tinkling, melodious phrases in ascending groups of 3 short notes.

NEST: In spruce trees at any height but generally well up; a globular hanging structure woven into the pendant twigs of a branch at the densest part near the tip. Both nest and eggs are virtually indistinguishable from the golden-crowned's.

RANGE: (P.M.) Breeds from w.c. Quebec, n. Manitoba, n.w. Mackenzie, and n.w. Alaska south to Nova Scotia, n. Ontario, c. New Mexico, and s. California. Winters from Virginia, Iowa, and s. British Columbia south to s. Florida, the Gulf Coast, and through Mexico to Guatemala.

PIPITS   Family MOTACILLIDAE

Water Pipit*   *Anthus spinoletta*—✳17

IDENTIFICATION: L. 6½. Pipits are invariably seen on the ground in open places. Their long bills, slender bodies, long dusky tails, and walking habits are distinctive. The birds nod as they walk and when resting frequently move their tails up and down. They are darker-backed and longer-legged than their common associate, the horned lark, which has a black tail more narrowly bordered with white. Spring birds are lighter and grayer above than the fall bird shown on the plate and are a more uniform and richer pink-buff below with narrower and less extensive streakings.

HABITS: In summer these pipits breed in the treeless tundra country of mountaintop and arctic. They migrate and winter in flocks that are sometimes enormous. They frequent open land and low wet places with standing water, old pastures or other areas of low vegetation, sand dunes and beaches, mud flats and burned or fallow fields. When flushed the flock jumps into the air simultaneously, uttering their distinctive call. Their flight is swift and buoyant, but erratic, and the flock strings out in a long, loose mass of undulating birds. Food consists of insects, mollusks, crustacea, seeds, and berries.

VOICE: Flight calls are of from one to many short, sharp, thin, high-pitched notes, generally paired. They are not unlike the horned lark's, but somewhat lower-pitched, more rolling, prolonged, and sibilant. The song, given from a perch on the ground, in a tree, or while soaring, is a weak, tinkling combination of single and double sibilant notes and trills.

NEST: On the ground in the shelter of a rock or bank or on the side of a moss-covered hummock; made of grass and twigs. The 4 or 5 pale gray eggs (.78 x .58) are thickly spotted with various shades of brown and marked with black lines.

RANGE: (M.) Breeds throughout the Northern Hemisphere; in North America from Greenland, n. Mackenzie, and n. Alaska south to Newfoundland, n. Manitoba, and New Mexico (mts.). Winters from s. New Jersey, s. Ohio,

Arkansas, New Mexico, and n. California south to n. Florida, the Gulf Coast, and through Mexico to Guatemala.

Sprague's Pipit*   *Anthus spragueii*—#17

IDENTIFICATION: L. 6¼. The generally paler appearance and the distinctly streaked head, neck, and back separate this bird from a water pipit in any plumage. The birds are very different in spring, Sprague's being almost white below, faintly tinged with buff, and finely and sparsely streaked.

HABITS: Although Europe has 8 other pipits besides the circumpolar water pipit we have only one—Sprague's, a bird of the western grasslands. When grasslands are plowed or burned it becomes scarce. Unless one detects their song, the birds are likely to be overlooked, as they stay hidden in grass when on the ground. If flushed they go off with a bounding, erratic flight. Nests have been located by the female's habit of rising off the nest to greet the male as it plunges earthward after a song flight. Insects and seeds are their chief foods, and in migration and winter the birds seem partial to weedy fields.

VOICE: The call as the bird takes wing consists of a series of single notes harsher than, and different from, the paired notes of the water pipit. The song, almost always delivered from several hundred feet in air, is occasionally given in fall and winter. The bird floats in circles for sometimes as much as an hour, singing at frequent intervals. Each song is a descending series of 7 or 8 double notes, high-pitched and clear, with a tinkling, metallic quality, the regular repetition of an accented note suggesting the veery's song.

NEST: In a hollow in the ground or in a tuft of coarse grass; a woven cup of grass, more or less concealed by a loose arch of grasses. The 4 or 5 pale gray eggs (.82 x .60) are uniformly blotched with purplish-brown.

RANGE: (M.) Breeds from s. Manitoba and c. Alberta south to n.w. Minnesota and Montana. Winters from s. Mississippi (occasionally South Carolina) and Texas south to s. Mexico.

WAXWINGS   Family BOMBYCILLIDAE

Bohemian Waxwing*   *Bombycilla garrula*—✳11

IDENTIFICATION: L. 8. This species is characterized by rich brown under-tail coverts, grayer over-all appearance, and the white patch and yellow edging on the wings.

HABITS: There are many mysteries connected with this bird of the boreal forests. Its appearance in civilized areas is sporadic and unpredictable. Few breeding areas are known, but the flocks which invade the United States in winter are frequently enormous. When nesting the birds often form loose colonies in favorable areas, to which they may or may not return in subsequent years. They depend upon fruits and berries for the bulk of their food much of the year, and the varying success of regional berry crops is probably responsible for their erratic behavior. Some insects are eaten, and the birds do some fly-catching. In winter they are attracted by mountain ash and hawthorn, crab apples, rose hips, cedar and juniper berries. Like other fruit eaters, they can be brought to feeding shelves by raisins and cut pieces of other dried fruits.

VOICE: Its only call is a rough buzz or chatter. A flock appears to keep up a constant twittering.

NEST: From 4 to 50 feet up in a pine or isolated spruce or tamarack in open muskeg; a flat structure of twigs, usnea lichen, and grasses placed on a horizontal branch near the trunk. The 4 to 6 pale blue eggs (1.00 x .70) are profusely dotted with black and marked with irregular lines.

RANGE: (E.W.) Throughout the coniferous forests of the Northern Hemisphere. Breeds in North America from n.e.

Manitoba, n. Mackenzie, and w. Alaska south to n. Idaho. Wanders in winter south and east to Nova Scotia, Pennsylvania, Illinois, n. New Mexico, and s. California.

Cedar Waxwing* *Bombycilla cedrorum*—✳11

IDENTIFICATION: L. 7¼. The soft-colored, crested waxwings with their red-and-yellow trimmings and every feather in place are unique. Juveniles lack distinctive colors and are heavily streaked below. The species is characterized by its over-all brownish color, yellowish flanks, and white under-tail coverts.

HABITS: Throughout most of the year cedar waxwings roam the countryside in flocks from a dozen to well over a hundred. They stay close together in flight and alight in a bunch in the top of a tree, frequently sitting awhile before feeding. Their nesting season is late and variable, running from late June into August. Fruits, fresh and dried, are their chief food the year round. Insects are eaten in summer, when some are caught flycatcher-fashion from a tree-top perch.

VOICE: The only sounds are high-pitched whistled hisses or wheezy lisps and a somewhat louder, more rattling or broken hiss. These are heard at all seasons and are given continuously in flight and when feeding.

NEST: From 6 to 35 feet up in the horizontal branches of a deciduous or coniferous tree or shrub. Preference is for orchards, shade trees, swamps, and open stands of scattered trees; dense forests are avoided. The large nest is loosely constructed of almost any available fibrous material. The 4 to 6 gray-blue eggs (.86 x .61) are well spotted with black and brown.

RANGE: (P.M.) Breeds from Cape Breton Island, s. Quebec, n. Ontario, c. Manitoba, and c. British Columbia south to n. Georgia, n. Arkansas, n. New Mexico, and n.w.

California. Winters from about Massachusetts, s. Ontario, s. Minnesota, and Oregon (irregularly farther north) south to the West Indies and Panama.

SHRIKES   Family LANIIDAE

Northern Shrike*   *Lanius excubitor*—❋11

IDENTIFICATION: L. 10¼. The distinguishing characteristics of this species are its finely barred or scaly under parts, its absence of black feathers at the base of the upper half of the bill, and the pale basal portion of its lower mandible. Females are duller and slightly olive. Young are similarly marked in various shades of brown.

HABITS: In the North this bird frequents open growths and brush-bordered swamps and bogs. In winter its habitat preferences and feeding methods are like the loggerhead's. At this season it is largely dependent upon mice and birds for food. Every fourth year numbers of northern shrikes occur well south of their breeding grounds. As wild mice have a population cycle of about this period, it seems likely that they are the most important winter food, the shrikes finding it necessary to come south when the mouse cycle on their normal wintering grounds is at its low point.

Because they take higher animals, many people are prejudiced against shrikes as "butcher-birds." Actually, like every other wild animal, shrikes simply harvest a crop produced for, as it were, the purpose of enabling them to live. Apparently every animal has a reproductive rate high enough to produce a surplus for such uses.

VOICE: The rarely heard call is a harsh whistle or scream. Frequently the birds start singing on their wintering territory. The song suggests that of the catbird-thrasher family. It is delivered from a treetop perch and continues indefinitely. Harsh notes, squeaks, and mews are interspersed with fairly melodious trills, liquid warbles, and whistled notes repeated several times, many of the latter notes suggesting the songs and calls of other birds.

NEST: Well hidden in the branches of a tree, generally a dense conifer, at moderate heights from the ground. The large nest is a matted affair of twigs, mosses, lichens, feathers, and fur. The 4 to 6 grayish eggs (1.08 x .80) are spotted with browns and grays.

RANGE: (E.W.) Throughout the Northern Hemisphere. In North America breeds from n. Ungava, n. Mackenzie, and n.w. Alaska south to New Brunswick, s. Quebec, s.c. Ontario, c. Saskatchewan, and n. British Columbia. Wanders in winter south to Virginia, Kentucky, Missouri, Texas, New Mexico, and n. California.

Loggerhead Shrike*   *Lanius ludovicianus*—※11

IDENTIFICATION: L. 9. Shrikes are plump, big-headed, slim-tailed birds. They generally fly close to the ground, a rapid series of wingbeats followed by a short sail being the usual pattern. In flight the white area in the center of the black wings flashes at each wingbeat. At the end of a flight the birds glide up suddenly to a conspicuous perch. After lighting they frequently tilt their tails. Adults are clear white below and black-billed and have black feathers across the forehead at the base of the bill. Juveniles are brownish above and barred below, but immatures are about like adults.

HABITS: This is a bird of open country with woody growths for nest sites and lookout perches. Rural areas with fields, hedgerows, scattered trees, fence and public-utility poles, and wires afford the ideal habitat. Although they can hover in one spot as they scan the ground, most loggerheads spend their time on conspicuous perches, searching the ground with remarkably keen eyes. Their chief foods are large insects like grasshoppers and crickets, but snakes, lizards, frogs, mice, and birds are taken. To tear up large prey into pieces for swallowing, the shrike usually wedges it into a crotch or impales it on a thorn or fence wire barb.

VOICE: Calls and notes are similar to the northern's. No one seems to be familiar enough with both species to describe the differences.

NEST: From 2 to 20 feet up in a tree or thorny shrub, generally well into the center of the plant; a deep cup of twigs, stems, and grasses heavily lined with matted plant downs, wools, and feathers. The 4 to 6 white eggs (.96 x .72) are thickly marked with browns and grays.

RANGE: (P.M.) Breeds from New Brunswick, s. Quebec, s. Ontario, s. Manitoba, n. Saskatchewan, and c. British Columbia south to s. Florida, the Gulf Coast, and s. Mexico. Winters from Virginia, s. Missouri, New Mexico, and n. California (rarely farther north) south through Mexico.

STARLINGS   Family STURNIDAE

Starling*   *Sturnus vulgaris*—✳33

IDENTIFICATION: L. 8½. The starling is a chunky, short-tailed "blackbird" with a long pointed bill and pointed wings. In spring the bills are yellow, at other seasons dusky-brown. The white and buffy tips to the body feathers, conspicuous in fresh fall plumage, wear off by spring. Juveniles are gray-brown, streaked with white on chin and throat. In flight the starling's stubby appearance and short triangular wings, paler beneath, are distinctive.

HABITS: This immigrant from Europe has thrived in North America and is still increasing its range. Most rural areas with plowed croplands, hayfields, and pastures provide ideal habitat. During summer nest sites must be available near such lands, and later places to roost ⸱t night must be within reasonable flying distance. For the latter tree groves are acceptable until the trees shed their leaves, after which starlings seek beds of cattails or other rank marsh vegetation. When coldest weather comes the preferred roost for those that have not gone south seems to be on or about buildings in towns and cities.

Starlings are quite gregarious, except when nesting, and often associate in flocks with red-winged and rusty blackbirds, cowbirds, and grackles, but they do not share their town roosts with these species. The maneuvering of a flock of starlings is remarkable. How an apparently leaderless mass of individuals can achieve such perfect timing and co-ordination is an unsolved mystery. Starlings do most of their feeding on the ground, where their short legs give them a distinctive waddling gait as they search for weevils, beetles, and grasshoppers. These and other insects supply over half the starling's food, the balance consisting of fruits, mostly wild, although they take cherries and mulberries and some seeds.

VOICE: The common call is a drawn-out rising whistle. Starlings are noisy at all seasons, and the song is a jumble of squeaks, rattles, wheezes, loud whistles, and imitations (often excellent) of other birds.

NEST: Generally from 10 to 25 feet up in a natural or woodpecker hole in a tree, or in any other cavity about buildings, cliffs, or rocks. Sometimes a number of pairs nest close together. The nest cavity is loosely filled with sticks, stems, grasses, and like material with a lining of finer grass and feathers. The 4 or 5 pale blue eggs (1.19 x .83) are unmarked; 2 broods and occasionally 3 are raised.

RANGE: (P.M.) Native to Europe, Asia, and n. Africa. Introduced into North America in 1890 in New York City. Has now spread as far as s. Quebec, n. Manitoba, c. Alberta, California, n. Florida, the Gulf Coast, and n. Mexico.

VIREOS   Family VIREONIDAE

Black-capped Vireo*   *Vireo atricapillus*—✳20

IDENTIFICATION: L. 4½. The black-and-white head markings are distinctive, though in females they may be more slaty-black. Young have the same pattern in dull brown and buff.

HABITS: Low brushy growths in rough dry country seem to be the preferred habitat. The birds occur in dense scrub oak of hilltops and ridges as well as in the more scattered thickets in the numerous ravines of the semi-arid country, to which the species is confined. The black-capped is unusually quick and active for a vireo. It stays so close to cover that it is generally hard to see. Usually the best clue to its presence is its song, which rings out in the narrow canyons.

VOICE: The song consists of deliberate 2- and 3-note phrases, recalling at times a white-eyed vireo's. The quality varies from harsh and vehement to sweet and bell-like, giving the effect of a gentle warble. The delivery is rather deliberate, and often 2 slightly different phrases are alternated. The bird is a persistent singer from early spring to late summer.

NEST: Usually about 4 feet up in the center of a thick shrub clump. The nest is thick-walled for a vireo's and is often decorated on the outside with bits of lichen. The 4 white eggs (.71 x .53) are unmarked.

RANGE: (M.) Breeds from s.w. Kansas south to c. and w. Texas. Winters in Mexico.

White-eyed Vireo*   *Vireo griseus*—✳20

IDENTIFICATION: L. 5. If the white iris is not visible, the combination of wing bars and eye ring, uniformly colored upper parts, and white under parts washed with yellow are distinctive. This species is more commonly heard than seen, and the song is distinctive.

HABITS: Dense thickets, often briary and overgrown with vines, in low moist areas are the favorite habitat of this bird, which seldom ranges far from the ground. Heavy stands of young second growth on uplands and hillsides are also occupied. While largely insectivorous, this vireo in winter eats such fruits as sumac, grapes, and wax myrtle. Active and inquisitive, it comes readily to a series of squeaks.

VOICE: The white-eye has several calls—a harsh mewing note, a short tick, and a single loud whistle. The song is an emphatic series of 5 to 7 sharply separated notes. These vary greatly, and each individual has several songs. The bird, a persistent singer, repeats a given song over and over. Most variations suggest a series of words or syllables like *chip-whee-oo*, or *chick-per-weo-chick*.

NEST: About 3 to 6 feet aboveground, well hidden in thick, low growths. The nest is fairly bulky for a vireo and more cone- than cup-shaped. It is often ragged-looking because of the leaves, moss, wasp paper, and sticks woven in with its soft woody fibers. The 4 white eggs (.74 x .55) have a few scattered small brown dots.

RANGE: (P.M.) Breeds from Massachusetts, Ohio, s. Wisconsin, and s.e. Nebraska south to s. Florida, the Gulf Coast, and c. Mexico. Winters from South Carolina, s. Alabama, and s. Texas south to Honduras.

Bell's Vireo*   *Vireo bellii*—⚹21

IDENTIFICATION: L. 4¾. The rather stout, slightly hooked, typical vireo bill separates this plainly colored species from a kinglet. It has two wing bars like the white-eye but only a narrow, interrupted eye ring and a dark eye. It is slenderer than the white-eye, grayer above and paler yellow below, only its rump being bright olive-green.

HABITS: Bottom-land thickets of willow and cottonwood seem to be the preferred habitat, but almost any low woody growths may be utilized for nesting or feeding. The birds are seldom seen more than 6 feet aboveground. They depend upon insects for food and take more grasshoppers than any other vireo.

VOICE: This bird has a distinctive scolding call of 3 rapid notes. The song, an unmusical warble, suggests a white-eye's but is a more rapid jumble of chattering notes, alternately ending first with an upward, then with a downward inflection. Occasionally the song is a series of scolds, squeaks, and sputters. The bird sings into September and is a persistent day-long performer. Its most surprising habit is singing on the nest.

NEST: Height from 1 to 10 feet, commonly about 3 feet up in a dense tree or shrub. The nest is often fairly deep and purse-shaped. The outside is frequently decorated with blossoms and multicolored cocoon silks. The 4 white eggs (.68 x .49) have a few fine brown dots.

RANGE: (P.M.) Breeds from n.w. Indiana, s. South Dakota, n.e. Colorado, s.w. New Mexico, s. Arizona, and n. California south to c. Texas and Guatemala.

Yellow-throated Vireo* *Vireo flavifrons*—❋20

IDENTIFICATION: L. 6. The clear bright yellow throat, breast, and "spectacles," the well-defined white wing bars and gray rump are distinctive. A pine warbler is slenderer, with a finer bill, dusky streaks on the under parts, and all greenish upper parts.

HABITS: Open stands of tall, mature deciduous trees along streams, roadsides, and in residential areas seem to be preferred. The species also frequents orchards and woodland borders but avoids conifers and dense second growth. Feeding is in the leafy crowns of trees, with insects almost its only food. When feeding the bird is slow and deliberate, very unlike the active warblers. It is so hard to see that identification is usually based upon the song. Fortunately it is a persistent singer.

VOICE: The scolding call is very harsh. The song is like a red-eye's but more deliberate, huskier, and lower-pitched. It is composed of rich, reedy notes slurred together and is pleasanter than a red-eye's, although the phrases are shorter and less varied. A 2-note falling slur is quite distinctive and occurs frequently.

NEST: In a forked twig, generally off a main branch not far from the trunk of a tree. The height varies from 12 to 30 feet. Much spider-web silk is used in the deep, sturdily built cup, which is beautifully decorated with lichens, moss, and spider egg cases. The 4 white to pink eggs (.82 x .59) are heavily spotted and blotched with browns.

RANGE: (M.) Breeds from Maine, s.w. Quebec, s.e. Ontario, s. Manitoba, and e.c. Saskatchewan south to n. Florida, c. Alabama, c. Louisiana, and c. Texas. Winters from s. Mexico south to Venezuela.

Blue-headed Vireo*   *Vireo solitarius*—⚹20

IDENTIFICATION: L. 6. The white "spectacles," conspicuous against the dark slate-gray head, are the best field mark. The pure-white throat contrasts strongly with the dark face.

HABITS: The blue-headed is a bird of coniferous or mixed conifer-deciduous woodlands. It prefers the vicinity of openings in the forest canopy, where, in response to greater illumination, young trees and other low vegetation are thicker. This species is remarkably fearless. The birds feed in low growths and treetops and eat little except insects.

VOICE: One call is a trumpetlike series of nasal notes; another is 2 pleasingly soft notes, the second a descending trill. The song is usually a typical vireo series of short phrases broken by pauses, higher-pitched, clearer, and sweeter than the red-eye's. Each bird has a number of different 2- to 4-note phrases which it sings at random. Abrupt changes of pitch are common, as are slurs, both often occurring in a single short phrase. Occasionally pauses are omitted and a beautiful rich warble pours forth.

NEST: The usual basketlike vireo nest. Ordinarily it is 5 to 10 feet high on a forked twig well toward the center of a small tree. The 4 white eggs (.77 x .57) are sparingly spotted with browns.

RANGE: (P.M.) Breeds from Cape Breton Island, s. Quebec, n. Ontario, c. Manitoba, s. Mackenzie, and c. British Columbia south to Connecticut, n. Georgia (mts.), Michigan, c. Minnesota, and c. Mexico (mts.). Winters from South Carolina and the Gulf Coast south to n. Nicaragua.

Black-whiskered Vireo*   *Vireo altiloquus*—✳20

IDENTIFICATION: L. 6½. The fine dusky streaks on either side of the throat are distinctive. The slightly larger bill is not much help in the field. The immature bird is browner above, with a pale yellowish wing bar and a somewhat buffy chin and throat.

HABITS: In Florida this vireo is found chiefly in the mangrove forests that fringe the coast and in the dense vegetation of the keys. Elsewhere it ranges widely through scrub growth and the shade trees of plantations and towns. The birds feed from treetops down almost to the ground. Berries and seeds appear to be as common in their diet as insects.

VOICE: The song is composed of rather short, abrupt 1- to 4-note phrases broken by pauses. One note is often strongly accented, the others weak. Its local names, whip-Tom-Kelly, John-to-whit, or cheap-John-stir-up, suggest the cadence.

NEST: A cup suspended from a forked horizontal twig from 6 to 15 feet aboveground. The fibrous material used in its construction varies with the locality. The usual site in Florida is in red mangrove over water. The 3 pale pinkish eggs (.89 x .61) have a few fine dots.

RANGE: (P.M.) Breeds from the Bahamas and c.w. Florida south through the Greater and Lesser Antilles. Winters from Hispaniola east and south to n. South America.

Yellow-green Vireo* *Vireo flavoviridis*—✳20

IDENTIFICATION: L. 6½. This bird is much greener above than a red-eye, and the markings on the sides of the head are less distinct. The clear yellow under-tail coverts and bright greenish sides are also diagnostic.

HABITS: This bird is abundant throughout Middle America, and many regard it as a race of the red-eyed vireo. It prefers light open woodland and second growth with plenty of low shrubbery. About settlements it likes shade trees. Low ground near streams or swamps also attracts it. Insects as well as small berries and fruits are taken as food.

VOICE: The scold note is like a red-eyed vireo's. The song is similar except that the phrases seem shorter, the intervals longer.

NEST: From 4 to 10 feet up in the fork of a small branch where it is well sheltered by leaves; a deep cup of weed fibers, bark, and leaves bound together with cobwebs and often decorated with white and yellow spider egg cases. The 3 white eggs (.81 x .57) are sparingly spotted with brown.

RANGE: (M.) Breeds from extreme s. Texas and Sinaloa south to the Canal Zone. Winters in e. Peru and e. Ecuador.

Red-eyed Vireo* *Vireo olivaceus*—✳20

IDENTIFICATION: L. 6¼. A clear white line over the eye bordered with black on a gray-headed greenish bird without wing bars is distinctive. The red eye is of little value as a field mark. Under parts are a cleaner white than those of any other vireo, only the sides and flanks being lightly washed with dirty greenish-yellow.

HABITS: The red-eye occurs wherever trees grow, even in isolated prairie groves. It nests low but belongs essentially to the forest canopy far overhead. The summer food is insects, but in fall these birds relish blueberries, the berries of dogwood, spicebush, sassafras, and magnolia, as well as a great variety of small fruits. Undoubtedly the red-eye was once the most abundant bird in North America, and it may still enjoy this distinction, despite the fact that vast areas that were once good red-eye habitat have been cleared and are now occupied by birds requiring more open types of country. Today on the average there is probably a pair of red-eyes for every acre of woodland within their range.

VOICE: The call is a harsh mewing note. The song is a monotonous and almost endless series of slightly varied phrases with sharp pauses between. Each phrase is of from 2 to 6 notes rapidly run together and ending with an upward or downward inflection. The whole effect suggests a long monologue, and the bird is often called "preacher." It sings all day long as it feeds.

NEST: The red-eye prefers to nest within 5 feet of the ground but will go up to 25 feet. All vireo nests are much alike—a well-made thin-walled ridged cup suspended by the rim in the fork of a horizontal twig. Soft, flexible woody fibers from weathered bark and weed stems firmly bound together with spider and caterpillar silk hold in place wasp paper, plant downs, and leaves. The center usually has a lining of fine grasses, rootlets, or hair. The outside is camouflaged with spider cocoons, lichens, or bits of blossoms, leaves, or moss. The nests withstand the weather for several years and are often taken over by the arboreal white-footed mouse. The 3 or 4 white eggs (.85 x .55) are sparsely spotted with dark brown.

RANGE: (M.) Breeds from Anticosti Island, c. Ontario, c. Manitoba, c.w. Mackenzie, and c. British Columbia south to c. Florida, s. Alabama, n. Coahuila, e. Colorado, s. Montana, and n. Oregon. Winters from Venezuela and Colombia south to s. Brazil and Ecuador.

Philadelphia Vireo* *Vireo philadelphicus*—✳20

IDENTIFICATION: L. 4¾. This is the only vireo with a line over the eye, plain wings, and extensively yellow under parts. Although not as bright a yellow as the throat and breast of a yellow-throated vireo, virtually the entire under parts of this species are a pale yellow. The area between eye and bill is dark, while in the similar warbling vireo it is light.

HABITS: On its breeding grounds this vireo favors woodland edges, young deciduous second growth in old clearings and burned-over areas, and willow and alder thickets along streams or about ponds and lakes. The birds feed both in treetops and in the dense shrubbery of moist areas. When feeding they are quite active for a vireo, often hanging upside down or fluttering before a tuft of leaves to pick out insects. From time to time they dart into the air to snap up flying insects. In fall their diet is supplemented with wild fruits.

One of the best tests of a field ornithologist's ability is the number of Philadelphia vireos he identifies in migration. It is not an uncommon bird, but through most areas it moves rapidly with the last wave of warblers in spring and goes south with the main warbler movement in fall. One should keep careful watch on road- and streamside thickets and investigate any red-eye song that doesn't sound quite right.

VOICE: The song is like a red-eye's with recognizable differences. The Philadelphia's is higher-pitched, some of its phrases weaker, and the whole much more slowly and disconnectedly uttered. Frequently a rising liquid phrase of 2 notes connected by a slight trill occurs.

NEST: Apparently this species chooses a deciduous tree even in woodlands that are predominantly coniferous. Sites vary from 10 to 40 feet high and are either in the crown of a small tree or on the horizontal branches of a tall one. Paper-birch bark, willow downs, and shreds of usnea lichen are usually conspicuous in the cuplike nest. The 4 white eggs (.74 x .55) are sparsely spotted with browns.

RANGE: (M.) Breeds from New Brunswick, n. Ontario, and n. Alberta south to n. New Hampshire, n. Michigan, and n. North Dakota. Winters in Central America.

Warbling Vireo*　　　　　　　　　　　　*Vireo gilvus*—✳20

IDENTIFICATION: L. 5¾. This is the grayest and palest of our vireos and has the weakest head markings. Occasionally the sides and flanks have a yellow tinge, but the area between the eye and bill is white. The song is unmistakable.

HABITS: Open woodlands, river-bottom stands of mature cottonwoods and willows, borders of woodland clearing, and isolated prairie groves are typical haunts. The bird is often common in elms and other shade trees, as well as in orchards and rows of trees between fields and along roads in farming country. It feeds high up in the leafy crowns of trees and, except for its song, would be hard to identify.

VOICE: The calls are catbird-like mewings. The song is a clear, pleasant warble of 12 to 20 notes run together, unhurried, not overly loud, and with considerable variation in pitch. The song is reminiscent of the purple finch, and it has been estimated that the warbling vireo utters it some 4,000 times a day during the breeding season.

NEST: Usually high up and out near the end of a slender, drooping branch of a large, well-developed tree growing in the open, occasionally within a few feet of the ground; a typical vireo cup suspended from a fork in a twig. The 4 white eggs (.72 x .52) are sparingly spotted with brown.

RANGE: (M.) Breeds from Nova Scotia, c. Ontario, s. Manitoba, n.c. Alberta, s.w. Mackenzie, and s. British Columbia south to North Carolina, s. Louisiana, New Mexico, n. Sonora, and s. Lower California. Probably winters in c. and n. South America.

HONEY CREEPERS Family COEREBIDAE

Bahama Bananaquit* *Coereba bahamensis*—#21

IDENTIFICATION: L. 5. The curved bill, the white line over the eye, and the yellow rump and abdomen are distinctive. Young birds are similar but paler and duller.

HABITS: These birds are at home wherever there are flowering plants or ripening fruit. The many flowering trees and shrubs of the tropics attract them as strongly as they do hummingbirds. Lacking the ability to hover, they hang on as best they can while probing blossoms for the nectar and small insects inside. They also pierce ripening fruits to feed on the juices.

VOICE: The common call is a sharp chirp, and they also make a chattering sound. The song is a series of low crackling notes with a marked sibilance.

NEST: Out near the end of a limb a few to more than 30 feet aboveground; a globular mass of leaves and fibrous material with the entrance in the side. The 3 white eggs (.69 x .51) are spotted with brown. Throughout the year the birds use these nests for night roosts.

RANGE: (R.) Resident in the Bahamas and Cayman Islands. Occasionally seen in s. Florida.

WOOD WARBLERS   Family COMPSOTHLYPIDAE

Black and White Warbler*   *Mniotilta varia*—✳29

IDENTIFICATION: L. 5¼. The striped black and white all-over appearance and the creeper-like habits are distinctive. Females are similar to males but duller, with a trace of brown on the sides and indistinct streakings below. Juveniles have the distinctive head stripes, but the body stripes are two shades of brown. Immatures in fall retain much of the brown body plumage.

HABITS: This warbler is found in all types of wooded areas from mature forests to second growths. In deciduous and mixed woodlands it is generally common. It also occurs in northern conifer forests but is not as abundant there, nor as evenly distributed. Insects are its only known food, and its method of feeding like a creeper or a nuthatch on the main branches and trunks of trees enables it to find egg masses and pupae in cracks in the bark.

VOICE: This bird has 2 call notes, a weak *tsip* and a louder *chink*. When alarmed it gives a loud, hissing *chee-chee-chee*. The common song is a monotonous series of 6 to 12 double syllables, the second note of each lower than the first, which gives it a rolling sound. The quality is clear but buzzy and not very musical.

NEST: On the ground in a depression at the foot of or under a stump, log, or rock; made of dead leaves, bark fibers, grass, and rootlets and lined with hair or fern down. The 4 or 5 white eggs (.66 x .53) are thickly spotted with browns and purples.

RANGE: (M.) Breeds from Newfoundland, n. Ontario, c. Manitoba, and c.w. Mackenzie south to n. Georgia, c. Alabama, and e. Texas and west to South Dakota and Kansas. Winters from Florida and n. Mexico south to Guadeloupe, Venezuela, and Ecuador.

Prothonotary Warbler*　　　*Protonotaria citrea*—❋21

IDENTIFICATION: L. 5½. Females differ from males only in being duller and paler—the yellow of the head less intense. In fall males become dusky across the back of the head while immatures resemble females.

HABITS: Swamp woodlands, willow-grown banks, and frequently flooded wooded bottom lands are the home of these birds. Where nest sites near or over water are lacking they go several hundred feet inland but continue to feed near water in the low shrubs, fallen trees, and flood debris characteristic of the habitat.

VOICE: A soft *tchip* call note and a sharp alarm note like that of a Louisiana water-thrush. The song is a vigorous, ringing repetition (4 to 8 times) of a single *peet* or *tweet*, not unlike that of a solitary sandpiper. The flight song starts like the others but ends in a pleasing warble.

NEST: This is the only eastern warbler that nests in a tree cavity. A rotted-out hole in a dead willow stub 5 to 10 feet above water is typical. Old woodpecker holes are much used and properly placed birdhouses are readily accepted, as are all manner of odd crannies about man-made structures. The cavity is always stuffed, often chiefly with moss, to form a nest cup. The 6 creamy-white eggs (.70 x .57) are heavily marked with browns and purples.

RANGE: (M.) Breeds from c. Delaware, s. Ontario, s.e. Minnesota, and n.e. Nebraska south to n. Florida and e. Texas. Winters from Nicaragua to Colombia.

Swainson's Warbler*　　　*Limnothlypis swainsonii*—❋30

IDENTIFICATION: L. 5. Adults are alike and unmistakable. Immatures are olive-brown above with reddish-brown wings, a strongly yellowish eye stripe, and yellowish under parts.

HABITS: This bird lives in two rather different habitats. In the low country along the coast it is restricted to the cane-breaks bordering the streams that intersect pine flat woods. It seems doubtful that it uses the adjacent tangled shrubby growth and deciduous trees. In mountainous country it is found in rhododendron tangles in valley bottoms, stream banks, and swamps.

VOICE: Call note is a clear-ringing *chirp*. The song is clear, pleasing, and often ventriloquial. It starts with 2 or 3 even or falling notes followed by an emphatic 4-syllabled phrase like the song of a white-eyed vireo. Often it suggests the songs of the hooded warbler and the Louisiana water-thrush.

NEST: From 2 to 10 feet up in dense cover which varies from canebrakes to shrub and vine tangles; a loose, bulky mass of dead leaves lined with fine fibrous material like rootlets, pine needles, and hair. The 3 bluish-white eggs (.77 x .59) are unmarked.

RANGE: (M.) Breeds from s.e. Virginia, s. Indiana, and n.e. Oklahoma south to n. Florida and Louisiana. Winters in Jamaica and s. Yucatan.

Worm-eating Warbler*   *Helmitheros vermivorus*—✳30

IDENTIFICATION: L. 5½. These birds can always be identified by the bold head striping and plain body plumage. Juveniles are brownish instead of olive, and their head stripes are brown. Immatures are like adults except for a touch of rusty-brown on the wing.

HABITS: Second-growth deciduous woodlands of comparatively young trees provided with a vigorous shrubby understory are preferred, but the birds are also fond of hillsides above brush-grown swamps or watercourses. They do most of their feeding on or near the ground. They are not very active and move quietly. On the ground they walk with the tail high.

VOICE: A rapid trill like a chipping sparrow's, but louder and richer. A given song may fluctuate in volume as it progresses. The rarely heard flight song is twittery and goldfinch-like.

NEST: On the ground, most commonly on a hillside in a thick drift of old leaves. The nest is of dead or skeletonized leaves, lined with reddish moss stalks. The 4 or 5 white eggs (.69 x .53) are variably marked with browns.

RANGE: (M.) Breeds from s. New England, w. New York, n. Indiana, and s. Iowa south to Virginia, n. Georgia, and s. Missouri. Winters in the Bahamas, the w. West Indies, and Central America from Chiapas to Panama.

Golden-winged Warbler   *Vermivora chrysoptera*—❋24

IDENTIFICATION: L. 5. The male's black-and-yellow markings are distinctive. In fall olive-green feather tips obscure the yellow and give the back a greenish appearance. The female looks like a fall male, except for gray instead of black head markings. Juveniles are grayish olive-green above and pale olive-yellow below with greenish wing bars.

HABITS: This warbler is always associated with openings in deciduous woodlands well grown up with woody plants and rank weeds and grasses. These openings may be along the borders of streams and wet low spots or in abandoned pastures or overgrown lumbering sites. The birds feed chickadee-fashion, hanging upside down near the twig ends, picking insects from the undersides of leaves. Feeding is carried on from treetops to dense brush near the ground.

VOICE: A series of 4 or 5 dry, insectlike, buzzy notes, the first higher than the rest, which are all on the same pitch—like *seee, buzz-buzz-buzz-buzz.*

NEST: On or near the ground, hidden in the stems of a rank weed like goldenrod. The bulky nest consists of a foundation of dead leaves and a cup of coarse fibers, e.g., grape-

vine bark. The 5 white eggs (.66 x .51) are well speckled
and blotched with browns and purples.

RANGE: (M.) Breeds from Massachusetts, c. Michigan, and c.
Minnesota south to n. New Jersey, n. Georgia (mts.), n.
Indiana, and n. Iowa. Winters from Guatemala south to
Colombia and Venezuela.

Blue-winged Warbler*   *Vermivora pinus*—⚹24

IDENTIFICATION: L. 4¾. The black line from bill to eye and
beyond and the gray wings with two strong wing bars are
distinctive. Females are duller and have less yellow on the
crown and less white on the tail. Juveniles are olive-green,
darkest on the back and throat, with wings like adults.

HABITS: The blue-winged, a bird of weed-grown brushlands, is
most commonly found in abandoned fields or semi-wild
pastures with scattered clumps of briars and young trees.
Woodland openings and borders, stream and swamp margins are frequent haunts. Occasionally it is found in the
heart of the forest if there is plenty of undergrowth. The
male sings from a high treetop perch, but the birds do most
of their feeding in small trees and shrubs. They are vireo-
like in the deliberation of their feeding movements.

VOICE: The common song is a double buzz, the first note generally higher in pitch than the second—*seeeee, buzzzzzz.*
Another is a series of short notes ending first with a rising
buzz, then a falling one—*tsee, tsee, tsee, tsee, tsee, tsee,
buzzz-see-see-buzzz.*

NEST: On or very near the ground in dense vegetation. The
small deep cup is supported by surrounding stems and is
made of dead leaves and coarse grass with small quantities of other fibers. The 5 white eggs (.64 x .51) are finely
speckled with brown.

RANGE: (M.) Breeds from s. Massachusetts, w. New York, s.
Michigan, and s.e. Minnesota south to Maryland, n.

Georgia (mts.), Kentucky, c. Missouri, and n.e. Kansas. Winters from s. Mexico south to Guatemala.

Golden-winged x Blue-winged Warbler Hybrids
Vermivora chrysoptera x Vermivora pinus—✳24

IDENTIFICATION: These birds are somewhat variable in appearance. Brewster hybrids may have the gray back more or less washed with olive-green, and the white under parts may show yellow, especially on the breast. The wing bars may be broadly yellow or white. The duller females usually have more green on the back and more yellow on the under parts than the average male. Lawrence hybrids run closer to type, but the wing bars may be broad and either yellow or white, or narrowly white. Females are like female blue-wingeds with dusky olive instead of black cheek and throat markings and occasionally a broad yellow wing bar.

HABITS: So far as is known, the hybrids behave like the two parent species which, in turn, have similar habits.

VOICE: Some individuals have a song like the golden-winged's, others like the blue-winged's, or the song may be a mixture of the two, each bird having its own variation. Generally Brewster's sing more like golden-wingeds, Lawrence's like blue-wingeds.

RANGE: (M.) See range of the two preceding species. These hybrids are the result of interbreeding where the ranges of the parent species overlap. Their winter range is unknown.

COMMENT: Hybrids in nature are rare, and when they occur it is usually between closely related species. Among North American birds the most notable hybrids are produced when golden-winged and blue-winged warblers interbreed. The bird that results from the initial cross is different from either parent. Originally it was described as a distinct

GOLDEN-WINGED × BLUE-WINGED WARBLER HYBRIDS

Golden-winged Warbler
Blue-winged Warbler

White under parts genes W-W
Unplain throat (black) genes p-p

Unwhite under parts (yellow) genes w-w
Plain throat genes P-P

Parents (P₁) — Normal body cells

Wp Wp
wP wP

F₁ gametes — Sperm or Egg cells

Wp   wP

Brewster Hybrid

First generation (F₁)

Wp wP — White under parts W-w   Plain throat P-p

F₁ gametes ♂

WP   Wp   wP   wp

FIRST GENERATION OFFSPRING OF BREWSTER HYBRIDS

♀	WP	Wp	wP	wp
WP	WP WP *Brewster Type*	Wp WP *Brewster Type*	wP WP *Brewster Type*	wp WP *Brewster Hybrid*
Wp	WP Wp *Brewster Type*	Wp Wp *Golden-Wing Warbler*	wP Wp *Brewster Hybrid*	wp Wp *Golden-Wing Type*
wP	WP wP *Brewster Type*	Wp wP *Brewster Hybrid*	wP wP *Blue-Wing Warbler*	wp wP *Blue-Wing Type*
wp	WP wp *Brewster Hybrid*	Wp wp *Golden-Wing Type*	wP wp *Blue-Wing Type*	wp wp *Lawrence Hybrid*

Lawrence Hybrid — Unwhite under parts w-w   Unplain throat p-p

R+S

species and called Brewster's warbler. Occasionally, when one hybrid breeds with another, a new and distinctive plumage results. Birds of this type were originally described as Lawrence's warblers.

The basic genetics of these interesting crosses is set forth here in graphic form. Every normal living cell has within it pairs of bodies known as chromosomes, each of which contains a series of individual inheritance units known as genes. Each pair of genes controls the development of color, form, or other attribute of some part of the body of the individual. As one gene in each pair came from the male parent and the other from the female, the genes for a given character may or may not be alike in the two chromosomes of a given pair. When they are alike they jointly regulate the development of a given character; i.e., they pull together. But when a gene from one parent is entirely different from the corresponding gene from the other, one gene is commonly stronger and dominates. The stronger is called the "dominant" and the weaker the "recessive" gene.

The color gene of the blue-winged warbler which produces a plain throat is always dominant when paired with a golden-winged's black throat-color gene: therefore, the hybrid's throat is plain. Similarly the golden-winged's under-part-color gene which produces white under parts is dominant over the yellow under-part-color gene of the blue-winged. The result, then, of this initial cross is always a plain-throated bird with largely white under parts; i.e., Brewster's warbler. Occasionally in second or subsequent generations an individual hybrid inherits from both parents the weak or recessive genes for throat and under-part color, in which case it becomes a black-throated bird with yellow under parts; i.e., Lawrence's warbler.

For simplicity the result of a pure Brewster mating is shown. Whether such matings occur is unknown, but the chances are against it. Most Lawrence's hybrids probably result from matings of Brewster's with impure blue-winged

or golden-winged birds: in this way an occasional offspring
could obtain both of the necessary pairs of recessive genes.

Bachman's Warbler   *Vermivora bachmanii*—#22

IDENTIFICATION: L. 4¼. The male could be confused only
with the much larger hooded warbler in which the black on
breast and crown are connected along the neck. The gray-
headed female differs from the more extensively gray-
headed Nashville warbler in having the forehead and eye
ring yellowish. Immature males have a smaller, partly obscured throat patch, and immature females are less yellow and have grayer backs.

HABITS: These warblers have generally been found breeding
in heavily wooded swamps and bottom lands, where they
nest in tangled brush on the higher areas. In migration
they seem to keep to the tops of the tallest trees along
swamp-fringed rivers. At other times, especially when nesting, they feed in lower swamp levels. During the nesting
period, which often starts in March, they are persistent
singers. This bird hàs suffered from the cutting of swamp
timber and from agricultural drainage. Many of its former haunts are gone, and the demand for further lumber
and drainage bode ill for what is perhaps the rarest of
North American warblers.

VOICE: The song is a rattly trill of some 8 notes on the same
pitch. It resembles the song of a worm-eating warbler or
chipping sparrow, but the pitch is higher and the quality
nearer that of a lazy parula warbler. Another song much
like a prothonotary's vigorous *tweet, tweet, tweet* has been
noted.

NEST: One to 3 feet off the ground among upright stalks of
cane, blackberry, or other low shrubs; a cup of stems and
leaves lined with fine black fibers. The 3 or 4 eggs (.63 x
.48) are pure white.

RANGE: (M.) Probably breeds, or once bred, from e. North
Carolina, s. Indiana, and s.e. Missouri south to South Carolina, c. Alabama, and n.e. Arkansas. Winters in Cuba and
the Isle of Pines.

Tennessee Warbler   *Vermivora peregrina*—✳30

IDENTIFICATION: L. 5. Except for its smaller size and thin,
fine-pointed bill, this bird looks a good deal like a vireo,
but its quick, nervous activity is in strong contrast with
the vireo's slow deliberation. Among warblers the light
line over the eye is distinctive. Only the spring male has
clear gray on the head, a clear white eyeline, and fairly
white under parts. In all other plumages the birds are
rather uniformly bright olive-green above; eyeline and
under parts are rather yellow or greenish-yellow, except
for the pure-white under-tail coverts.

HABITS: The summer home is about openings and clearings in
northern woodlands. The birds seem to need grassy or
boggy areas mixed with dense brush and clumps of young
second-growth timber. In such areas they are often so
abundant as to seem colonial in their nesting habits. Their
normal food is small insects, but they do pierce ripe grapes
to drink the juice. Some berry eating is reported, and at a
feeding station they displayed a liking for bananas. In
spring they feed in treetops, but in fall they are everywhere in weed tangles and hedgerows.

Audubon saw only three Tennessees, a fact hard to
reconcile with their present abundance. The increase in
population is probably due to the increase (because of
forest destruction) in the brushy, semi-open country which
the species requires for nesting.

VOICE: The songs are variable but are all of a sharp quality
like the chatter of chimney swifts. A common song is a
rapid series of notes followed by a lower-pitched series of
shorter and more rapid notes—*zit-zit-zit*, etc., *zi-zi-zi-zi*,

etc. Another is in 3 parts, each higher or lower than the preceding series. The first part is a trill, then a double-noted *chipa-chipa*, etc., followed by a rapid series of single notes. In flight it utters a series of sharp double notes—*zeep-zeep*.

NEST: In sphagnum moss, under a sedge tussock, or on the ground under a small shrub; made of coarse sedge and grass lined with finer grass; invariably well hidden. The 5 or 6 white eggs (.60 x .47) are speckled with brown.

RANGE: (M.) Breeds from Anticosti Island, c. Quebec, n. Manitoba, and c. Yukon south to n. Maine, n. New York, n. Michigan, s. Manitoba, and s. British Columbia. Migrates east of the Rockies and in spring chiefly west of the Appalachians. Winters from s. Mexico south to Colombia and Venezuela.

Orange-crowned Warbler*   *Vermivora celata*—✳30

IDENTIFICATION: L. 5. These birds are characterized by their dull olive-green color, slightly lighter and yellower below than above. The under parts always show indistinct dusky streaking. The concealed orange crown patch is valueless as a field mark. In fall when the birds are a duskier olive there is usually little difference between upper and under parts.

HABITS: In the Arctic this bird breeds as far north as dwarf woody growths occur along stream bottoms. Throughout its range it strongly prefers thickets and does most of its foraging at moderate heights. It frequents dense new growths on cutover lands, is found in open woodlands where underbrush is heavy, and is especially attracted to steep shaded slopes and streamside thickets. In the northern states it is a late fall migrant.

VOICE: The song is a varied, rather musical short trill. The opening notes are often slow, followed by a more rapid series higher in pitch. At the end the notes decrease in volume and rise or fall in pitch as they become richer in tone. Call note a sharp *chip*.

NEST: On the ground under a bush, more rarely in a shrub or tree; a cup of long, coarse grass and bark fiber, lined with fine grasses, moss, downs, feathers, and fur. The 5 white eggs (.63 x .49) are finely spotted with reddish-brown.

RANGE: (P.M.) Breeds from n. Manitoba, n. Mackenzie, and n.w. Alaska south to s. Manitoba, New Mexico, and n. Lower California. Winters from South Carolina, Arkansas, s.c. Texas, and s. California south to s. Florida and Guatemala. Found east in migration to Massachusetts, especially in late fall.

Nashville Warbler*   *Vermivora ruficapilla*—✳22

IDENTIFICATION: L. 4¾. The clear, bright yellow under parts and gray head of spring adults are distinctive. The white or buffy eye ring is a good character, but the chestnut crown patch is hard to see and is often lacking in the female. In fall adults and immatures the head is brownish, the back grayer, and the breast tinged with brown.

HABITS: This bird is an inhabitant of one of the earlier of the many successive stages through which land passes as it returns to forest after being clear-cut, burned, or abandoned for agriculture or grazing. Such an area is at the right stage for Nashvilles when clumps of young trees, especially birches, are 10 to 12 feet high and plenty of low brush cover is available. Once established, the bird usually persists as a breeder until the trees have formed a woodland with an overhead canopy which excludes sunlight and kills the brush. The Nashville is one of the many birds that has prospered through man's activities, but it continues to occur, as it must always have done, on undisturbed lands where because of either swampy conditions or aridity trees are present only in scattered clumps interspersed with brushy areas. In migration they feed in the tall treetops as well as in the lower growths, their normal foraging grounds. On the breeding grounds the song is usually given from a perch in or near the top of a small tree.

VOICE: The common 2-part song is pleasingly musical. The first half is a series of several 2-note phrases followed by a trilled series of lower, short, single notes that fade toward the end.

NEST: On the ground, hidden at the base of a shrub or stump or worked into the side of a mossy hummock; made of grasses, moss, and leaves lined with fine grass, pine needles, rootlets, or similar material. The 4 or 5 white eggs (.61 x .48) are speckled with brown, usually in a wreath.

RANGE: (M.) Breeds from Cape Breton Island, s. Quebec, c. Ontario, and c. Saskatchewan south to Connecticut, n. Pennsylvania, n. Illinois, and Nebraska. Also s. British Columbia south to s. California and east to Idaho. Winters from s. Florida and s. Texas to Guatemala.

Parula Warbler   *Compsothlypis americana*—✳25

IDENTIFICATION: L. 4½. The adult male is unmistakable. Fall males, females, and immatures have increasing amounts of green washed over the blue and less of a band across the yellow breast.

HABITS: This warbler is most commonly found breeding in the vicinity of swamps, ponds, and lakes, around woodland openings, or other areas where trees are festooned with either Spanish moss or usnea lichen, but it may occur anywhere in wooded areas. The species is insectivorous and does most of its feeding in treetops.

VOICE: The song is a wheezy or buzzy high-pitched ascending trill ending abruptly with a louder, explosive final note. The trill may or may not be preceded by a few even-pitched staccato notes of the same distinctive quality.

NEST: At varying heights from rather low to 50 or more feet up. In the North the nest is always in the center of a hanging tuft of usnea lichen, commonly known as "old man's beard moss." In the South, Spanish moss, which has a similar manner of growth, is used. In both cases the living "moss" is woven into a basketlike nest which is sparingly lined. Where no hanging moss is available the bird is generally rare as a breeder, but it does occur in hemlocks and spruces, the drooping twigs of which will support a woven basketlike nest of grasses, bark shreds, and downs. The 4 or 5 white eggs (.67 x .48) are speckled and spotted with browns.

RANGE: (M.) Breeds from Anticosti Island, c. Ontario, n. Minnesota, and e. Nebraska south to c. Florida, the Gulf Coast, and s.c. Texas. Winters from c. Florida and the Bahamas south to Barbados and from s. Mexico to Nicaragua.

Pitiayumi Warbler   *Compsothlypis pitiayumi*—#25

IDENTIFICATION: L. 4½. The almost black areas along the sides of the face and the absence of a distinct band across the breast are good field marks. Other differences from a parula are the shorter wing bars and the lack of white around the eye. Females are greener and duller.

HABITS: This bird is found in dense woodlands and thickets along river bottoms. It does most of its feeding in the tops of the tallest trees and would be hard to find were it not for its song.

VOICE: Similar to that of a parula warbler.

NEST: Anywhere from 8 feet to well up in a treetop. The nest is built into a clump of hanging moss or other air plant, the fibers of which are woven together to make the nest cup. The 3 or 4 white eggs (.60 x .45) are speckled and spotted with brown.

RANGE: (R.) Occurs from extreme s. Texas south to Brazil.

Yellow Warbler

Dendroica petechia—✳21

IDENTIFICATION: L. 5. This is our only bird which has an all-yellow appearance in the field. Males of some tropical American races, including that of the Florida Keys, have a reddish-brown patch on the top of the head. Females and immatures are a darker, more greenish-yellow above and paler below with fewer streaks—sometimes none. Juveniles are pale olive-brown above with yellow-edged dark brown wings and pale, plain yellow under parts.

HABITS: The yellow warbler frequents lowlands grown up to scattered small trees or dense shrubbery. Its common wild haunts are willows and alders along streams and ponds, but it is almost equally at home in orchards, gardens, hedgerows, and shade trees. In the Far North and in dry western grasslands it nests wherever small patches of woody plants persist in sheltered areas or low spots.

VOICE: This bird has a sweet, high-pitched, musical voice. The song is generally a series of about 4 introductory *weet* or *sweet* notes followed by a variable ending, which is sometimes a descending series of notes; at other times it drops at first and ends high. The goldfinch-like quality of the ending is distinctive.

NEST: Generally from 3 to 5 feet aboveground, occasionally higher; placed in an upright fork of a small tree or shrub. The nest has a deep foundation and is solidly built of long bark and plant fibers and grass and plant downs; it is lined with similar material. If a cowbird places an egg in the nest, the yellow warbler often covers it with a new nest cup and lays a fresh clutch. The 4 or 5 blue-white eggs (.70 x .50) are thickly speckled with brown.

RANGE: (P.M.) Breeds north to the limit of trees and from coast to coast from n. Quebec, n. Ontario, n. Mackenzie, and n.c. Alaska south to n. South Carolina, n. Alabama, s. Missouri, and c.w. Texas on south through Mexico to

n. Colombia. Also in the Florida Keys and throughout the West Indies. Winters from s. Mexico to Peru and east to the Guianas and Brazil.

Magnolia Warbler   *Dendroica magnolia—*❄26

IDENTIFICATION: L. 5. In all plumages the black band on the end of the largely white tail is distinctive. The breeding female is a less brilliant counterpart of the male, and in the quite different fall plumage adults and immatures are much alike. Juveniles are brown above, grayish and yellow below with brown streaks.

HABITS: Open stands of young conifers are the normal home, but scattered pairs are often found along woodland roads and about small, isolated openings in the forest. The species is generally abundant along swamps and shallow ponds where there are young trees. The second growth after a clean cutting of spruce is generally well suited to its needs, as are neglected pastures with scattered clumps of trees. Even in migration magnolias feed at rather low levels and tend to stay hidden inside a tree.

VOICE: The short, musical song begins with 2 slurred 2-note phrases followed by a variety of higher- (occasionally lower-) pitched endings. The whole suggests *weeta, weeta, weetee* or *weeta, weeta, weeto.*

NEST: In spruce, fir, or hemlock at almost any height but generally between 5 and 15 feet up. The loosely constructed shallow nest is made of twigs, plant stems, and grass and lined with black rootlets. The 4 white eggs (.65 x .48) are variably spotted or blotched with brown.

RANGE: (M.) Breeds from Newfoundland, c. Quebec, c. Manitoba, and s.w. Mackenzie south to n. Massachusetts, Virginia (mts.), n. Michigan, s. Saskatchewan, and c. Alberta. Winters from s. Mexico to Panama.

Cape May Warbler
Dendroica tigrina—✳28

IDENTIFICATION: L. 5. The handsome spring male is unmistakable, but in fall its bright colors are obscured by the feather tips—grayish above, white below. Females and immatures are much alike, with streaked under parts varying from white to yellowish. Their best field marks are the yellow to yellow-green rump, the light, often quite yellow, patch on the neck behind the ear, and the line over the eye.

HABITS: The Cape May is a bird of the mature spruce-fir forests of the North. It seems to prefer open parklike stands or those in which patches of birches occur. It feeds in low shrubbery and in treetops and in migration has an affinity for conifers. A favorite singing perch is the tip of a tall spruce. Its food consists chiefly of small insects, but in the fall it displays a great fondness for the juice of ripe grapes.

VOICE: The commonest song is a series of 6 to 12 identical staccato notes on the same high pitch and of even loudness. The quality is thin and rather buzzy. Other songs are composed of short 2-note phrases like those of a black and white warbler or are in several parts on different pitches like those of a Tennessee.

NEST: From 30 to 60 feet aboveground, hidden a few feet from the top in a spruce or fir. The bulky, compact nest is made of sphagnum moss held together with vines and twigs; it is lined first with grass, then with fur, feathers, and rootlets. The 4 white eggs (.65 x .50) are spotted and blotched with reddish-brown.

RANGE: (M.) Breeds from New Brunswick, n. Ontario, and s. Mackenzie south to n. New Hampshire and s. Manitoba. Winters in the West Indies, chiefly in the Greater Antilles and Bahamas.

Black-throated Blue Warbler
Dendroica caerulescens—✳27

IDENTIFICATION: L. 5¼. The small square white patch on the wing is the best character. Fall and immature males have the blue washed with green, the black flecked with white. Immature females are greenish above and washed with dusky yellow below; their white wing patch may be largely concealed.

HABITS: This warbler occurs during the breeding season in deciduous and mixed woodlands, provided they have a thick, shrubby undergrowth. Steeply sloping land with a ground cover of laurel or yew seems especially attractive. In migration they commonly stay close to the ground.

VOICE: There is considerable variation in the songs of this bird. The commonest is a series of 3 to 5 long, slow, husky notes on the same pitch, ending with a drawn-out, slurred, rising note—*quee, quee, quee, quee, quee-e-e-e.*

NEST: From a few inches to 3 feet aboveground in a shrub, tree or seedling, rank weed, or fallen branch. The nest cup is of fine bark shreds, grass, leaves, and often rotten wood, bound together with cobwebs and lined with black rootlets and hair. The 4 white eggs (.68 x .50) are variously marked with browns.

RANGE: (M.) Breeds from s. Quebec, c. Ontario, and n. Minnesota south to n. Connecticut, n. Georgia (mts.), s. Ontario, n. Michigan, and c. Minnesota. Occurs west to Kansas in migration. Winters from the Florida Keys and Bahamas through the Greater Antilles and in Guatemala and Colombia.

Myrtle Warbler
Dendroica coronata—✳27

IDENTIFICATION: L. 5½. The bright yellow rump and the yellow patches on the sides of the breast are the best field marks in all plumages. In fall an occasional immature female lacks the yellow breast patches.

HABITS: The myrtle is the most abundant northern warbler and wanders farther north than any other. It breeds throughout northern coniferous woodlands, showing preference for the more open stands and the borders of clearings. In migration myrtles occur everywhere and are especially abundant in brushy areas, hedgerows, field borders, and weedy tangles. When insects are not available they live on seeds and berries. Fruits of wax myrtle, bayberry, red cedar, and poison ivy are staple winter foods. At feeding shelves they are attracted by doughnut crumbs, suet, and sunflower seeds.

VOICE: The common song during migration is a jumbled series of 6 to 15 rapid, weak, and colorless notes varying irregularly in pitch. Later it has a song of 2-note phrases, the second note lower than the first, which usually trends upward in over-all pitch. The loud, harsh *tchip* call note is distinctive.

NEST: Generally in an evergreen from 5 to 50 feet up, most commonly about 15 feet. The loose, bulky nest is usually saddled on a limb part way out from the trunk. It is made of twigs, grasses, rootlets, moss, and plant fibers and is thickly lined with hair and feathers. The 4 or 5 white eggs (.70 x .52) are speckled or blotched with browns.

RANGE: (M.) Breeds from the northern limit of trees in c. Quebec, n. Manitoba, n. Mackenzie, n. Alaska, and e. Siberia south to Maine, n. New York, n. Michigan, s. Alberta, and n. British Columbia. Winters from New England, the Ohio Valley, Kansas, and on the Pacific coast from c. Oregon south to the Greater Antilles and Panama.

Audubon's Warbler *Dendroica auduboni*—✳27

IDENTIFICATION: L. 5. Differs from the myrtle warbler in having a yellow throat and white on 4 or 5 of the outer tail feathers instead of on 2 or 3. Occasionally an immature female does not show yellow on the throat.

HABITS: This abundant warbler takes the place of the myrtle as a breeder throughout the coniferous forests of our western mountains, ranging up to timber line. In fall and winter they are found everywhere from shade trees and garden shrubbery to brushy hillsides, open lands, and ocean dunes. Their feeding habits at this time become quite varied as they fly-catch, forage on the ground, search flowers for nectar and insects, and eat seeds and fruits, including feeding-shelf raisins.

VOICE: The thin, colorless song starts with several slow notes followed by a more rapid jumble of short notes rising or falling in pitch toward the end. The *tsup* call note is softer than a myrtle's.

NEST: From a few feet to 50 or more aboveground, usually part way out on a horizontal conifer limb but occasionally in a deciduous tree or shrub; made of fine twigs, rootlets, and other plant fibers and lined with hair and feathers. The 4 grayish-white eggs (.72 x .54) are sparsely but boldly marked with brown.

RANGE: (P.M.) Breeds from w.c. Saskatchewan, c. Alberta, and c. British Columbia south to Guatemala and east to w. South Dakota and w. Texas. Winters from s. Texas and w. Washington south to Guatemala.

Black-throated Gray Warbler
Dendroica nigrescens—✳29

IDENTIFICATION: L. 4¾. The black-and-white head pattern is distinctive. Females tend to be gray where the male is black, and their throats are often white. Fall birds are duller and slightly brownish on the back, the black markings somewhat obscured and the sides washed with brown.

HABITS: This warbler likes dense low growths interspersed with trees for singing perches. Otherwise it is tolerant of a wide range of conditions. In the North it occurs in and about openings in the fir forest, where tree seedlings or other undergrowth are present. Throughout most of its range it favors dry slopes grown up to oaks, pines, junipers, and manzanita. Much of its feeding is done in the low chaparral.

VOICE: The song is a lazy, low-pitched lisping which sounds like a rolling *wee-zy, wee-zy, wee-zy, wee, zee,* with a final syllable slurred up or down and strongly accented.

NEST: At heights of from 3 to 50 feet. The higher nests in conifers are generally on a limb out from the trunk, while the lower ones in oaks or shrubs are usually in a clump of leaves. The nest is a cup of well-bleached plant fibers lined with fur and feathers. The 4 white eggs (.69 x .50) are brown-spotted.

RANGE: (M.) Breeds from n.w. Colorado and s. British Columbia south to s. New Mexico and n. Lower California. Winters south from s. Texas and s. Lower California through most of Mexico.

Black-throated Green Warbler
Dendroica virens—⚹28

IDENTIFICATION: L. 5. The bright yellow cheeks are a good field mark, especially with young females, which, lacking the black throat, might be taken for pine warblers. The very different juveniles are dull brown above, dull white below, dusky on the throat, and spotted on the breast and sides.

HABITS: The black-throated green is essentially a woodland warbler although it inhabits old cedar-grown pastures and second growths. It is widely distributed and occurs in all types of forests but prefers open stands of large trees. Pines and hemlocks attract it, as do bog communities of spruce and larch. The bird spends much of its time in the treetops and is hard to detect except by its song.

Voice: In all its many forms the lazy, sibilant quality of the song is distinctive. Commonest is a series of about 6 identical high-pitched notes terminated by two lower notes—*zee, zee, zee, zee, zee, zee, so say*. Another common song consists of 4 or 5 notes, each on a different pitch.

Nest: From within a few inches of the ground to high up in a tree. The favorite site is among the branches of a conifer. The deep nest cup of grass, bark shreds, moss, fine twigs, and birch bark is bound together with cobwebs. The lining is generally of hair and feathers. The 4 or 5 white eggs (.65 x .46) are spotted and scrawled with browns.

Range: (M.) Breeds from Newfoundland, c. Quebec, c. Ontario, s. Manitoba, and c. Alberta south to coastal South Carolina, the mountains of n. Georgia and Alabama, n. Ohio, s. Wisconsin, and s. Minnesota. Winters from n.e. Mexico south to Panama, less commonly from s. Florida through the West Indies.

Golden-cheeked Warbler   *Dendroica chrysoparia*—✳28

Identification: L. 5. The black in the upper parts of both sexes, solid in the male and streaked in the female, is distinctive. Immature females resemble those of the black-throated green but lack yellow on the under parts.

Habits: This warbler, rare in terms of total range, is common in its chosen habitat—the dry upper slopes and ridges of the Edwards Plateau. Here it occupies a dwarf forest of cedar and oak, in which it seems especially attracted to the neighborhood of isolated old cedars which dominate the lower scrub oak.

Voice: A high-pitched sibilant song, usually short and hurriedly delivered. Often written as *tweah, tweah, twee-sy*.

Nest: From 6 to 20 feet up in an upright fork of a tree, generally an old cedar; made of shredded cedar bark, grass, and rootlets, with some cobweb material; lined with hair and feathers. The 4 white eggs (.66 x .51) are finely speckled with brown.

RANGE: (M.) Breeds in the Edwards Plateau of s.c. Texas. Winters from s. Mexico to Nicaragua.

Cerulean Warbler   *Dendroica cerulea—*✳25

IDENTIFICATION: L. 4½. The bluish male, with a narrow blackish line across the breast, is easily recognized. The female is dull blue-gray only on the head, the back being strongly greenish. Immatures resemble fall blackpolls but are brighter green above and less extensively yellow below.

HABITS: The cerulean, a treetop warbler, is partial to open stands of large trees. It is not a uniformly distributed species and tends to occur in small, widely scattered colonies in especially favorable spots. Old riverbank woodlands seem to be one of these. Its habits make it hard to see, but it is an incessant singer.

VOICE: A common song is a husky, rolling series of 4 or 5 short notes on the same pitch followed by a higher-pitched trill. This final trill is generally all on the same pitch but may rise like a parula's. It can be written *tse, tse, tse, tse, te-e-e-e-e-e-e.*

NEST: Twenty-five to 60 feet aboveground on a lower branch of a tall tree, generally on a branch that hangs well out over an opening. The shallow nest is neatly woven of bark fibers or old weed stalks and lined with moss stalks or hair. The 4 whitish eggs (.60 x .47) are variably marked with brown.

RANGE: (M.) Breeds from s. New York, s. Ontario, s. Wisconsin, s. Minnesota, and s.e. Nebraska south to Delaware, n. Georgia, c. Alabama, Louisiana, and n.e. Texas. Winters from Venezuela to c. Peru.

Blackburnian Warbler

Dendroica fusca—#26

IDENTIFICATION: L. 5¼. Females and fall males are marked like the vivid spring males, but the orange areas are duller or replaced by yellow and the black areas are masked by brown feather tips. Immatures have pale yellow in place of orange and are indistinctly streaked on the sides. The large amount of white in the tail is a good field mark in all plumages.

HABITS: Tall timber is the normal home. The bird is found in deciduous and coniferous forests but is generally most abundant in mixed woodlands with large hemlocks, spruces, or pines. Most feeding is high up in the forest canopy, and the males sing from treetop perches. Like many warblers, these are apt to be found in various habitats in migration, but treetops remain the best place to look for them.

VOICE: The song is variable in form and has considerable tone range, some of the notes being very high-pitched. The thin, wiry quality is distinctive. The general form is first a series of 4 double notes followed by a trill or a rapid run of short notes. The ending may be higher or lower in pitch and is occasionally slurred upward.

NEST: Anywhere from 6 to 60 feet up, generally in a large conifer and usually well out on a branch; made of fine twigs and soft plant down or usnea lichen, lined with bark shreds, rootlets, and occasionally hair. The 4 white eggs (.68 x .50) are spotted and blotched with rich browns.

RANGE: (M.) Breeds from Cape Breton Island, c. Quebec, c. Ontario, and c. Manitoba south to Connecticut, n. Georgia (mts.), n. Michigan, and c. Minnesota. Winters from Yucatan and Venezuela to c. Peru.

Yellow-throated Warbler*   *Dendroica dominica—*✳25

IDENTIFICATION: L. 5¼. Females of this gray-backed bird differ from males in having slightly less black about the head. All fall birds are washed with brown above and below.

HABITS: The big timber of bottom lands, swamps, and river-banks is a common habitat. The bird is especially frequent in stands of old sycamore and cypress. Mature pines in open stands or in mixed woods may be inhabited, but here the distribution is usually irregular. In the South it seems attracted by any woodland where Spanish moss drapes the trees. The birds stay in the treetops and are rather deliberate in movement as they creep along the upper limbs thoroughly searching each spot before moving on.

VOICE: The song has many variations but is generally fairly loud and musical. A common form is a series of clear double syllables that run down the scale and grow fainter, ending on an abrupt higher note. Others with more variation in pitch suggest the indigo bunting.

NEST: From 20 to more than 100 feet up on a horizontal limb of a large tree except where Spanish moss occurs, then invariably in a hanging clump of it near the end of a limb; made of bark shreds and grass lined with downs, feathers, and hair. The 4 dull greenish-white eggs (.69 x .52) are blotched with purplish and brownish marks.

RANGE: (P.M.) Breeds from s. New Jersey, Maryland, Ohio, s. Michigan, s. Wisconsin, and s.e. Nebraska south to c. Florida, the n. Bahamas, the Gulf Coast, and c. Texas. Winters from e. South Carolina through the Bahamas and Greater Antilles and from s. Texas to Costa Rica.

Sutton's Warbler*   *Dendroica potomac—*✳25

IDENTIFICATION: L. 5¼. The bright yellow throat and breast bordered with black on the side neck, together with the blue-gray upper parts and greenish back patch, separate this from other warblers. The female is much like the male except that the black markings are restricted.

HABITS: One of the two known specimens was collected on a dry hillside dominated by scrub pine mixed with oak, the other 18 miles away in a wet willow-sycamore woodland. The bird was unknown until these specimens were obtained in late May of 1939: the male 12 miles s.e. of Martinsburg, the female 4 miles n.w. of Shepherdtown, West Virginia. Little more is known except for subsequent sight records from the same area and a bird reported in migration near Tampa, Florida, in September 1944. Further collecting is forbidden.

The chances that this is a hybrid between two well-known species seem remote, but it is amazing that so striking a bird could so long remain undetected in a well-studied region like eastern North America. This lends support to the possibility that Audubon's carbonated warbler, collected at Henderson, Kentucky, in 1811 and figured on plate ☒60 of the elephant folio, may still exist. The same may be true of two other mystery warblers—the Blue Mountain and the small-headed. The first was described and illustrated by Wilson (plate ☒44) from specimens taken near the Blue Ridge of Virginia, close to where Sutton's warbler was found. The other, which Wilson called the small-headed flycatcher, was collected by him in New Jersey and Pennsylvania and by Audubon in Kentucky.

VOICE: Described as a rapid, buzzy, parula-like trill ascending the scale, then dropping abruptly to a lower pitch just before the end. The whole is repeated twice in rapid succession without a break.

NEST: Unknown.

RANGE: (M.) Apparently breeds in the n.e. "panhandle" of West Virginia but may occur in adjacent parts of Pennsylvania, Maryland, and Virginia.

Chestnut-sided Warbler*

Dendroica pensylvanica—#28

IDENTIFICATION: L. 5. The female is duller than the male, and the brown stripe is narrower or broken. Fall adults and immatures are much alike except that young birds lack any brown. In fall plumage the clear yellow-green of the upper parts, the white eye ring, and white under parts are distinctive.

HABITS: This warbler, which a hundred years ago was so rare that Audubon saw it but once, is now abundant. The brushy sprout growth that follows clear-cutting and the early stages of forest regeneration on abandoned farm- and pasturelands afford it ideal habitat. When the young trees finally form a dense second-growth woodland with a closed canopy the bird vanishes from the area.

The brief period that an area remains suitable illustrates the instability of bird populations on other than forested areas. In general, birds that do not inhabit deep woodlands are throughout the normally forested part of the continent dependent on man or fire to create their required habitats. Furthermore, in the absence of continuing or repeated disturbance, each species' tenure of an area is limited to the time it takes the plant community to mature into the succeeding stage of its transformation into forest. Thus weeds follow grass, brushland follows weeds, open second growth comes next, and so on, with each stage providing the habitat for a different set of birds.

VOICE: This warbler has a loud, clear, musical song not unlike a yellow warbler's. The spring song is a series of about 5 2-note phrases ending with a strongly accented phrase that starts high and is slurred down—like *tawee, tawee, tawee, tawee, tawee, ta-wee'-cha*. The less distinctive, more variable summer song is a longer run of slurred 2-note phrases that generally falls in pitch.

NEST: About 2 or 3 feet up in a shrub or small tree; a loosely built cup of grass, weed stalks, plant downs, and bark shreds lined with fine grasses, rootlets, and hair. The 4 white eggs (.69 x .50) are marked with brownish spots of varying size.

RANGE: (M.) Breeds from Newfoundland, s. Quebec, c. Ontario, c. Manitoba, and c. Saskatchewan south to n. New Jersey, n. Georgia (mts.), n. Ohio, Illinois, s. Missouri, and e. Nebraska. Winters from Guatemala to Panama.

Bay-breasted Warbler   *Dendroica castanea*—\#29

IDENTIFICATION: L. 5½. The richly colored males with conspicuous, buffy neck patches and the similarly marked but less extensively brown females are easily identified. Fall adults usually show a trace of brown on the sides, but immatures are much like blackpolls, except that they are a brighter, clearer green above with fewer dark streaks, have yellower wing bars, are buffier, and (at most) are very distinctly streaked below. Feet and legs are darker than the blackpoll's, but the surest mark is the buffy color of the under-tail coverts.

HABITS: This warbler is an inhabitant of spruce woodlands of the Canadian zone. Like so many species, it is attracted to small forest openings with a scattered growth of vigorous young trees. It is often common along the borders of clearings and in overgrown pastures and lumbered-off areas dominated by 6- to 10-foot trees. The borders of bogs and ponds also provide breeding grounds. The birds feed at all heights and are rather deliberate in movement. The bulk of them go south in fall considerably ahead of the blackpolls which they so closely resemble at this time of year.

VOICE: The common song in migration is an irregular series of notes of varying length on the same high pitch, thin and sibilant but rather pleasant. They have more varied songs on their northern breeding grounds. One starts like the preceding but ends in a warble.

NEST: On a limb or against the trunk of a conifer at heights of from 4 to more than 40 feet; loosely built of twigs, grass, and pine needles lined with rootlets and hair. The 5 white eggs (.72 x .52) are covered with brown markings of varying size.

RANGE: (M.) Breeds from Newfoundland, n. Ontario, c. Manitoba, and e.c. Alberta south to Maine, n. New York, n. Michigan, and n. Minnesota. Winters from Panama to Colombia.

Blackpoll Warbler   *Dendroica striata*—#29

IDENTIFICATION: L. 5½. The black-capped spring male is easily identified. The spring female lacks the cap and is somewhat greenish above, slightly yellowish below, and lightly streaked. In fall adults and young are alike. They differ from young bay-breasteds in being a duller green more thickly streaked with black above and in being yellowish rather than buffy below, with definite side streaks. The legs and feet are paler, and the belly and under-tail coverts are pure white.

HABITS: This abundant warbler is commonest in treetops in migration and is the latest of the spring migrants. Its breeding grounds are among the dwarfed spruces and firs of the northern part of the coniferous forest. Farther south it occurs chiefly where high altitudes or oceanic winds or bog conditions have created areas of stunted spruce and fir.

VOICE: The song is a series of 12 or more short, sibilant, staccato notes on the same high pitch; readily identified by the way it gradually increases in volume until the middle is reached and then fades out at the end.

NEST: Generally 4 to 12 feet up in a small conifer, occasionally on the ground; loosely made of grasses, twigs, rootlets, and moss, often with feathers in the lining. The 4 or 5 white eggs (.70 x .54) are spotted and blotched with browns.

RANGE: (M.) Breeds from the northern limit of trees in Newfoundland, n. Quebec, n. Manitoba, n. Mackenzie, and n.w. Alaska south to n. Maine, s.c. New York (Catskills), n. Michigan, s. Manitoba, and n. British Columbia.

Winters from the Guianas and Venezuela to Brazil.

Pine Warbler   *Dendroica pinus*—✳30

IDENTIFICATION: L. 5½. The male is not unlike a yellow-throated vireo in color but has a greenish rump, a faintly streaked breast, which is not as clear or as bright a yellow as the vireo's, and a line over the eye instead of yellow spectacles. Females and immatures are a plain, almost olive-brown above and are often dingy white below, with little if any trace of yellow.

HABITS: This bird is well named, as it is nearly always associated with pines. The birds feed on insects, searching the trees from top to bottom like creepers, and do some feeding on the ground. Pine seeds supplemented by other seeds and berries are staple winter foods.

VOICE: The song is a run of short notes varying slightly in pitch and almost rapid enough to be called a trill. It is like a chipping sparrow's but softer, lower-pitched, and not so rapid.

NEST: From 10 feet aboveground to the tops of the tallest trees, usually concealed in foliage out on a horizontal limb; made of bark strips, weed stems, twigs, and pine needles held together with silk and lined with fur and feathers. The 4 white eggs (.70 x .52) are wreathed with brown spots.

RANGE: (P.M.) Breeds from New Brunswick, s. Quebec, s. Ontario, n. Michigan, s. Manitoba, and c. Alberta south to s. Florida, the n. Bahamas, Hispaniola, and the Gulf

Coast to e.c. Texas. Winters from Virginia and s. Illinois south to Florida and into n.e. Mexico.

Kirtland's Warbler   *Dendroica kirtlandii*—#24

IDENTIFICATION: L. 5¾. This large, tail-wagging warbler is not easily confused with any other. Females are slightly duller than males, paler, and less sharply marked with black. In fall adults and young are strongly washed with brown above and on the sides.

HABITS: The only place this warbler seems willing to nest is in an open stand of young jack pines averaging 6 to 12 feet in height; it is therefore not likely to find any area suitable for more than a few years. Here we seem to have a species so dependent upon recurring fires for the creation of suitable habitat that it might conceivably be exterminated by rigid fire suppression over its very limited range. Although known as a breeder only from Michigan, it should be looked or listened for in similar jack-pine country in other areas.

VOICE: The song is a rapidly articulated jumble which suggests the songs of the northern water-thrush and the house wren. Its outstanding characteristics are its loudness (carries ¼ mile at times), its liquid, bubbling quality, and the lively, emphatic manner in which it is delivered. Lower-pitched than the song of any other eastern *Dendroica*, it starts low and rises to the end, becoming louder and faster as it progresses.

NEST: Sunk in the ground and well concealed, usually in a clump of small pines in an opening; made of strips of bark and weed fiber and lined with fine grasses, pine needles, and hair. The 4 white eggs (.72 x .56) are speckled with fine brown spots.

RANGE: (M.) Breeds in n.c. Michigan. Winters in the Bahamas.

Prairie Warbler   *Dendroica discolor*—✳31

IDENTIFICATION: L. 4¾. The male is distinctively marked. Females and immatures are similar, but the brown back patch is usually more or less obscured and the whole back washed with gray; the black side and flank streaks may be fainter or absent and the cheeks gray.

HABITS: This is not a bird of the prairie but of brushy land. It seldom feeds high and is notably active—constantly tilting its tail and often fluttering its wings. A cutover woodland, after many of the stumps have sent up vigorous sprouts, exactly suits the prairie warbler for a few years. It also breeds on abandoned agricultural lands and pastures that are growing up to shrubs and young trees. Probably because of the unstable and temporary character of the plant communities it inhabits, its distribution is very spotty. Even on apparently suitable lands there may be a considerable year-to-year fluctuation. Only in a few areas are they reasonably permanent breeders. One is among the mangrove tangles that fringe the Florida coast and Keys. Another is in the oak-pine barrens on highly impoverished soils or on areas where recurring fires preclude the development of a more mature woodland.

VOICE: The rather loud and distinctive song is a long, ascending series of rapidly uttered short notes. The tone is pleasingly musical but buzzy.

NEST: Between 2 and 5 feet off the ground, occasionally up to 20 feet; usually concealed in dense leafy vegetation in a low thicket or out near a branch tip in a small tree. Made largely of plant downs, held together with grass and leaves, and lined with rootlets, hair, and feathers. The 4 white eggs (.63 x .47) are wreathed with brown spots.

RANGE: (P.M.) Breeds from Massachusetts, s. Ontario, n. Michigan, and e. Nebraska south to s. Florida, n. Mississippi, and Arkansas. Winters from c. Florida south through the West Indies to Martinique.

Palm Warbler* *Dendroica palmarum*—⚹31

IDENTIFICATION: L. 5¼. The constant tail wagging serves to identify this species in any plumage. Immatures sometimes lack the distinctive reddish-brown crown and may be yellow only on the breast. The palm warblers that nest in the Northeast are always more completely and more brightly yellow below.

HABITS: The summer home is about open spruce-tamarack bogs in northern woodlands. At other seasons it is widely scattered and often common about towns and gardens. It likes bare or open areas, as it spends much of its time feeding on the ground or in low vegetation. Insects are the chief food, but it can survive for some time on seeds and fruits, e.g., bayberry.

VOICE: The song is a weak but pleasant, rapid, trill-like run of 2-note syllables. They are on the same pitch, but there is usually an increase in volume at some point and often a few added twittery notes at the beginning and end.

NEST: On the ground in a hummock of moss or sedge under a small tree; made of grass and bark shreds, lined with rootlets and often feathers. The 4 or 5 white eggs (.63 x .50) are speckled or blotched with brown.

RANGE: (M.) Breeds from Newfoundland, c. Quebec, n. Ontario, and s. Mackenzie south to s. Nova Scotia, Maine, n. Michigan, n. Minnesota, and c. Alberta. Winters from South Carolina and the Gulf Coast to Puerto Rico and Yucatan, rarely from New Brunswick south along the coast.

Ovenbird*   *Seiurus aurocapillus*—✳31

IDENTIFICATION: L. 6. This heavy-bodied warbler with its black-bordered, pale orange-brown crown patch and black-streaked, white under parts is the same in all but the juvenile plumage. Young are bright brown above and paler brown below, except for a white belly, and are streaked with black above and below.

HABITS: This is a bird of the forest floor and is generally evenly distributed through all reasonably mature woodlands. It is, as a rule, more abundant in dry woods not too thick with underbrush and other low growths. Most of its feeding is on the ground, but it uses a low branch for a lookout and singing perch. Many who know the bird well are unfamiliar with its wonderful flight song, which can be heard from May to September, most often in late afternoon or on moonlight nights, but sometimes in broad daylight or pitch dark.

VOICE: The common song is a series of 2-note phrases— *teacher, teacher, teacher, teacher, teacher*. The delivery is vigorous and the song, growing louder as it progresses, becomes very loud at the end. The flight song is an indescribable jumble of notes of various pitches, a combination of warble and twitter with, generally, a few *teachers* thrown in.

NEST: The completely arched-over nest with its side entrance is on the ground, usually in the open. It is constructed of dead leaves and plant fibers, lined with grass and hair. Usually it is so worked into the forest floor and covered with dead leaves like those around it that it is almost impossible to detect. The 4 or 5 white eggs (.79 x .63) are spotted with brown.

RANGE: (M.) Breeds from Newfoundland, c. Quebec, n. Ontario, and s.w. Mackenzie south to e. North Carolina, n.

Georgia, Arkansas, Colorado, and s. Alberta. Winters
from e. South Carolina and the Gulf Coast south to the n.
Lesser Antilles and through Mexico to Colombia.

Northern Water-thrush*   *Seiurus noveboracensis*—✳31

IDENTIFICATION: L. 6. The thrush-like appearance of the water-
thrushes, their presence near water, and their habit of
constantly teetering like the spotted sandpiper will always
identify them. In both species the birds are much alike in
all plumages. The northern differs from the Louisiana in
its strongly yellow under parts and eyeline, its black instead of brownish streaks, and its uniformly streaked
throat.

HABITS: The breeding grounds are the cool, shrub-grown bogs,
wooded swamps, and lake shores of the North. Shaded
surroundings and wet ground with open pools of shallow
water seem necessary at this season. Here it feeds on
aquatic insects, tiny mollusks and crustacea, worms, and
occasionally fish. At other seasons it is found in a wider
variety of habitats but continues to do most of its feeding
on the ground. In migration it is frequently encountered
in gardens and under tangles of shrubbery. In fall it leads
the southward warbler flight.

VOICE: The song is a series of short, ringing, emphatic notes
with a beautiful liquid quality. The series of 10 or 12 drops
in pitch, often rather irregularly. There is also a speeding
up of tempo toward the end.

NEST: In a cavity in a bank, on the side of a stump, or in the
upturned roots of a fallen tree; made largely of green moss
and lined with moss fruiting stalks. The 4 or 5 creamy-
white eggs (.75 x .58) are finely speckled or heavily
blotched with browns.

RANGE: (M.) Breeds from Newfoundland, n. Quebec, n.
Ontario, n. Manitoba, c. Mackenzie, n. Alaska, and e.

Siberia south to n. New England, West Virginia (mts.), s. Ontario, n. Minnesota, n.w. Nebraska, c. Montana, and s. British Columbia. Winters from the Bahamas, s. Florida, the Valley of Mexico and Lower California south to Colombia and the Guianas.

Louisiana Water-thrush*   *Seiurus motacilla*—❋31

IDENTIFICATION: L. 6¼. This, the larger of the two water-thrushes, has a white eyeline and white under parts, except that the sides and flanks are tinged with buff. The throat, but for a dark streak on the side, is unmarked.

HABITS: Where the breeding ranges overlap the Louisiana seems to prefer the vicinity of flowing streams, especially swift mountain brooks, while the northern prefers the quieter waters and pools of extensive low swamps or bogs. Farther south, the Louisiana is found in limited numbers in river-bottom lands near sluggish streams. In migration this is the shyer of the two species and is less commonly seen away from low, wet areas.

VOICE: The 2-part song is loud and forceful. It opens with 3 or 4 long, upslurred, rather slowly uttered notes, then breaks into a hurried jumble of short, almost explosive notes, some high, some low, but usually trending downward. The call note of both water-thrushes is a distinctive, loud, metallic *pink*.

NEST: In a cavity in a stump, among the roots of a tree, or, most frequently, in and under the overhang of a stream bank; made externally of dead leaves, then moss and twigs, and lined with grass, hair, or rootlets. The 5 white eggs (.75 x .60) may be plain or heavily blotched with brown.

RANGE: (M.) Breeds from Massachusetts, s. Ontario, s.e. Minnesota, and e. Nebraska south to c. South Carolina, n. Georgia, s. Alabama, and n.e. Texas. Winters from s. Florida and the Bahamas south to the Lesser Antilles and from n. Mexico to Colombia.

Kentucky Warbler   *Oporornis formosus*—✳23

IDENTIFICATION: L. 5½. The solid olive-green upper parts and bright yellow under parts, together with the distinctive black head markings, make this bird easy to identify. Females and immatures generally have the black markings more or less obscured by greenish or yellow feather tips.

HABITS: The summer home is in the luxuriant forests of low, moist, rich bottom lands, ravines, and swamp borders. Here in dense shade and often among thick, low growths it spends most of its time on the ground but goes into the lower branches of a tree to sing.

VOICE: The loud song is a series of 5 or 6 clear, whistled, identical double syllables like *tur-dle, tur-dle,* etc. It suggests the even louder song of the Carolina wren and the songs of the tufted titmouse and ovenbird. It is a persistent singer.

NEST: On or just off the ground (never sunk into it) at the foot of a small bush or hidden in a patch of leafy vegetation. Generally it is in a comparatively open spot in the woods. It is made of dead leaves and is lined with rootlets, grass, and hair. The 4 or 5 white eggs (.73 x .56) are usually finely speckled with brown.

RANGE: (M.) Breeds from s.e. New York, s. Ontario, s. Wisconsin, s. Minnesota, and s.e. Nebraska south to North Carolina, n. Georgia, s. Louisiana, and e. Texas. Winters from s. Mexico to Colombia.

Connecticut Warbler   *Oporornis agilis*—✳22

IDENTIFICATION: L. 5½. The conspicuous eye ring, white in adults, buffy in immatures, is the best field mark, although the under-tail coverts reaching almost to the end of the tail are distinctive. In females and young the gray hood is replaced by a less distinct brownish one, very pale on the throat, but sharply defined where its border crosses the lower breast. This sharp line of separation differs from the gradual merging of breast and belly color in immature mourning warblers.

HABITS: In the southern part of its breeding range the Connecticut is encountered in open bogs with scattered tamaracks and spruces. Farther northwest, where it seems more abundant, it prefers brushy openings in upland poplaraspen country. It is not particularly active and does most of its feeding on the ground or in low growths. In spring the birds, which are very late migrants, are found in brushy tangles in low or swampy woodlands. In fall they also occur among tall weeds, especially in moist areas. This warbler is seldom found unless definitely searched for in its special haunts.

VOICE: The song is a loud, shrill, penetrating series of identical 2- or 3-note phrases, suggesting a uniform repetition of the word *beecher* or the phrase *whip-pity*. It is something like a low-pitched yellow-throat song or an ovenbird's held at the same volume throughout.

NEST: On the ground, sunk into a mound of moss or in a hollow under a clump of grass; generally composed almost wholly of grasses. The 4 or 5 white eggs (.78 x .56) are usually boldly blotched with brown.

RANGE: (M.) Breeds in a narrow east-west belt along the southern edge of the northern coniferous forest zone from s. Ontario, n. Michigan, c. Minnesota, s. Manitoba to c. Alberta. Winters from n. Brazil to Colombia. In spring it migrates via Florida, moving directly northwest to its breeding grounds, but in fall it flies almost due east to the Altantic coast before starting south.

Mourning Warbler　　　　　*Oporornis philadelphia*—✳22

IDENTIFICATION: L. 5½. Both sexes have gray hoods but differ from Connecticut warblers in the lack of an eye ring, except for a more or less incomplete one in immatures. The male has a large black patch on the breast which is veiled by gray in the fall. Immatures have clear, but often pale, yellow throats and breasts which merge gradually with the bright yellow under parts.

HABITS: The essential habitat is an extensive, dense stand of shrubbery. The birds seldom leave such growths except to forage through near-by patches of coarse, rank weeds. Generally they stay well hidden, but the male regularly rises to the top of a bush or sapling to sing.

Mourning warblers are commonly found breeding in the zone of dense brush that commonly borders a bog or marshland and in the briary tangles of second growth that spring up on burned- or cutover forest lands. It is another of the many birds that have benefited from the bad forestry practices of the past century. Wilson, its discoverer, saw only one, Audubon very few, and Nuttall was never sure he saw it.

VOICE: The short, loud, musical song has 2 parts. The first consists of about 3 2-note phrases like *choree, choree, choree,* followed by 3 or 4 short, single notes uttered in rapid succession.

NEST: Usually on the ground but occasionally as high as 2 feet, and always in a tangle of briars, canes, weed stalks, or grass. The large nest is made of dead leaves and coarse fibers, then grass, and is finally lined with fine grass, rootlets, or hair. The 4 white eggs (.71 x .54) are generally rather evenly speckled with brown.

RANGE: (M.) Breeds from Newfoundland, c. Quebec, c. Ontario, c. Manitoba, and e.c. Alberta south to Maine, West Virginia (mts.), n. Michigan, and c. Minnesota. Winters from Nicaragua to Venezuela and Ecuador.

Macgillivray's Warbler   *Oporornis tolmiei*—✳22

IDENTIFICATION: L. 5½. Males differ from mourning warbler males in their white eye spots, blacker lores, and grayer breasts. The longer tails and complete eye rings of immatures are not of much value in the field.

HABITS: Extensive brushy areas on moist ground are favored, but the species also breeds on fairly dry hillsides where vegetation is very dense. It is often abundant in the new growth that comes up in the tangled confusion of fallen treetops or slash piles in a burned- or cutover forest. Its impenetrable habitat plus its quiet, retiring habits make it hard to see.

VOICE: The song consists of 2 rapidly delivered runs of identical phrases, the first part usually higher in pitch, the second more liquid in quality—*sweet sweet sweet, peachy peachy peachy*.

NEST: Anywhere from almost on the ground to about 5 feet up in a shrub; raggedly and loosely made of weed stalks and grass with a lining of finer grass and rootlets. The 4 white eggs (.70 x .53) are spotted with brown and often faintly scrawled with black.

RANGE: (M.) Breeds from s. Saskatchewan, c. Alberta, c. British Columbia, and s.e. Alaska south to n. New Mexico and c. California and east to w. South Dakota. Winters from n. Mexico to Colombia. Occurs in migration casually to the Mississippi Valley and regularly to c. and s. Texas.

Yellowthroat   *Geothlypis trichas*—✳23

IDENTIFICATION: L. 5¼. The adult male keeps its black mask the year round. The female has a brownish forehead, paler yellow throat, a whitish eye ring, and under parts that are washed with brown—darkest on sides and flanks, lightest on the white belly. Immatures are extremely non-descript, their throats sometimes being so buffy as to look hardly yellow at all. Their bellies, unlike those of similar warblers, remain fairly white, and the under-tail coverts are always quite yellow.

HABITS: This wide-ranging species varies considerably in appearance in different parts of the continent and has been divided into many subspecies. It is an active, inquisitive frequenter of dense, low cover on a variety of sites but is commonest near water and in the rank vegetation of marshy areas. Cattail, tule, and bulrush marshes, stream-side thickets of willows, and tangles of blackberries and weeds on old fields are common breeding habitats.

VOICE: The usual song is a short, vigorous series of clear, high-pitched, 3-note phrases, but there are variations with more notes. It is often written *witchity, witchity, witchity.* The flight song, delivered from a height of 10 to 15 feet, is a rapid jumble of short notes with an occasional *witchity* worked in.

NEST: On the ground or a short distance above it in a dense clump of coarse vegetation; always among or attached to the stems of the plants. The loose, bulky structure is made of grasses, sedges, and bark strips with a lining of finer grasses, rootlets, or hair. The 4 white eggs (.71 x .54) are variably spotted with browns and black.

RANGE: (P.M.) Breeds from Newfoundland, s. Quebec, c. Ontario, c. Alberta, and s.e. Alaska south to s. Florida, the Gulf Coast, and s. Mexico. Winters from North Carolina, Louisiana, n. Mexico, and c. California south to Puerto Rico and Costa Rica.

Mexican Ground-chat *Chamaethlypis poliocephala—✳2ɔ*

IDENTIFICATION: L. 5½. The black-lored males with slaty heads washed with olive are unmistakable. Females and young are often nondescript, but their stout, strongly down-curved bills distinguish them at once from yellow-throats.

HABITS: Dense stands of tall, coarse grasses seem to be essential. Scattered shrubs for singing perches are also important. Thickets, weed-grown fields, and fernbrakes are less frequent habitats. Very little is known about this bird, and chances to learn more should not be missed.

VOICE: The short song is a low-pitched, rather pleasant warble.

NEST: A foot or 2 from the ground in dense vegetation, usually in a clump of coarse grass; made of grasses with a lining of finer grasses and often hair. The 4 creamy-white eggs (.69 x .55) are lightly marked with brown.

RANGE: (R.) Occurs from extreme s. Texas and n.w. Mexico south to Panama.

Yellow-breasted Chat*   *Icteria virens*——❋23

IDENTIFICATION: L. 7½. The chat is classified as a warbler, but its large size, heavy bill, unwarbler-like behavior, and loud voice set it apart from its kind. Immatures and adults are almost identical.

HABITS: The chat is a bird of dense shrub and vine tangles scattered with young trees. In pre-settlement days it was probably found chiefly on streamsides and pond borders, but now it also inhabits the young growth on cut- or burned-over forest land, old pastures, and abandoned fields. Few birds are harder to see or easier to detect by ear. The song is usually given as the bird moves about inside the crown of a tree or a dense thicket. Occasionally it jumps into the air and, flying slowly or hovering with dangling legs and deep wingbeats, pours out a flood of sound. It supplements its normal warbler diet of insects with considerable fruit.

VOICE: Instead of singing in the ordinary sense, the chat utters a disjointed series of noises, often at widely spaced intervals—whistles, mews, scolds, trumpeting sounds, squeaks, and cackles, delivered singly or repeated several times in rapid succession. The performance is unmistakable, and several of the sounds are absolutely distinctive.

NEST: From 3 to 5 feet aboveground in a small tree, clump of bushes, or vine tangle. The bulky nest is made of dead leaves, grasses, and bark shreds with a lining of finer grass. The 4 white eggs (.86 x .66) are variably but evenly spotted with brown.

RANGE: (P.M.) Breeds from Connecticut, s. Ontario, Iowa, Montana, and s. British Columbia south to n. Florida, the Gulf Coast (where it is rare), and e. Mexico. Winters from n. Mexico south to Costa Rica.

Hooded Warbler   *Wilsonia citrina*—#23

IDENTIFICATION: L. 5½. Males need no description. Females generally show a trace of black about the head, but immatures are quite plain. Their best field marks are their broad yellow forehead and the white in the tail.

HABITS: A mature woodland in a low, moist site which favors well-developed shrubbery is a typical haunt. In the South hooded warblers are common in heavily forested swampland with a dense tangle of shrubs. In the North cool stream bottoms and ravines are favorite breeding grounds. The bird does most of its feeding in the lower strata of the forest, chiefly under 10 feet, but is not often seen on the ground. It is an expert flycatcher and a generally active bird, with a trick of snapping its tail open and shut, revealing the white areas.

VOICE: The short song is loud and clear with a rich, ringing quality. It consists of a series of identical 2-note phrases followed by a closing phrase that falls in pitch, suggesting the syllables *peet-to, peet-to, peet-to, weet-too.*

NEST: Usually between 2 and 3 feet up in a fork in a shrub or small tree; made of dead leaves held together with plant fibers and spider webs; neatly lined with grass and fine bark shreds. The 3 or 4 creamy-white eggs (.69 x .55) are spotted with brown.

RANGE: (M.) Breeds from Connecticut, c. New York, s. Michigan, n. Iowa, and s.e. Nebraska south to n. Florida and the Gulf Coast west to Louisiana. Winters from s. Mexico to Panama.

Wilson's Warbler   *Wilsonia pusilla*—⚹21

IDENTIFICATION: L. 5. Many females are black-capped like males. Immatures often lack any trace of cap and are best distinguished by their yellow foreheads and big, black, beady eyes which stand out against the bright yellow cheeks.

HABITS: The Wilson's warbler has an extraordinarily broad north-south range, breeding from the shores of the Arctic Ocean south almost to Mexico. Its habitat preferences are much the same everywhere—low, shrubby growths in open, moist areas along streams and ponds or in bogs and brush-grown swamps. Willows and alders are the plants with which it is most often associated. Although it is one of the most active of all warblers and engages in much fly-catching, it usually stays within about 10 feet of the ground.

VOICE: The song is a weak, chattery series of short, rapidly uttered notes, usually all on the same pitch until near the end, when they generally drop in tone and may increase or decrease in volume.

NEST: On the ground, well hidden in a moss hummock, or under a sedge tussock in a moist, shrubby area or a few feet up in dense vegetation. The bulky nest is often almost a ball of leaves, moss, grass, and rootlets, with a lining of fine grass and hair. The 4 white eggs (.64 x .49) are spotted with browns.

RANGE: (M.) Breeds from Newfoundland, c. Quebec, n. Manitoba, n.w. Mackenzie, and n. Alaska south to Nova Scotia, n. New Hampshire, n. Minnesota, s. Saskatchewan, c.w. Texas, and s. California. Winters from n. Mexico to Panama.

Canada Warbler *Wilsonia canadensis*—※24

IDENTIFICATION: L. 5½. Immatures lack the necklace, but the yellow spectacles and solid gray upper parts are distinctive.

HABITS: The usual home is in the luxuriant undergrowth of mature woodlands. The bird likes cool, moist areas and is found about swamp borders and in streamside shrubbery. Like the preceding species, it is a very active fly-catching warbler and does most of its feeding near the ground. In migration it frequents brushlands and young second growth in clearings. In the North it occasionally breeds in such areas if they are sufficiently moist.

VOICE: The song is loud, rich, and strongly accented but hard to describe, as it is an irregular series of notes, varying in length and pitch. Often they are slurred together to produce phrases that suggest the yellowthroat's *witchity*.

NEST: On or near the ground, well concealed in a mound of moss, a rotten stump, the upturned roots of a fallen tree, or under a fern clump. The locality is generally moist, and the nest is sometimes above water. It is generally a rather formless mass of dead leaves, bark shreds, and grass, lined with similar finer material, including rootlets and hair. The 4 white eggs (.67 x .52) are rather evenly speckled with brown.

RANGE: (M.) Breeds from Newfoundland, c. Quebec, c. Ontario, c. Manitoba, and s. Alberta south to Connecticut, n.

Georgia (mts.), s. Ontario, and c. Minnesota. Winters in Ecuador and Peru.

Common Redstart   *Setophaga ruticilla*—※26

IDENTIFICATION: L. 5½. The pattern is the same in both sexes —black and orange-red in the male, grayish olive-green and pale yellow in the female. Young males are little, if any, brighter than females during their first breeding season. Fall young are like females but more olive to brown above, with less yellow especially in the wings and tail.

HABITS: The redstart, the most animated of our warblers, is rarely still. It has a characteristic habit of drooping its wings, fanning out its tail, and jumping into the air after insects. Deciduous woodlands, open enough to support a good understory of young trees, or open second growth on moist lowlands are common habitats. The bird is so abundant and so widely distributed that few woodlands are without them, especially near openings or swampy spots.

VOICE: The song is thin and not very loud, with a distinctive, high-pitched, sibilant quality. A common form consists of a series of 5 or more short notes, or 2-note phrases, ending in a strongly accented upward or downward slur. There are many variations, and a singing bird often alternates among two or three.

NEST: In an upright crotch of a tree or shrub from 6 to 25 feet aboveground; made of bark shreds and grass, bound with weathered plant fibers and spider webs. The lining is of fine grass, rootlets, and hair. The 4 whitish eggs (.68 x .50) are speckled or blotched with brown.

RANGE: (M.) Breeds from Newfoundland, s. Quebec, c. Manitoba, c.w. Mackenzie, and n. British Columbia south to North Carolina, n. Georgia, s. Alabama, Arkansas, Colorado, n. Utah, and n.e. Oregon. Winters throughout the West Indies and from c. Mexico to Ecuador and the Guianas.

WEAVER FINCHES   Family PLOCEIDAE

English Sparrow   *Passer domesticus*—♯42

IDENTIFICATION: L. 6⅓. (Remember this length and use it as a yardstick in estimating the size of other small birds.) The friendly English sparrow is too well known to need description. It molts only once a year, in late summer, and in the new plumage the male's color is partially concealed by gray feather tips. The wearing off of these tips makes its breast brighter in spring. Young are like females but browner above and buffier below, with rather pinkish bills, legs, and feet.

HABITS: The environment produced by the establishment of urban or agricultural civilization in any temperate area exactly suits this bird, which in Europe is known as the house sparrow. Small colonies build up even on isolated farms in the wilderness. Man has transplanted the bird all over the world. Whether or not he acted wisely, the fact remains that today the so-called English sparrow is his constant companion in the temperate zone of every continent.

The birds are always gregarious. Except when nesting, they assemble in large flocks which gather at night into communal roosts in protected spots, e.g., in or on a building, in a tree, or on a vine-covered wall. Summer food is chiefly insects, plus green vegetables, fruits, and seeds. The greater part of the fall and winter diet consists of weed seeds and waste grain.

The history of the introduction of the English sparrow (1850) into North America provides excellent proof of the automatic checks and balances that control wildlife populations. Within less than a century the original few thousands have increased to millions. So long as acceptable habitat remained unoccupied, the extra birds produced as a result of the sparrow's very high reproductive rate, spread into it. A pyramiding of the total population followed, and a prodigious rate of increase was achieved. Today the available habitat is carrying all the English sparrows it can accommodate, and the same high reproductive rate produces no year-to-year increase in total population. The extra birds become surplus population and are eliminated so unobtrusively by natural mortality factors that we are seldom conscious of the process.

VOICE: Just about all one ever hears is a monotonous *cheeep,* a harsh alarm note, and an occasional twittering song which is little more than a series of chirps.

NEST: Varies in form depending upon location. The commonest site is a cavity, usually in a building or bird box, which the bird stuffs with grass, feathers, and trash. When they build in trees, bushes, or vines they construct a bulky domed nest of grass, straw, string, rags, paper, and feathers with a small entrance hole at the side. The 5 or 6 grayish-white eggs (.88 x .60) are evenly speckled with brown, and several broods are raised annually.

RANGE: (R.) Occurs naturally throughout Europe, Asia, and North Africa and has been introduced by man all over the world. In North America has spread over all but the Far North and s. Mexico.

European Tree Sparrow*   *Passer montanus*—※42

IDENTIFICATION: L. 6. Adults and young are about the same. The best field marks are the rich chestnut top of the head, the black ear spot on the gray cheek, and the small black throat patch.

HABITS: These very gregarious birds are found in farming country near St. Louis and in the city parks. They show no great attachment for dwellings and are scattered over the countryside. The niche which they occupy in Europe is in this country apparently already occupied by indigenous species well equipped to hold their own against new-comers. As a result it has made little progress since its introduction into St. Louis in 1870.

VOICE: The commonest call is a *chip*, shorter and higher-pitched than an English sparrow's. It also has a shrill *chur* call and a twittering song.

NEST: In a tree cavity, a hole in a wall, or in a bird box. Very seldom does it build a domed nest like the English sparrow's. The 5 slightly buffy eggs (.76 x .55) are thickly spotted with brown.

RANGE: (R.) Native to Europe and much of Asia. Established in Missouri and e. Illinois in the vicinity of St. Louis.

BLACKBIRDS   Family ICTERIDAE

Bobolink   *Dolichonyx oryzivorus*—✳34

IDENTIFICATION: L. 7¼. A June male bobolink needs no description, but in late winter when this nuptial plumage is new the black feathers are almost obscured by long buffy feather tips. The tips begin to wear off in spring migration, and by the time the bird has reached Florida in mid-April they are almost gone. The white back and the buffy head patches are much darker at first, but as the season progresses they bleach into the shades with which we are familiar. After breeding the males molt into plumage like that of females and young. This is like the female's spring plumage except that the back is darker olive-green and the head and under parts distinctly buffy.

HABITS: Breeding territory is always in an extensive field of tall grass or grain or similar crop. The bird is thus a direct beneficiary of man, since such areas have largely supplanted the original forests of eastern North America. Early cutting of hay and grain (i.e., before July 15) is its worst hazard, and its abundance is largely dependent upon local mowing dates. In spring and summer bobolinks are highly insectivorous, but in fall they turn to weed and grass seeds, and large migratory flocks can be quite destructive to unharvested grain.

VOICE: The bobolink's famous song, given on the wing or from a perch, is a loud, bubbling series of irregularly arranged higher and lower notes with a metallic quality. As the song progresses the pitch goes higher and higher and the notes tumble out faster and faster. It also has several call and alarm notes, and in migration the birds of a flock call back and forth with a sharp metallic *pink* which identifies them even when they are high overhead.

NEST: On the ground in a heavy stand of tall grass, clover, alfalfa, or similar vegetation; a flimsy cup of grass, plant stems, and rootlets placed in a slight depression. The 5 to 7 eggs (.85 x .62) vary in ground color from a bluish-gray to a reddish-brown and are spotted with brown and purples. One brood is raised.

RANGE: (M.) Breeds from Cape Breton Island, s. Ontario, s. Manitoba, c. Alberta, and s.e. British Columbia south to Pennsylvania, Indiana, n. Missouri, Colorado, and n.e. California. Winters in South America south to n. Argentina and Paraguay.

Eastern Meadowlark*   *Sturnella magna*—❋34

IDENTIFICATION: L. 10¾. Meadowlarks are much the same in all plumages, but females are markedly smaller and paler and have a narrower breastband. In winter both young and adults are browner: the black is masked and the white areas are buffy. The bird can always be identified in flight by the white outer tail feathers which are also visible on the ground, as it constantly jerks open its tail with a nervous flick as it walks along.

HABITS: Open country with sufficient grassy covering for nesting is required. Where this obtains, the birds are generally common. Beetles, grasshoppers, and similar insects are eaten in summer, weed seeds in winter. The bird is low-flying and alternates between vigorous flutterings of its short wings and brief sailing periods with wings stiffly outstretched and carried slightly downward. Meadowlarks like to sing from the top of a tree or similar vantage point.

VOICE: The song usually consists of 3 to 5 clear, high-pitched, whistled notes—*tsee-you, tsee-ear*. Delivery is slow and the notes long. No two are on exactly the same pitch, and they are often slurred together. The bird has a number of loud, distinctive calls of rough quality, some little more than a chatter.

NEST: A partially domed-over and loosely built structure of grass and plant stems placed in a slight hollow in the ground in dense grassy or weedy cover. The normal 5 white eggs (1.10 x .80) are spotted with browns and purples.

RANGE: (P.M.) Breeds from New Brunswick, s. Quebec, and c. Ontario south to Florida, the Gulf Coast, and n. Mexico; west to e. Minnesota, w. Nebraska, n.w. Texas, n.c. Arizona, and Sonora. In winter most birds retire south from the area north of s. New Jersey, the Ohio Valley, and Kansas.

Western Meadowlark* *Sturnella neglecta*—❋34

IDENTIFICATION: L. 9½. From the prairie country of the Midwest to the Pacific coast this species replaces the eastern meadowlark. It is slightly paler, the yellow of the chin extends up on to the cheeks near the base of the bill, and the black markings on the flanks are spots rather than streaks.

HABITS: Habits and habitat requirements of the two are essentially the same.

Voice: The song of the western meadowlark which is heard the year round is its best field character: a deep, rich melody of 6 or 7 notes with a clear, bubbling quality. The almost flutelike notes become hurried toward the end. The call note, a sharp, penetrating *chuck* followed by a rolling sound, is strikingly different from the eastern's.

Nest: Nest and eggs are like those of the eastern species.

Range: (P.M.) Breeds from s. Manitoba, c. Alberta, and s. British Columbia south to n. Mexico and east to Minnesota, s. Wisconsin, n. Illinois, Oklahoma, and c. Texas. Absent in winter, except for stragglers, from the area north of Nebraska and Utah.

Yellow-headed Blackbird
Xanthocephalus xanthocephalus—✳34

Identification: L. 10. Fall males have the yellow of the head and hind neck obscured by dusky feather tips. Fall females become brighter, with chests of deeper yellow, heads of richer buff, and breasts less streaked. The young are at first a uniform tawny-buff, deepest on the head and throat, but slowly acquire distinctive yellow throats and breasts during the late summer. In a flock with other blackbirds the white wing patch is the best field mark.

Habits: This species nests in the sloughs and marshes of the West, where tall vegetation grows in fairly deep water. Loose colonies, sometimes numbering thousands, are formed with adults spreading out over adjacent uplands to feed. During the rest of the year they travel in flocks, often with other blackbirds. They feed on insects and weed seeds, adding grain when they can get it.

Voice: The yellow-head's song starts with a few harsh, distinct notes and deteriorates into a jumble of sounds which ends in a long, rasping squeal. Its call is a hoarse, rattling *rroak*.

NEST: A deep basketlike structure woven out of old reed leaves or cattails taken from the water; usually placed one to several feet above water and supported by growing reeds. The 4 grayish or greenish eggs (1.00 x .70) are speckled with brown.

RANGE: (P.M.) Breeds from n.e. Manitoba, s. Mackenzie, and s. British Columbia south to c. Mexico and east to c. Wisconsin, n. Indiana, and w. Texas. Winters south from s. California and s.w. Louisiana.

Red-winged Blackbird   *Agelaius phoeniceus*—⚹34

IDENTIFICATION: L. 9½. Adults molt once a year in late summer, and until the brownish feather edges wear off their colors are somewhat dull. Young look like females but are buffier above and slightly pinkish-buff below. Young males develop a mottled orange shoulder patch but remain quite brownish during their first year.

HABITS: Red-wings commonly breed wherever fresh-water marshes occur. Here they nest over or near water, foraging up to a mile away in croplands, hayfields, orchards, or woodlands. The male's red-and-buff epaulets are much more conspicuous at this season, especially when he shows them in courtship display. At other times the birds wander in flocks that often become enormous. They feed on many crop-destroying insects, and a big flock rolling over a field can significantly reduce their numbers. In fall the birds turn to weed seeds and unharvested grain.

VOICE: Song, a gurgling, liquid *conk-kar-ree*, running up the scale and ending in a trill. It also has a long, high-pitched, whistled alarm note and a harsh *cack*-like call which is usually accompanied by much flicking of the tail.

NEST: A loosely woven cup of coarse marsh grasses or cattail leaves lined with finer grass and roots; most often suspended from the stems of growing marsh reeds a foot or two above water but sometimes higher in a bush or tree or down on a sedge tussock or even on the ground in dense grass or similar cover near water. The 3 to 5 pale bluish eggs (1.00 x .70) are marked with blackish-purple dots, blotches, and zigzag lines.

RANGE: (P.M.) Breeds from Nova Scotia, Quebec, Keewatin, c. Mackenzie, and Alaska south to Florida, and the Gulf Coast to c. Mexico. Winters south from Pennsylvania, the Ohio River Valley, Kansas, Utah, and British Columbia to Costa Rica.

Orchard Oriole   *Icterus spurius*—#35

IDENTIFICATION: L. 7¼. A fully adult breeding male (i.e., in its second breeding season) is unmistakable. In the fall after the annual molt its colors are somewhat obscured by greenish and buffy feather edges. Young are like females but browner above and more uniformly colored except for a buffy rump. In their first breeding season the sexes are similar except for the male's black chin and throat.

HABITS: Rural country with an abundance of scattered trees along roads and streams or in orchards and about houses is the normal habitat. The bird is either not strongly territorial or the defended territory is small, as they often nest so close together as to suggest a loose colony.

The male sings a great deal on the wing, often delivering its song during a short vertical flight from the top of a tree, to which it returns. Insects are almost the only food, but mulberries are relished.

VOICE: Robin-like in quality. The loud, clear, short song is a fairly high-pitched hurried burst of varied notes that ends with a series of like notes terminated by a slurred, falling note. It has a blackbird-like *cluck* and a squeaky, chattering call.

NEST: An open pouch about as deep as wide, generally woven out of fresh green grass stems and suspended in the forked branch of a tree or shrub 10 to 20 feet from the ground. Fine grasses and plant downs are used as lining. The 4 to 6 eggs (.82 x .57) are spotted and scrawled with browns and purples.

RANGE: (M.) Breeds from Massachusetts, s.e. Ontario, Wisconsin, and North Dakota south to n. Florida, the Gulf Coast, and s. Mexico and west to w. Kansas. Winters from s. Mexico to n. Colombia.

Black-headed Oriole*   *Icterus graduacauda*—✳35

IDENTIFICATION: L. 9. The greenish-yellow back is the outstanding characteristic. Females differ in being smaller and duller and even greener on the back. Immatures lack the black head and are greenish-yellow above, pale yellow beneath.

HABITS: These lemon-yellow birds prefer rather secluded areas with thick woody vegetation. They are generally found in pairs throughout the year. Mesquite thickets, stream- and pondside growths and tangles in forest openings attract them. They are infrequent singers and stay hidden in the foliage. They do most of their feeding in low growths, eating insects and small fruits like hackberries. This oriole is frequently imposed upon by its relative, the red-eyed cowbird.

VOICE: The whistled song is a soft, sweet, and rather melancholy *peut-pou-it*, with each note on a different pitch.

NEST: Usually between 6 and 14 feet aboveground in a dense shrub or tree. The semi-pensile nest is attached at the top and sides to upright terminal branches and is woven of fresh green grasses. The 4 dull white eggs (.97 x .71) are dusted and mottled with brown and scrawled with black lines.

RANGE: (R.) Occurs from s. Texas south through e. Mexico to Chiapas.

Lichtenstein's Oriole*   *Icterus gularis*—⚹35

IDENTIFICATION: L. 9. These birds vary regionally from cadmium yellow to deep orange and are uniformly colored.
They resemble male hooded orioles, but the orange-yellow
shoulders are distinctive. Young are pale yellow below,
rather greenish on the back, and have a more restricted
throat patch.

HABITS: This appears to be a treetop species of the forest and
of scattered groves in the open or along streams.

VOICE: The song is a rapid repetition of 2 or 3 notes lacking
the clear tone of most orioles.

NEST: Placed fairly high, the nest is a hanging cylinder sometimes 2 feet long and only 6 inches in diameter, woven of
long, tough fibers, and suspended from a drooping branch.
The 3 or 4 eggs (1.16 x .75) are laid in a cup of grass and
downs.

RANGE: (R.) Occurs from Tamaulipas and occasionally s
Texas south through e. Mexico to Nicaragua.

Hooded Oriole   *Icterus cucullatus*—⚹35

IDENTIFICATION: L. 8. The long curved bill and graduated tail
are distinctive. As with many orioles, the bird varies in
color in different parts of its range. In some regions the
hood, rump, and under parts of the male are fiery orange,
in others cadmium yellow. Above the female is a yellowish-olive which becomes gray on the back; it is uniformly
dull yellow below. The wings retain the two white bars of
the male. Young males are like females except for the
black throat.

HABITS: This is a widely distributed and adaptable species,
equally at home in thickets of semi-arid country and heavy
timber of river bottoms and other moist areas. Shade trees

often attract it, and it is often common about towns. Most of its food appears to be insects, and it does much of its feeding in low growths.

VOICE: Common calls are a high, thin note or a series of longer chattering syllables. The infrequent song is a warbled series of throaty whistles interspersed with chatter notes.

NEST: At heights from 4 to 20 feet. A favorite site is in the cluster of drooping old leaves below the growing head of a yucca, palm, or palmetto, but some nests are woven into the heart of a living bunch of hanging Spanish moss or in a clump of dense foliage out near the end of a limb. The thin-walled structure is woven of long, wiry fibers, usually of a single kind. It is often semi-pendant and lined with downs and feathers. The 4 white eggs (.85 x .61) are blotched and scrawled with brown, purple, and black.

RANGE: (P.M.) Breeds from extreme s. Texas, s. Arizona, and s.w. California south to s.e. Mexico. Not found in the United States in winter.

Baltimore Oriole   *Icterus galbula*—✳35

IDENTIFICATION: L. 7½. The handsome male in Lord Baltimore colors is known to everyone. Females are extremely variable. Some look like a faded male with the black flecked with olive-brown; others are yellowish-olive above with a brighter yellow rump and tail, and yellow below with only a suggestion of orange. Young are like dull females with no black on the throat. Even in the drabbest plumage there is usually enough orange below and in the tail to set the birds apart from orchard orioles. Their distinct wing bars separate them from the shorter, heavier-billed young and female tanagers.

HABITS: This species likes tall shade trees in towns and along country roads, where it often nests in elms. It also occurs on the edges of fairly open mature deciduous woodlands and along streams. Its food is largely insects but includes some fruits.

VOICE: A rich, mellow whistle, loud, clear, and rather low-pitched. A single or double whistle is used as a call note, and a loud rattle serves as an alarm note. The song is a disjointed composition of whistled 2-note phrases and shorter, softer single notes broken by long pauses. There is not only a wide variation in the pattern of the song but in the tone and quality of the bird's voice. As a rule, each individual has a recognizably different song.

NEST: A woven bag about 6 inches deep, constricted at the top and suspended from small twigs at the outer end of a usually drooping upper branch of a tall tree. It is made of long fibers from old weed stalks and bark supplemented with horsehair, twine, etc. Light-colored materials are favored, and the nest is generally light gray and quite conspicuous. The 4 to 6 grayish eggs (.92 x .61) are blotched and scrawled at the large end with black and brown.

RANGE: (M.) Breeds from Nova Scotia, Ontario, s. Manitoba, and c. Alberta south to n. Georgia, c. Louisiana, and s. Texas; west to c. Montana and e. Colorado. Winters from s. Mexico south to Colombia.

Bullock's Oriole   *Icterus bullockii*—✳35

IDENTIFICATION: L. 8. The head pattern and white wing patch set the brilliant male apart from other orioles. The duller female has no black, but its saffron-yellow cheek, chest, and tail areas usually contrast strongly with the dirty white of the flanks and belly. Young males resemble females but have a black streak running down the throat from the base of the bill.

HABITS: Bullock's is the common oriole of most of the West. It frequents river valleys and agricultural land up into the lower mountains, nesting in a variety of sites from streamside shrubbery to the tops of tall trees around buildings. Feeding birds search treetops and fields, taking mostly insects, but they eat large quantities of cherries and other small fruits when they can get them.

VOICE: Alarm note, a loud rattle. Calls a clear, piping whistle and a softer double note. The song is a series of deliberately spaced, clear, whistled single and double notes.

NEST: A deep, loosely woven bag of grass, horsehair, string, etc., expanded at the bottom and heavily lined with feathers, plant down, or wool; suspended by the rim well out on a branch or woven more completely into a group of ascending twigs in a cottonwood, willow, or in a clump of mistletoe. The 5 grayish-white eggs (.94 x .63) are intricately scrawled with an apparently continuous purplish-black line.

RANGE: (M.) Breeds from s. Saskatchewan and s. British Columbia south to n. Mexico and east to e. South Dakota and s. Texas. Winters in Mexico.

Rusty Blackbird   *Euphagus carolinus*—❋32

IDENTIFICATION: L. 9½. The pale yellow-eyed "rustys" get their name from the brown edges of their feathers. These when new give both sexes a reddish-brown appearance, especially around the head and forward part of the body. By spring the edges have worn off and the birds are a solid color—the male black glossed with greenish, the female slaty with only a hint of gloss. Fall young are browner than adults.

HABITS: Generally solitary during the nesting season, but in large flocks, often with other blackbirds and grackles, at other times of the year. They prefer wet woods and swamps thick with trees or alders and full of shallow pools. They feed mostly on the ground and walk and wade very actively, the unseen flock keeping up a constant babble of squeaks, clucks, and whistles. When flushed they fly

as a unit to continue the chorus from the top of a tree. Insects, many of them aquatic, plus weed seeds, grains, and
wild fruits, are their chief food.

VOICE: Call, a hoarse *cack* or lower *cuk*. Its unhurried song is
a broken series of high, squeaky notes alternating with several rather musical notes run together in a gurgle.

NEST: These early nesters start out with a bulky mass of
sticks and grass mixed with moss and lichens; this supports a well-molded cup of dried duff lined with fresh
green grass. Nests are up to 10 feet high in dense clumps
of conifers or shrubs near or over water. The 4 or 5 pale
blue-green eggs (.92 x .80) are blotched with brown.

RANGE: (M) Breeds from n. Quebec, n. Mackenzie, and
Alaska south to n. New England, c. Ontario, c. Manitoba,
and c. British Columbia. Winters from New Jersey and
the Ohio River Valley south to the Gulf Coast and west to
c. Texas.

Brewer's Blackbird　　　　　*Euphagus cyanocephalus*—✳ 3℟.

IDENTIFICATION: L. 9½. The male's head and neck are
strongly glossed with purple; in good light this distinguishes it from the equally pale-eyed and black-plumaged
spring rusty blackbird. In fall males stay almost solid
black. The dark brown-eyed females are smaller and
lighter than the yellow-eyed female rustys and are more of
a gray-brown. They are also quite pale over the eye and on
the throat, and the glossy iridescence shows but faintly.
Until the fall molt, young are similar to females.

HABITS: Civilization has favored this species. It nests in colonies of from 6 to 30 pairs in hay meadows and in trees
and bushes along lakes and streams. The rest of the year
the birds wander in flocks, often with other blackbirds,
over all sorts of open country and roost at night in groves.
They are common about towns and farmyards, fearless in

tracking the plow and feeding under cattle. Their food is insects and all kinds of seeds, including grain.

VOICE: Squeaks, trills, whistles, and cacks (some hoarse, some musical) combine to produce a noisy but pleasant chatter when a flock performs in unison.

NEST: Coarse twigs, stems, and grasses enclose a cup of hardened mudlike material lined with hair, rootlets, and fine grass. Site variable, from the ground to well up in trees, but often fairly uniform within a given colony. The 4 to 6 grayish eggs (1.00 x .75) are blotched with browns, often very heavily.

RANGE: (P.M.) Breeds from c. Manitoba and c. British Columbia south to n. Mexico and east to Wisconsin. Winters from s. British Columbia and Wisconsin south through Mexico to Guatemala. Casual in winter east to South Carolina and Florida.

Boat-tailed Grackle *Cassidix mexicanus*—✳33

IDENTIFICATION: L. male 16½, female 12½. The big male is some 4 inches longer than the similarly colored common grackle, and its 7-inch tail seems disproportionately large and broad, as does its long, heavy bill. The smaller clove-brown female is totally unlike females of the other species, and young birds are even paler and browner.

HABITS: This bird is seldom found far from tidal marshes and coastal lowlands. In Florida the extensive low-lying, often marshy terrain, many lakes, and sluggish rivers produce an ideal habitat over much of the state. Boat-tails breed in loose colonies and move about in small flocks the rest of the year. They feed on mud flats along the edge of the water and often wade for food. They take shrimps, crabs, snails, fish, and other aquatic animals; they follow the plow for grubs and they eat corn and rice.

These grackles, together with fish crows and black vultures, often prey upon the eggs and newly hatched young of the great coastal heronries. Such depredations (unless increased by human disturbance which causes the herons and ibis to leave the nests unguarded) must be regarded as nature's way of placing a check upon the heron population.

VOICE: A variety of loud notes, mostly harsh, guttural clucking and chattering sounds interspersed with deep, whistled notes and squeaks.

NEST: Generally low, 2 to 10 feet up in bushes or canelike growths in or adjacent to a marsh; occasionally high in a tree. The bulky nest is made of coarse, non-woody material with a cup of decayed vegetation and mud in the center lined with fine grass. The 3 or 4 pale blue eggs (1.32 x .90) are spotted and scrawled with dark purple.

RANGE: (R.) Occurs on the south Atlantic and Gulf coasts (including all Florida) south to n. Colombia and on the west coast of Mexico from Arizona south.

Common Grackle　　　　　　　*Quiscalus quiscula*—✳33

IDENTIFICATION: L. 12. The long wedge-shaped tail, which the males often "keel" in flight by depressing the central feathers, is the best field mark. The iridescent sheen on the black plumage varies from green or blue to purple. The smaller females are duller, being iridescent only on the fore part of the body. Young are a uniform dull brown with brown instead of yellow eyes.

HABITS: As these grackles feed on open ground, the conversion of vast acreages to cropland and closely grazed pastures has favored them. Ornamental evergreens now grown to tall trees are also helpful, since they offer ideal sites for nesting colonies. The birds invade cities to feed on lawns, nest in parks, and roost at night in huge flocks in shade trees. They are also attracted to wet areas, where they feed along the water's edge or wade out for food. Originally they were probably more or less confined to such areas.

Grackles feed on all kinds of ground-dwelling insects such as beetles, grasshoppers, and weevils, digging out a great many in their larval or "white grub" stage. Acorns, beechnuts, and wild fruits are eaten, but much of the fall and winter food is drawn from waste grains, especially corn. In late summer flocks can be quite destructive to unharvested crops. Many other foods are taken in small quantities—fish, crayfish, shellfish, snakes, lizards, mice, nestling birds, and eggs.

VOICE: Harsh *cacks* and a series of ascending squeaky notes with a pronounced metallic quality.

NEST: A bulky but compact mass of small twigs, stalks, and grasses deeply cupped and often cemented with mud and lined with fine grasses. It may be high in a tree or almost on the ground. Dense evergreens are favored, but low bushes, deciduous trees, and cavities in buildings or old trees are used. Most nesting is in colonies of up to 25 or more pairs. Sites near water are preferred, but favorable clumps of tall evergreens in open farming country often harbor colonies. The 5 pale bluish eggs (1.14 x .82) are spotted and scrawled with brown or black.

RANGE: (P.M.) Breeds from Newfoundland, n. Ontario, and s. Mackenzie south to s. Florida and the Gulf Coast to s.e. Texas. Winters from Maryland, the Ohio River Valley, and Kansas south.

Brown-headed Cowbird   *Molothrus ater*—✳32

IDENTIFICATION: L. 8. The coffee-brown head of the male is always distinctive, although in fall it has a faint purplish tinge. Its shorter bill, longer tail, and paler under parts distinguish the female from a similarly colored but chunkier young starling. Juveniles are dark olive-brown above scaled with pale buff, dull white below streaked with brown.

HABITS: Cowbirds are of South American origin. Of the 7 known species, 4 have parasitic breeding habits. But since the birds they most frequently impose upon continue to be about as abundant as their habitats permit, it is evident that the cowbird does not have an appreciable effect upon their population level.

Originally this species attended the great herds of bison on the prairies of the Midwest and was known as the "buffalo bird." Now they attend cattle and are common about the man-made grasslands that cover much of the once-forested East. During the breeding season each pair usually has a fixed territory within which the female lays its eggs. The rest of the year they travel in flocks, often with other "blackbirds." Their basic food is seeds of grasses, weeds, and grains. Where available the seeds of yellow foxtail grass (*Setaria glauca*) form a high proportion of their vegetable diet. Grasshoppers and leaf hoppers, stirred up by cattle as they feed, form the bulk of their animal food.

VOICE: The song is a squeaky rattle with musical, liquid quality uttered as part of an interesting courtship performance. It also gives a harsh rattle and a squeaky 3-note whistle.

NEST: These cowbirds lay their eggs in the nests of other birds and allow the foster parents to raise their young. The open nests of vireos, warblers, sparrows, and flycatchers, especially of the red-eyed vireo, redstart, yellow warbler, and song sparrow, are most frequently chosen. Four or 5 white eggs (.86 x .65) evenly speckled with brown are laid a day apart, each in a different nest. Robins and catbirds puncture them and throw them out, chats desert the nest, and yellow warblers often cover them with a new nest bottom, but most birds tolerate them. The incubation period is very short, and the young cowbird throws out any remaining unhatched eggs and kills any other nestlings. It grows fast and is ready to leave the nest in ten days.

RANGE: (P.M.) Breeds from Nova Scotia, s. Ontario, s. Manitoba, s.w. Mackenzie, and c. British Columbia south to c. Virginia, c. Tennessee, Louisiana, and s. Mexico. Winters from Maryland, the Ohio River Valley, Texas, and c. California south to s. Mexico.

Red-eyed Cowbird   *Tangavius aeneus*—✳32

IDENTIFICATION: L. 8½. The erectile ruff across the back of the neck and the slightly rough-looking plumage are the most distinctive characters. The female is similar to the male but duller, only slightly glossed with bluish-green, and has a smaller ruff. Juveniles are sooty-gray, palest below, where they are faintly streaked with olive.

HABITS: The red-eyed cowbird feeds and migrates in flocks with the brown-headed cowbird and various blackbirds. Habitat preferences and habits are similar to those of its more northern relative, but the red-eyed is not as promiscuously parasitic as the brown-headed. The closely related orioles are its chief victims. In South America another cowbird, the screaming, is parasitic only on a cowbird, the bay-winged. The bay-wing in turn, while it incubates its own eggs and feeds its own young, usually steals an already completed nest from some other bird. Thus we see by what stages the interesting parasitic nesting habits of our brown-headed cowbird probably developed.

VOICE: The song is lower-pitched and wheezier than that of the brown-headed cowbird. It is uttered during a courtship performance that usually takes place on the ground.

NEST: The light blue-green eggs (.91 x .71) are usually laid in the nests of orioles. As young orioles are as large as young cowbirds, they are often raised successfully together.

RANGE: (P.M.) Breeds from c.s. Texas and s. Arizona south to Panama. Winters from the Rio Grande Valley south.

TANAGERS   Family THRAUPIDAE

Western Tanager   *Piranga ludoviciana*—✳36

IDENTIFICATION: L. 6¾. In fall the male loses most of its distinctive red face but keeps its black back and yellow wing bars. These bars, which females and young also have, set this species apart from other tanagers. The larger female orioles have wing bars but are differentiated by their sharp-pointed bills and larger size. Young males usually have little red the first year but are otherwise almost like older males.

HABITS: This is a bird of the upper canopy in mature but open woodlands. It feeds chiefly on insects, many of which it catches on the wing. It also likes fruit and during migrations sometimes finds ripening cultivated varieties very attractive.

VOICE: The rough song is much like a scarlet tanager's. The bird constantly utters a colorless chattering call of 2 or 3 notes—*pit-ick* or *pit-er-ick*—and a rather plaintive, soft, purring *tu-weep*.

NEST: At outer ends of pine and oak limbs from 10 to 25 feet up; loosely made of coarse stems, small twigs, grasses, and pine needles with a cup lined with hair or rootlets. The 3 or 4 blue-green eggs (.90 x .65) are lightly marked with small gray-green spots.

RANGE: (M.) Breeds from s.w. South Dakota, s.w. Mackenzie, and n.w. British Columbia south to c.w. Texas, s. Arizona, and n. Lower California. Accidental farther east. Winters from c. Mexico to Costa Rica.

Scarlet Tanager   *Piranga olivacea*—✳36

IDENTIFICATION: L. 7¼. In the fall molt, the male loses its red plumage and its new black feathers are edged with green. Its fall body plumage is not unlike the female's, although somewhat brighter—the back a cleaner green, the top of the head yellowish, and the under parts a richer, almost orange, yellow. Males in the middle of this change have an odd patchy appearance as the color plate shows. In fall the female, instead of growing duller, becomes brighter above and more orange-yellow below.

Juveniles just out of the nest are olive-green above and dull white below (yellowish on belly and yellow under tail), streaked with dusky gray. They have two yellowish-olive wing bars. Immatures look like females, but the males have jet-black wing coverts in the fall. They assume the red body plumage (slightly paler and more orange than an old male's) for their first breeding season.

HABITS: The scarlet tanager is common in mature woodlands throughout its range. As it does most of its feeding in tree-tops, it is not often detected unless one is familiar with its distinctive call note and song. Suburbs abundantly planted with large shade trees are frequently inhabited by breeding tanagers. Leaf-eating insects of the treetops are the chief food.

VOICE: The most frequent sound is a soft, low-pitched, buzzy tip-churr given by both sexes. The song is robin-like but has a hoarse undertone or burr that distinguishes it.

NEST: A shallow, flat, loose mass of twigs, stems, and grass lined with rootlets, grass, or pine needles; placed from 10 to 50 feet up, well out on a horizontal limb. The 3 or 4 greenish eggs (.94 x .66) are spotted at the large end with brown.

RANGE: (M.) Breeds from Nova Scotia, s. Ontario, s. Manitoba, and s. Saskatchewan south to South Carolina, n. Alabama, n. Arkansas, and s. Kansas. Winters from Colombia to Bolivia and Peru.

Summer Tanager   *Piranga rubra*—※36

IDENTIFICATION: L. 7½. The male stays a rosy red all year and could only be confused with a cardinal. Females differ from female scarlet tanagers in having greener wings and much richer (almost yellow-orange) under parts, brightest under the tail. Young males in fall are even more orange than females; both are separated from orioles by the lack of wing bars. In their first spring young males often do not become fully red but show a strange mixture of red and green patches.

HABITS: The open, drier southern woodlands of pine, oak, and hickory are the preferred habitat. Even fairly young second growth is acceptable, and the bird frequently nests in the outskirts of southern towns. Flying insects are important in its diet, and it is expert at catching them on the wing.

VOICE: The common call note is a rapid, chattery *chick-tucky-tuck*. The song, delivered like a scarlet tanager's, is richer and more melodious.

NEST: Out near the end of a limb 10 to 15 feet aboveground; shallow and often loosely built of stalks, bark, leaves, and like materials, the center lined with fine grasses. The 3 or 4 pale bluish or greenish eggs (.96 x .68) are variously marked with brown.

RANGE: (M.) Breeds from Delaware, c. Ohio, s.e. Wisconsin, s.e. Nebraska, c. New Mexico, and s.e. California south to s. Florida, the Gulf Coast, and n. Mexico. Winters from c. Mexico south to Peru and the Guianas.

SPARROWS   Family FRINGILLIDAE

Cardinal   *Richmondena cardinalis*—⚹37

IDENTIFICATION: L. 8¼. Its crest, big conical bill, and black face set the male apart from any other red bird. The brown female always has some patches of red and a very conspicuous red bill. Young are like females but may be darker (little or no red) and have a darker bill.

HABITS: This bird is at home in any habitat that includes dense thickets and tangles near open areas—field edges, woodland borders, stream banks, open swamps, parks, and residential districts. It is non-migratory, but individual birds wander extensively, and in many sections it is gradually spreading northward.

Wild seeds and fruit are the chief foods, supplemented by a variety of insects. The birds' fondness for sunflower, melon, and squash seeds will bring them to feeding stations, and a steady supply will help establish wanderers as local residents.

VOICE: Rich, powerful, and pleasantly musical. The song, which often starts softly, is a repetition of short, whistled phrases in which some notes are usually run together. After a few phrases on one pitch the bird generally changes to another. A common song is written *wet-year, wet-year, weet-weet-weet-weet-weet*, another *whurty, whurty, whurty, whurty*. Call note is a sharp *clink*.

NEST: Low, generally 6 to 8 feet up in a bushy thicket or vine tangle; a loosely constructed but fairly deep cup of twigs, stems, leaves, and fibers lined with rootlets, grasses, and often hair. The 3 or 4 white or greenish eggs (1.00 x .70) are variably spotted with reddish-brown, one often quite unlike the others. Two broods are raised.

RANGE: (R.) Occurs from n. New Jersey, s. Ontario, n. Illinois, s.e. South Dakota south to Florida and the Gulf Coast and from c. Texas and s. Arizona south to s. Mexico.

Pyrrhuloxia   *Pyrrhuloxia sinuata*—✳ 37

IDENTIFICATION: L. 8. The short curved, parrot-like, yellow to horn-colored bill and gray back are characteristic. Females and young are buffy below and have little or no red about the face and under parts.

HABITS: Streamside thickets and dense patches of brush are essential. The bird seldom ventures far from good cover, but a whistled imitation of its call may bring it into sight. Much of its feeding is on the ground, where it takes both seeds (like mesquite beans) and insects, but it is not as terrestrial as the cardinal. Outside the breeding season the species is quite gregarious.

VOICE: The song suggests a cardinal's but is not as loud and clear. The call is a series of thin, flat notes.

NEST: Well up in a dense or thorny shrub; made of twigs, grass, and bark. The 3 or 4 white eggs (.90 x .70) are finely speckled with brown.

RANGE: (R.) Occurs from s. Texas and s. Arizona south to c. Mexico.

Rose-breasted Grosbeak   *Hedymeles ludovicianus*—✳ 38

IDENTIFICATION: L. 8. The breeding male is unmistakable. In fall males look more like females but retain their black tail and wings and have some pink on the breast. First-year males breed in similar plumage. The sparrow-like female's large size, big pale bill, bold head pattern, and white wing bars are distinctive. Young birds look like females, but buff usually replaces white.

HABITS: During the breeding season many species of birds are evenly distributed throughout a uniform habitat representing a single vegetative type like forest, field, or marsh, but the rose-breasted grosbeak is one (there are many) which is found only where two types of vegetation come together. The number of breeding pairs that can be accommodated depends upon the total length of the zone of contact between the types. A woodland of fairly large trees beside an open area densely grown up with tall shrubs is ideal. In nature such an edge occurs where a stream, pond, or marsh has created an opening in the forest. But we also find these grosbeaks breeding in parks, residential neighborhoods, and farming country where patches of woodland and shrubby areas are so interspersed as to produce the maximum possible amount of edge. The male has the curious habit of singing softly while incubating the eggs. During summer the bird's food is evenly divided among wild seeds and fruits and insects. It feeds in treetops and close to the ground. Its visits to gardens has led to its name of "potato-bug bird." Its deliberate actions are at times almost parrot-like.

VOICE: Robin-like but sweeter and more liquid. The song is a melodious warble of a dozen or 2 dozen notes uttered quite rapidly, usually in a loud whistle but occasionally in quite a soft tone. The distinctive and frequent call note is a sharp, almost metallic clink.

NEST: Generally 6 to 15 feet up, in a low tree branch or crotch, usually not far from water; a frail and loosely woven cup of twigs, stems, grass, and rootlets. The 3 to 5 eggs (.90 x .69) are spotted with brownish or purplish.

RANGE: (M.) Breeds from Cape Breton Island, c. Ontario, c. Manitoba, and s.c. Mackenzie south to c. New Jersey, n. Georgia (mts.), c. Ohio, s. Missouri, and c. Kansas. Winters from s. Mexico south to Venezuela and Ecuador.

Blue Grosbeak   *Guiraca caerulea*—⚹38

IDENTIFICATION: L. 7. The deep purplish-blue males look
black at a distance or in bad light. They have a much
heavier bill than any blackbird and two brown wing bars,
the upper wider and paler than the lower. Young males of
the smaller indigo bunting frequently have brown on the
wing, but they are usually brown elsewhere above and
whitish below. In fall the male's blue is somewhat masked
by brownish to buffy feather edges. The dull brownish
females and young often have a few telltale patches of blue
in the body plumage. The species' most distinctive characters in any plumage are its large size, big heavy bill, and
pale wing bars.

HABITS: Originally a bird of dense, low streamside shrubbery
and weed tangles, the blue grosbeak now occurs in agricultural areas in thick hedgerow vegetation, on woodland
borders and ditchbanks, and in roadside plantings, but
still displays a marked preference for relatively low moist
areas. The male often sits motionless on top of the tallest
available bush to sing for a considerable period. The birds
feed in open crop fields but disappear into cover at the
least disturbance. Large insects—many taken from the
ground—seeds, and grains are the normal foods.

VOICE: The call note is an explosive, sharp *spink*. The song,
which does not carry far, is a finch-like jumble of sweet
notes run together into a warble.

NEST: A loosely made cup of weed and grass stems into which
leaves, paper, and often snakeskins are worked; lined with
hairlike rootlets and hair. Tall, coarse weed clumps, thick
shrubbery, or low trees are the usual nest site, which varies
in height from 3 to 12 feet. The 3 to 4 eggs (.84 x .65)
are a pale bluish-white.

RANGE: (M.) Breeds from Maryland, s. Illinois, Nebraska,
and n. California south to Florida, the Gulf Coast, and n.
Mexico. Winters from Mexico to Honduras.

Indigo Bunting   *Passerina cyanea*—⚡40

IDENTIFICATION: L. 5½. The male's blue requires sunlight to bring out its full intensity, and a singing bird against the sky can look quite dark. The nondescript female is one of the most uniformly colored of all our sparrow-like birds. In fall much of the male's blue is obscured by brown feather edges above and paler, often almost white, ones below. Old females and immature and molting males are usually a variable mixture of blue and brown. Some males in first breeding plumage are fully blue except for brown wing coverts and should not be confused with the larger, darker, heavier-billed blue grosbeak.

HABITS: This species requires dense ground cover of brushy growths with an occasional tree or telephone wire for a singing perch. It is found about old pastures and abandoned farms, woodland clearings and old burns, and along forest edges adjacent to fields, streams, and lakes. In summer it is chiefly an insect eater; in fall it turns to weed seeds.

VOICE: The call note is a sharp, brittle *tsick*. The song, delivered from a treetop perch, is composed of well-spaced units of 1 to 3 (usually 2) high-pitched, thin, strident notes. Each group is on a different pitch, and the song descends in pitch and becomes weaker toward the end. The bird is a persistent singer throughout the day and sings into late summer.

NEST: A compactly woven cup of grass, stems, bark strips, and dead leaves placed in a crotch, generally only a few feet from the ground in a dense patch of cover formed by low woody growths, coarse weeds, or vines. The 3 or 4 eggs (.75 x .52) are pale blue. Two broods are raised.

RANGE: (M.) Breeds from s. New Brunswick, s.e. Ontario, n.w. Michigan, and c.e. North Dakota south to c. Georgia, s. Louisiana, and c. Texas. Winters from s. Mexico and Cuba to Panama.

Varied Bunting   *Passerina versicolor*—❋40

IDENTIFICATION: L. 5. Males look almost black at a distance or
in poor light. A closer view reveals a dusky-blue bird
washed with reddish-purple on under parts and back. After
the late-summer molt the male's colors are obscured by
brownish feather tips. The plain female lacks the faint
streaks one finds on a female indigo and has only a light
eye ring.

HABITS: Wherever dense shrubby tangles are present in otherwise open country one may expect this species. The birds
like streamside thickets, mesquite chaparral, and brushy
pastures. Most of the time they are on the ground or hidden in vegetation, but the song is delivered from a conspicuous perch.

VOICE: A thin, rather crisp but pleasing song typically bunting
in form.

NEST: Low, usually only a few feet up in a shrub in a thicket;
a cup of grass, bark, and rootlets. The 3 or 4 eggs (.78 x
.58) are a plain bluish-white.

RANGE: (R.) Occurs from extreme s. Texas and s.e. California
south to s. Mexico.

Painted Bunting   *Passerina ciris*—❋40

IDENTIFICATION: L. 5¼. In their first spring young males are
like females except for a few patches of blue on the head.
The full color may not be acquired for several years. Males
wear their gaudy dress the year round but are noticeably
darker after the fall molt. Females and immatures are our
only green sparrow-like birds. Young just out of the nest
are dusky gray-brown above, grayer below, and almost
white on the belly.

HABITS: Brushy and weedy tangles, hedgerows, woodland
borders, and stream banks are the normal habitat. The

bird frequently nests in well-planted areas in southern towns. Until forbidden by Federal law the species was often kept as a cage bird under the name of "nonpareil." In the wild it is hard to see, as it is extremely shy and its habitat affords good protection. Insects and seeds are eaten, the latter apparently predominating. The birds are known to eat cotton worms and boll weevils and they are very fond of the seeds of foxtail grass.

VOICE: The call is a sharp 2- or 3-note chirp. The bird often sings from a tree- or bush-top perch. The song has been described as a loud, clear chant: *pew-eata, pew-eata, J eaty you too*, deliberately spaced and uttered in a sweet, musical voice.

NEST: In the thick foliage of a clump of bushes or low trees, normally about 3 feet aboveground, occasionally higher; a deep thin-walled cup placed in a crotch or fork and compactly woven of grass, weed stems, bark strips, and dead leaves and lined with hair, rootlets, and other fine material. The 3 or 4 white eggs (.76 x .56) are marked with reddish-brown.

RANGE: (M.) Breeds from s.e. North Carolina, n. Mississippi, and s. Kansas south to n. Florida, s. Louisiana, and s.e. New Mexico. Winters from c. Florida and c. Mexico south to Panama.

Dickcissel   *Spiza americana*—#43

IDENTIFICATION: L. 6¼. In most plumages the reddish-brown wing patch is a good field mark, although it is absent in juveniles and often restricted in females. Dickcissels are always grayer than bobolinks and females are paler than English sparrow females, with sharper back streaks, sharp-pointed tail feathers, and a whiter eye stripe which, like the breast, is usually touched with yellow. The black throat patch of fall males is obscured by pale feather tips. Young birds in fall are like females but usually more definitely streaked below.

HABITS: This is a bird of open country. During the nesting season upward of a dozen or more pairs may form a loose colony. In migration the birds travel in flocks that are sometimes of great size. Most birds have a strong attachment for the place where they first bred, returning, if not to the same nest site, at least to the same general area. Dickcissels seem to lack this attachment and often shift breeding grounds from year to year in a most erratic manner. One year they may be abundant, the next absent. More than a century ago they were common on the Atlantic coast, but they have not bred in numbers in this area for more than 65 years. Food requirements seem easily met, as they eat a variety of insects, weed seeds, and waste grain. Apparently suitable habitats exist in abundance in most agricultural areas.

VOICE: From a conspicuous perch on top of a weed stalk, bush, or telephone wire the refrain *dick, dick, dickcissel* is repeated over and over, the number of *dicks* and *cissels* varying. The bird sings incessantly into late summer. The opening notes are loud and sharp, the end a buzzy hiss that is lost at a distance.

NEST: Usually on or close to the ground in open fields which support dense vegetation. Fields of clover, alfalfa, hay, grain, or weeds are used. Occasionally they nest in open brushland with scattered trees, and the nest may be well up in a bush or tree. It is a bulky cup of plant stalks, grass, and leaves lined with hair, rootlets, and grass. The 3 to 5 eggs (.80 x .60) are pale blue.

RANGE: (M.) Breeds from s.e. Ontario, n.w. Minnesota, n.w. North Dakota, and n.e. Wyoming south to c. Alabama, s. Mississippi, and s. Texas. Formerly bred from Massachusetts to South Carolina. Winters from Guatemala to Colombia and Trinidad.

Evening Grosbeak   *Hesperiphona vespertina*—✳38

IDENTIFICATION: L. 8. The huge pale bill and short tail are good
characters in any plumage. In flight the wings are prom-
inently black and white and the chunky birds fly with an
undulating motion. Females and young show little of the
yellow that makes the male so distinctive.

HABITS: The summer home is in the boreal zone of fir, spruce,
and other conifers. Highly gregarious, the birds are seen
together in small groups, even when nesting. In fall and
winter they gather in large flocks. Some remain on their
breeding grounds throughout the year; others wander erratically. Increasing numbers in recent years have been
returning regularly to certain New England feeding stations. The species feeds on buds, fruits, seeds, and (in
summer) insects. In winter they are partial to seeds of the
box elder or ash-leaved maple. They come readily to feeding stations, where they prefer sunflower seeds, and, like
all northern finches, they are strongly attracted by salt
or salt-impregnated earth.

It is interesting to speculate upon the possible long-
range effect of the extensive artificial feeding of a species
like this one. The winter season, when food supplies are at
a minimum, is the most critical period of the year for many
birds. The annual year-to-year population of such a bird
may be largely determined by the number of individuals
that can be carried through the winter by the available
food. If enough winter bird-feeding stations are established
to free the evening grosbeak from dependence on natural
foods its population might increase greatly in years to
come.

VOICE: The song is a series of short, abruptly terminated
musical warbles, the last ending in a shrill whistle. They
also make a chattering sound and utter a number of single-
or double-note chirping calls in a loud, ringing whistle.

NEST: Loosely woven out of small twigs, the shallow cup heavily lined with fine rootlets. Twenty to 60 feet up, usually in a conifer in a dense leaf cluster near the end of a branch. The 3 or 4 blue-green eggs (.90 x .65) are lightly marked with gray, olive, and dark brown.

RANGE: (E.W.) Breeds from n. Michigan and c. British Columbia south in the mountains to s. Mexico. In winter they occur east to New England, south to Maryland, Kentucky, and Missouri and in lowlands throughout the West.

Purple Finch   *Carpodacus purpureus*—☀41

IDENTIFICATION: L. 6¼. Their small size, conical bills, and reddish wing bars separate the raspberry-headed males from the larger, pinker pine grosbeak. In fall dull feather edges somewhat reduce the intensity of the color. Females and young are best distinguished by the broad white line over the eye and their heavy streaking. Young males breed and sing in plumage like the female's, but they may be more yellowish or olive-yellow, especially on the rump.

HABITS: The original breeding grounds were in the openings in northern forests created by swamps, streams, and ponds, where an occasional conifer towered above its neighbors. Now they breed also about man-made clearings and invade parks and residential areas where evergreens have been planted.

The males have regular singing perches in tall treetops and perform for long periods morning and evening. Their courtship is intense, males often rising in the air in full song and executing an elaborate fluttering dance before the female.

After nesting the birds wander erratically in flocks in which females and young far outnumber adult males. They are often abundant in an area one year and rare the next. Purple finches come readily to feeding stations and like sunflower seeds, hemp, and the various millets.

Their normal foods—buds, seeds, wild fruits, and insects—
vary with the season.

VOICE: The song is a rapid, high-pitched warble with a beautiful liquid quality. Generally the notes run together, but
the song may be broken into sections. Sometimes individual notes do not vary much in pitch and the song becomes
almost a trill; at other times it is in short snatches, broken
by long pauses. The metallic call note is short and distinctive.

NEST: Five to 60 feet aboveground, usually in an evergreen,
occasionally in a deciduous bush or hedge; a neatly made
cup of fine twigs, grasses, and rootlets, often well lined
with hair or wool. The 4 to 6 blue eggs (.79 x .56) are
spotted about the larger end with brown.

RANGE: (P.M.) Breeds from Newfoundland, s. Quebec, n.
Ontario, and n.w. British Columbia south to n. New Jersey,
Maryland (mts.), n. Illinois, c. Minnesota, s. Alberta, and
on the Pacific coast to Lower California. Winters from
Nova Scotia, s. Ontario, s. Minnesota, Nebraska, and s.
British Columbia in varying numbers south to Florida,
Texas, s. Arizona, and Lower California.

House Finch   *Carpodacus mexicanus*—❋41

IDENTIFICATION: **L. 5½.** The male's color is generally a
brighter and purer red than that of the purple finch but
is more restricted in area. The best character is the heavy
brown streaking of the lower under parts. In female and
young the less streaked gray-brown back and less contrasting head pattern are generally diagnostic.

HABITS: This gregarious species is at home in sunny open
country if water is available. Building, agriculture, and
irrigation—in fact, almost all the changes wrought by man
—seem to suit this bird, since today it is widespread and
abundant both in town and country. In the West it occu-

pies a niche similar to the one the English sparrow has usurped in the East. Although generally a resident species, there is some movement in winter, individuals wandering as far east as south Texas. The bird is chiefly vegetarian, depending primarily upon weed seeds, but it is fond of wild and cultivated fruit.

VOICE: A clear, rolling warble of notes which vary greatly in pitch but run together. It is a longer song than a purple finch's and higher-pitched. The call notes are varied, but the most distinctive is a harsh chatter.

NEST: In a wide variety of places, usually the one that provides the best shelter at hand. Bird boxes, tree cavities, crannies in buildings, dense vines, shrubs and cactus clumps, and even old nests of cliff swallows and orioles are used. The nest is well built out of whatever soft and fibrous substances are available. Often an entire nest is made of one type of material. The 4 or 5 pale blue eggs (.73 x .54) are lightly spotted with black.

RANGE: (R.) Occurs from n. Wyoming and s. Washington south to s. Mexico and east to w. Kansas and c. Texas.

Morellet Seedeater *Sporophila torqueola*—※44

IDENTIFICATION: L. 4. These tiny finches with their heavy, blunt, curved bills are extremely variable in plumage. The males seem to require at least several years to develop a clear black-and-white pattern, and some may never develop it. Until then the black markings are less extensive and are masked with gray. The bill is the best clue to the identity of the dull brownish female.

HABITS: Throughout northern Middle America this is the commonest of the many little seedeaters. When not nesting the birds are quite gregarious. Brushy or weedy cover appears to be essential, and they are usually hard to see. The borders of pastures or cultivated land and the banks of irrigation ditches are favorite haunts.

VOICE: The call is a *clickty* note. The loud bunting-like song is composed of a monotonous series of high notes followed by several lower notes.

NEST: A few feet up in a small shrub, usually suspended from several small twigs; a compact cup of fine rootlets or grass sometimes lined with hair. The 4 or 5 blue-green eggs (.65 x .48) are evenly spotted with brown.

RANGE: (R.) Occurs from extreme s. Texas south to Costa Rica.

Pine Grosbeak *Pinicola enucleator*—❋ 39

IDENTIFICATION: L. 9. This species, the largest of the grosbeaks, is larger than the purple finch or either of the crossbills, the only birds with which it might be confused. Its narrow white wing bars, stout bill, and long tail are distinctive. The male's red plumage is similar in shade to that of the white-winged crossbill. The female is much grayer than females of either crossbill and has brighter but more restricted greenish areas. Young males are like females, with enough red in the green on the head and rump to produce a rusty to orange effect.

HABITS: The summer home is usually along the border of an open area in the coniferous forest. Habitats adjacent to streams or ponds seem preferred, but the birds are also found on the borders of hayfields and pastures. After nesting they are gregarious and travel in search of food in flocks of up to a hundred birds, in which the fully adult rosy red males are much in the minority. Grosbeaks appear to travel only when it becomes necessary to do so in order to find food. Some years they hardly leave the breeding region; in others they go hundreds of miles south.

In summer they take a few insects but they live chiefly on buds and seeds. Beechnuts and the seeds of all the conifers are special favorites. During their southern wanderings, apple seeds, ash fruits, and mountain ash berries seem to attract them.

VOICE: The song is a beautiful melody of whistles, warbles, and trills, sometimes loud, sometimes soft and ventrilo-quial. The call is 2 or 3 loudly whistled mellow musical notes suggesting the call of a greater yellow-leg. In flight they give a low, trilled whistle.

NEST: In a lower branch of a conifer or in a shrub 6 to 30 feet from the ground. The flat nest is made of twigs and moss lined with grass and fine rootlets. The 3 or 4 pale greenish eggs (1.05 x .73) are spotted with purplish-brown.

RANGE: (E.W.) Breeds in the boreal forests of the whole Northern Hemisphere, south in North America to s. Nova Scotia, n. New Hampshire, s.c. Ontario, and Manitoba. In western mountains breeds south to n. New Mexico and c. California. In winter wanders south to Pennsylvania, Indiana, and Nebraska.

Gray-crowned Rosy-finch*

Leucosticte tephrocotis—⚹41

IDENTIFICATION: L. 6¼. The amount of gray on the head varies. In one race only the back and sides of the crown are gray; in another the cheeks and sometimes even the throat are gray. Females are paler and duller. The brown-capped rosy-finch, which currently is considered a distinct species, lacks the gray altogether. In another species—the black rosy-finch—the brown of the body is so dark as to seem almost black. Both may well be only races of the gray-crowned.

HABITS: These rosy-finches are found up to the tops of our highest mountains. They generally nest above timber line in sheer rock faces and talus slopes above the snow fields, where they do the greater part of their feeding in early summer. They are active birds, foraging widely over alpine meadows and along the edges of snow pools. Seeds and insects, which they sometimes catch in the air, are standard foods. In winter wandering flocks are found on bare wind-swept areas from high in the mountains to far out on the Great Plains. The large compact flocks restlessly swirl into the air at frequent intervals.

VOICE: The call note is a high-pitched *zee-o* or a short twitter. The song is a long series of chirps that vary in length and intensity, rather like an English sparrow chorus.

NEST: Under boulders or in rock crevices; a substantial cup of moss and grass lined with fine grasses and occasionally with feathers and down. The 4 or 5 eggs (.89 x .61) are pure white.

RANGE: (P.M.) Breeds from c. Yukon and s.w. Alaska south to n.w. Montana and s.c. California. Wanders in winter east to s. Manitoba, w. Iowa, and south to New Mexico.

European Goldfinch*   *Carduelis carduelis*—✳42

IDENTIFICATION: L. 5½. The red-faced adults are unlike any native species. Young birds are gray-brown above and whitish below, variably spotted and streaked with brown. They lack red and black head markings but have the distinctive yellow wing areas, which in this plumage are crossed by two brownish bars.

HABITS: These birds like hedgerows in open farming country and weeds and thickets on abandoned land. In Europe there is a marked migration, although in some parts of its range it seems more nomadic than migratory. In this country they seem very sedentary and are seldom seen far from the areas where they are known to breed. Weed seeds are the chief food, plus insects in spring and summer.

VOICE: Call, a liquid *twit* uttered frequently in flight and as it feeds. The song is a clear, liquid warble.

NEST: Made of grass and fine roots mixed with down and wool and lined with the same material; placed in small conifers or hedges. The 4 or 5 pale blue eggs (.72 x .50) are lightly speckled with browns.

RANGE: (R.) Occurs all over Europe, North Africa, and part of Asia. Introduced into North America near New York City in 1878 and St. Louis, Missouri, in 1870. Now a well-established resident in southwestern Long Island, New York.

Hoary Redpoll   *Acanthis bornemanni*—✻41

IDENTIFICATION: L. 5. The chief differences between this species and the next are the smaller bill, the predominately white ground color of the body, which gives it a lighter appearance, the unstreaked rump, and usually unstreaked sides. The pink on the under parts of the male never runs up onto the cheek and extends farther down in the center of the breast than on the sides.

HABITS: The breeding grounds extend to the farthest reaches of the Arctic tundra. In places its range overlaps that of its more southern relative. The habits of the two redpolls do not differ significantly, but the hoary seldom comes as far south in winter or appears in such great numbers as the common redpoll. When hoarys do occur it is usually with a flock of the latter.

VOICE: The notes are sharper than those of the next species.

NEST: On the ground in the lee of a rock or sparse vegetation. Where low trees are available it may be several feet up. The nest is a cup of grass, downs, and bark shreds lined with feathers. The 5 or 6 bluish-green eggs (.73 x .53) are dotted and scrawled with brown.

RANGE: (P.M.) Breeds on the tundra bordering the Arctic Ocean south to the tree line in both hemispheres. Wanders south in winter, occasionally getting as far as Connecticut, s. Ontario, Illinois, and Montana.

Common Redpoll

Acanthis flammea—#41

IDENTIFICATION: L. 5¼. The red cap present in all plumages, except the juvenile, is the best mark. Females lack the rosy breast and rump. This redpoll is quite brownish and well streaked compared with the hoary redpoll.

HABITS: The bird inhabits forest openings, scrub and second growths, swamps of tamarack, willow, and alder, and stream banks throughout the northern part of the spruce forest and ranges well out into the barren lands wherever dwarf willow and birch maintain a foothold. Varying numbers wander south in winter in compact flocks. In summer they feed chiefly on insects, but in winter seeds, especially alder and birch, are their staple food. They are active birds, clinging and hanging in every possible position as they alternately open seed heads and fly to the ground to pick the seeds off the snow.

VOICE: The flight call is a series of rattling, metallic chirps. A feeding flock keeps up a continual twitter. The song is a rippling trill preceded by a twitter not unlike the flight song. It is delivered from a treetop perch or during a display flight as the bird loops and circles with hesitant wing-beats.

NEST: At almost any height but generally low in the forked branches of a willow or birch. Occasionally on the ground in a sedge tussock. Loose colonies are usually formed in favorable sites. The nest has a foundation of twigs, mixed with grass, moss, and other soft material. The cup is lined with downs, fur, and feathers. The 5 or 6 blue-green eggs (.65 x .53) are spotted with reddish-brown.

RANGE: (P.M.) Breeds in the Northern Hemisphere from the tundra south; in North America to s. Newfoundland, n.c. Quebec, n. Manitoba, and n. British Columbia; in Europe to the Alps and Carpathians. In winter irregularly south to North Carolina, n. Oklahoma, Colorado, and n. California.

Pine Siskin*   *Spinus pinus*—❋42

IDENTIFICATION: L. 5. The uniformly streaked appearance above and below, the rather narrow pointed bill, wing bars, and concealed yellow patches in wings and tail are distinctive. Young are like adults but more yellowish all over and the streaks a richer brown. It can be identified dozens of times by its call note for every time it is seen well enough to distinguish any of the above characters.

HABITS: Conifers are essential to any acceptable breeding ground, and siskins have followed their planting into new areas. Throughout northern or high-altitude evergreen forests they are well distributed but in any given locality much more common some years than others. Like so many birds of the boreal forest, they are erratic both as breeders and as winter visitors to the south. They travel in flocks that may number hundreds and include goldfinches, redpolls, and crossbills. Flocks of apparently non-breeding birds are found all summer. The siskins' summer foods are insects, buds, tender leaves, and seeds. In winter they depend on the seeds of conifers, annual weeds, and especially on those of alder, birch, and white cedar.

VOICE: Song and calls are goldfinch-like but lower in pitch, with a buzzy, husky quality. It has a distinctive penetrating *ze-e-e-e-e-m* note rising in pitch and intensity at the end.

NEST: A platform of twigs with grass, bark, and moss worked into the mass; the shallow inner cup is lined with down, fur, and feathers. The nest is always in a conifer about 10 to 20 feet aboveground and saddled well out near the end of a branch, where it is protected by foliage. The 3 or 4 pale blue-green eggs (.67 x .48) are dotted with brown and black.

RANGE: (P.M.) Breeds from c. Quebec, s. Mackenzie, and c. Alaska south to Nova Scotia, North Carolina (mts.), n. Michigan, s.e. Nebraska, and s. Mexico (mts.). In winter south to s. Florida, the Gulf Coast, and Mexico.

Common Goldfinch   *Spinus tristis*—¥42

IDENTIFICATION: L. 5. The extremely undulatory flight is distinctive but not diagnostic, as many finches have a similar flight. The uniformly unstreaked olive-brown plumage and the pale bills of females and young are unlike any other finch. Winter males resemble females except that they keep their jet-black wings and bright yellow shoulder patches.

HABITS: During the summer the "wild canary" likes open country with weedy fields and scattered woody growths to provide nest sites. It is one of the latest nesters and is found in flocks until well into midsummer. Winter flocks are often quite large and may include some of the more northern finches. The basic food is weed seeds, which in partially digested form are fed by regurgitation to the young. The birds eat some insects, especially in spring, also buds and succulent vegetation. Birch, alder, and conifer seeds supply them with considerable winter food, and they are more often in woodlands at this season.

VOICE: The songs and calls have a distinctive high-pitched, sweet, twittery quality. On the wing it utters a call like *per-chic'-o-ree*. It also has a *zwe-zeeeee* call. The song is an endless series of trills and twitters, interspersed with *wee* or *swee* notes with an upward inflection.

NEST: An open cup of grass, bark, and plant stems well lined with down, placed in an upright fork in a bush or small tree from a few feet to 20 or more aboveground. The 5 unspotted eggs (.65 x .48) are a very pale blue.

RANGE: (P.M.) Breeds from Newfoundland, s. Quebec, s. Manitoba, and s. British Columbia south to n. Georgia, c.

Arkansas, s. Colorado, c. Nevada, and n. Lower California.
Winters south to the Gulf Coast and s. Mexico.

Dark-backed Goldfinch   *Spinus psaltria*—✳42

IDENTIFICATION: L. 4. In different parts of their range the
back color of the males varies from olive-green to solid
black and the under parts from pale to bright yellow. The
heads, however, are always black. Females and young are
much like those of the common goldfinch but are olive-
green instead of olive-brown above and olive-yellow instead
of yellowish-gray below. In flight this species shows a conspicuous and distinctive white patch on the wing.

HABITS: These are abundant throughout all types of reasonably open country, whether humid or dry. Although they
usually nest in trees, especially along watercourses, they
occasionally nest out in the sagebrush. This species seems
very fond of thistle seeds. These and other weed seeds
compose its diet. The birds seldom feed in treetops even
in winter, when they roam in large flocks in which mated
pairs seem to stay together.

VOICE: Sweet and plaintive. The flight call is a brittle, rattling
note. The bird also has a single or double *tee* or *tee-yee*
call. The twittery, exuberant song often includes notes
suggestive of other birds.

NEST: A deep cup rather loosely made of grasses, plant fibers,
and downs, placed variously from moderate heights in
trees to low bushes or weed tangles close to the ground.
The 4 or 5 pale blue-green eggs (.61 x .45) are unmarked.

RANGE: (P.M.) Breeds from n. Colorado and Oregon east to
c. Texas and south through Central America to Venezuela
and c. Peru. Winters from Texas, New Mexico and n. California south.

Red Crossbill   *Loxia curvirostra*—#39

IDENTIFICATION: L. 6. Except for very young birds, the long narrow bill with its crossed tips at once distinguishes a crossbill. The brick red of the adult male is unlike the color of any other northern finch. Females are more extensively greenish than pine grosbeaks, and the rump color, which is quite yellow, is much brighter than the head. The less streaked appearance and the plain wings separate females of this species from the next. Juvenile birds are more streaked, and immature males are a mottled mixture of bright yellows, dull reds, and green.

HABITS: This bird is always associated with conifers; its normal home is in the boreal forests of northern latitudes and mountaintops. Its food is conifer seeds extracted from the cones with a bill which has become peculiarly adapted for this one purpose. For some reason, possibly the periodic failure of the cone crop, the birds are erratic in time and place of nesting and in seasonal movements. They nest from January to August, and in certain winters roving flocks occur far outside their normal habitat. Occasionally they nest in extensive pitch-pine areas far south of their normal breeding grounds. Red crossbills eat some insects and, away from conifers, a wide variety of seeds, buds, and wild fruits, which they hunt in treetops and on the ground. As they feed they clamber about in trees, using bills and feet like a parrot. They are quite fearless.

VOICE: Call note, a sharp chick-like *pip* repeated 2 or 3 times. It also has a high-pitched, thin, twittery trill. One of its songs is a series of short, ascending 2-note phrases forcefully delivered in a warbling voice followed by a trill.

NEST: A foundation of twigs supports a shallow cup of bark fibers, rootlets, and grasses padded and lined with moss and downs. The location may be 5 to 80 feet up, saddled in thick foliage, frequently well out on the branch of a conifer. The 4 or 5 pale green-blue eggs (.75 x .55) are finely spotted with brown.

RANGE: (E.W.) Breeds over the Northern Hemisphere; in North America from Newfoundland, c. Quebec, n. Mackenzie, and c. Alaska south to Maine, n. Georgia (mts.), Michigan, and through the mountains of Mexico to Guatemala. In winter wanders south to n. Florida and the Gulf Coast.

White-winged Crossbill   *Loxia leucoptera*—#39

IDENTIFICATION: L. 6. The male's rosy red is quite different from the brick red of the preceding species, but the conspicuous white wing bars are the best identification mark in any plumage. Females are grayer and more streaked than female red crossbills. Juveniles are gray, thickly streaked with rich brown. Immature males are a patchwork of yellows, greens, and reds.

HABITS: Like the red, this is a bird of conifer forests but is more northern in distribution and seldom wanders as far south. It travels in smaller flocks and does not mix as freely with other species. Seeds from spruce and fir cones provide its staple food in the North. When it comes south it is attracted by Norway spruce and hemlock but not by pitch pine.

Our two crossbills present an interesting problem. They are closely related, similar in habits and the ecological niche they occupy, yet they apparently thrive in the same area without one tending to displace the other. Nor do they appear to hybridize. The matter is all the more remarkable in that three other pairs of boreal species—the three-toed woodpeckers, the redpolls, and the Cryptoglaux owls—present an essentially similar problem. In each case, although one ranges farther north and the other farther south, the greater part of the range is occupied by both members of the pair.

Voice: The song is a vigorous and varied outburst of loud canary-like *sweets*, frequently dying away into a low warble, then swelling again into a loud, musical trilling. Frequently the song continues unbroken for a minute or more, the bird launching itself into the air from its treetop perch to finish it on hovering wings. A common call is a series of plaintive sandpiper-like *peeps*, also a series of dry, unmusical notes.

Nest: Similar to that of the red crossbill, sometimes constructed largely of twigs and usnea lichens. The height is variable, but frequently it is quite low. The nest is generally in the thick foliage of a spruce or similar conifer. The 2 to 4 pale blue-green eggs (.80 x .55) are blotched with browns.

Range: (E.W.) Breeds in the boreal forests of the Northern Hemisphere; in North America from the northern limit of trees south to s. Nova Scotia, n. New York, c. Ontario, s. Alberta, and s. British Columbia. In winter wanders irregularly to North Carolina, s. Illinois, Colorado, and n. Oregon.

Olive Sparrow*   *Arremonops rufivirgatus*—✳37

Identification: L. 5¾. This little olive-green sparrow differs from the larger green-tailed towhee in its striped crown and buffy breast. Young are uniformly dull brown above with only the wings and tail showing a trace of green. They are paler below, becoming buffy on the belly, and have pale wing bars.

Habits: Although frequently abundant this is a hard bird to find, as it stays close to the ground under brushy cover. It sings from a low perch, where it is hidden by leaves. Overgrown abandoned fields are a favorite habitat, but it also frequents field borders, forest clearings, and tangles of rank weeds and tall grasses in low, moist areas.

VOICE: The call is a loud cardinal-like *clink*. The song is a simple repetition of a single note that becomes a trill at the end.

NEST: A large, round, domed structure of twigs, grass, stems, and leaves, placed 2 to 5 feet up in a bush, low tree, or cactus plant. The 4 eggs (.84 x .65) are pure white.

RANGE: (R.) Occurs from s. Texas south through e. Mexico to Oaxaca.

Green-tailed Towhee*　　　*Oberholseria chlorura*—✻37

IDENTIFICATION: L. 6¾. Only in strong light do the upper parts of this bird look green. Its pure-white throat, in strong contrast with its gray breast, is its most distinctive character. The edge of the wings and the underwing surfaces are bright yellow and the wing and tail feathers fairly bright yellowish olive-green. Young are streaked all over with dusky and are dull olive or brownish-gray above, dingy white below.

HABITS: Areas well grown up with low brush are the normal home. Scattered trees are tolerated, but when the forest encroaches the bird disappears as a breeder. It seems to prefer hilly to flat land and occurs way up in the drier mountains. It feeds on and near the ground, subsisting chiefly on weed seeds and insects.

VOICE: The common call is a soft, plaintive series of *mews*. The rich, melodious song has been likened to a fox sparrow's but is more varied. A common form begins with a *wee churr*, followed by some high notes or a rough burr and ending with a feeble trill.

NEST: In dense foliage of a shrub near or almost on the ground; a bulky structure of twigs, grasses, and stems with a fairly deep cup lined with rootlets and hairs. The 3 or 4 eggs (.82 x .61) are pale blue to white, evenly spotted with reddish-brown.

RANGE: (M.) Breeds from s.c. Montana and c. Oregon south to c.w. Texas and s. California. Winters from w. Texas and s. California south to c. Mexico.

Eastern Towhee   *Pipilo erythrophthalmus*—✳37

IDENTIFICATION: L. 8. Their large size and the extensive white areas at the corners of their long, rounded tails help identify these birds as they flit through the underbrush and disappear. Juveniles are rich brown above and buffy below, streaked all over with darker brown. Their tail is like the adult female's. Northern birds have red eyes, but in a southern race the eyes are white.

HABITS: Dense brushy cover is essential. Suitable conditions soon develop on poorly kept pastureland or abandoned fields as shrubs and young trees crowd out the grass. Towhees generally persist in a locality until the forest canopy eliminates the last brushy opening. Parks, roadsides, field borders, and even isolated forest openings are occupied by this abundant species if the desired cover is present. The species is fairly solitary. It feeds almost entirely on the ground, vigorously scratching away the dead leaves to get at the heavy insect population of the moist humus layer. It eats insects and other small animal life and seeds and fruits.

VOICE: Call, a 2-note *to-wheee* or *jor-hee*. Its song is very distinctive—2 clear notes generally on different pitches, the first higher, followed by a uniformly medium-pitched trill, often given as *drink your teeeeeee*. The quality is variable, but the effect is usually musical.

NEST: On the ground in the shelter of a small shrub, clump of grass, stump, or brush pile or up to 5 feet above the ground in a bush or small tree. Two broods are raised, the first often in a ground nest, the second in one above the ground. The loosely built nest is made of coarse stems, leaves, and bark lined with fine grasses, rootlets, and hair. The 4 to 6 white eggs (.90 x .70) are finely dotted with reddish-brown.

RANGE: (P.M.) Breeds from s. Maine, s. Ontario, s. Manitoba, and s.e. Saskatchewan south to Florida, s. Mississippi, n. Louisiana, and Oklahoma. Winters from Maryland, Ohio, s. Wisconsin, and s.e. Nebraska south to Florida, the Gulf Coast, and c. Texas.

Spotted Towhee   *Pipilo maculatus*—※37

IDENTIFICATION: L. 7½. The chief character which distinguishes this slightly smaller towhee from its eastern relative is the white spotting on the wings and back which is present to some degree in all plumages. The amount of spotting varies in different races, as does the white in the tail. Generally the tail is whiter than in the eastern bird.

HABITS: Dense shrubby cover is common in the low rainfall areas of the West, but this towhee seldom occupies it unless the ground is well carpeted with dead leaves and leaf mold in which it can forage. The bird seldom ventures far from the ground except to sing from a convenient bush top. In the eastern part of its range there is some north and south migration (as well as an eastward movement), but farther west in more mountainous areas this becomes chiefly an altitudinal shift—up in summer and down in winter.

VOICE: The different local races into which this wide-ranging species is divided have noticeably different calls and songs. Common calls are a double mewing note and a single, more nasal one. The song generally starts with one or more clear, high-pitched notes, then runs off into a lower-pitched, buzzy trill.

NEST: Approximately like that of the eastern towhee. The 4 or 5 eggs (.90 x .68) of the palest shade of blue-green are fairly uniformly speckled with few to many red-brown dots.

RANGE: (P.M.) Breeds from s. Alberta and c. British Columbia east to w. Nebraska and w. Texas and south to Guatemala. Winters from e. Nebraska, Utah, and s. British Columbia south.

Lark Bunting   *Calamospiza melanocorys*—#40

IDENTIFICATION: L. 7. In fall males lose their distinctive plumage and look much like females and young. The young are slightly buffier than the female, and in their first breeding season the male's inner wing and center tail feathers remain brown. The white shoulder patch, conspicuous in flight, is present to some extent in all plumages, although it may be tinged with buffy. It is the best field mark.

HABITS: Grasslands of the drier, more barren type seem to be preferred. Occasionally the species breeds in the moister tall-grass prairies and cultivated clover fields east of its normal range, suddenly appearing in considerable numbers and as suddenly vanishing after one or more years. The birds are usually seen in compact flocks when not nesting. Sometimes the flocks are enormous, yet the birds move in unison as they wheel, turn, or settle to the ground. They eat insects and weed seeds and show special fondness for grasshoppers.

VOICE: The male sings from a prominent perch or more often from the air as it hovers on fluttering wings. The song is a series of trills warbled in a rich, musical voice. On the wing the birds have a distinctive soft, sweet *boo-ee* call note.

NEST: On the ground, usually in a slight depression under the shelter of a clump of vegetation; a loosely built cup of grass, stems, and rootlets, often lined with hair. The 4 or 5 pale blue eggs (.85 x .65) are generally unmarked. The bird is somewhat gregarious even in the breeding season, and nesting pairs tend to form loose colonies in especially favorable cover.

RANGE: (M.) Breeds from s.w. Manitoba to s. British Columbia south to n.w. Texas and s.e. New Mexico, and from w. Minnesota and e. Nebraska west to w. Colorado. Winters from s. Texas, s. Arizona, and s. Lower California south to c. Mexico.

Ipswich Sparrow*   *Passerculus princeps*—❄47

IDENTIFICATION: L. 6¼. This looks like a big and very pale Savannah sparrow with a proportionately longer tail. The yellowish line over the eye is pale and prominent in spring but in winter is almost white. The legs are a pale pinkish straw color.

HABITS: This, the only land bird of Sable Island, a narrow 20-mile strip of sand dunes 100 miles off Nova Scotia, is an insular form of the Savannah sparrow. Whether it should be regarded as a full species is questionable.

Some individuals winter on Sable Island; others scatter down the Atlantic coast along the outer beaches and sand dunes. Its name came from the Ipswich dunes of Massachusetts. A favorite feeding ground is along the wrack line on the upper beach. Here they can be more readily observed than in the beach grass of the dunes. They usually walk or run, seldom hopping like a Savannah. They take insects when available, turning to beach-grass seeds only in winter.

These sparrows are the descendants of what could hardly have been more than a few pairs of Savannah sparrows that originally colonized Sable Island. No such small sample is likely to be typical and carry with it all the genetic factors which produce individual variability within a species. As this small, isolated group interbred it probably lost most of the variant genes it did bring with it and in time became almost completely homogeneous. However, a small population such as this favors the rapid dissemination among its members of such spontaneous variations or mutations as may occur from time to time. If, as it seems reasonable to assume, the habitat available to the birds on Sable Island differs in certain respects from the typical mainland habitat of the Savannah sparrow, certain mutations of no survival value on the mainland might here be sufficiently favorable for them to persist and become diffused through the entire population on the island.

Whether the sum total of these factors has yet produced a bird that would not interbreed with mainland Savannahs, no one knows. It is merely assumed on the basis of the differences which we observe between them that they would not. Should Sable Island eventually wash completely away, as seems likely, forcing the Ipswich sparrow to breed on the mainland or perish, it will survive as a distinct form only if it has actually achieved reproductive isolation from the Savannah. Should this be lacking (in which case it is not a species), interbreeding with mainland Savannahs would soon obliterate the distinctive Ipswich characteristics. Many biologists now believe that new species develop almost exclusively under conditions such as these, where a population is cut off and isolated geographically from the parent species for a period long enough to enable it to develop differences sufficient to prevent any interbreeding when the isolating barrier eventually breaks down.

VOICE: Except when nesting, their only utterance is a sharp, dry *tsip*. The song is slightly lower-pitched and less buzzy than a Savannah's, the second trill ending with a sound like a common tern's *tee-arr*.

NEST: A cup of coarse plant stems and grasses lined with fine grass and hair; placed in a hollow in the ground in the shelter of vegetation. The 4 or 5 eggs (.77 x .65) are either white, bluish, or olive, very heavily splashed with brown.

RANGE: (P.M.) Breeds on Sable Island, Nova Scotia. Winters south to Georgia on the outer beaches of the Atlantic coast.

Savannah Sparrow*   *Passerculus sandwichensis*—❋47

IDENTIFICATION: L. 5¾. The Savannah has a short, slightly forked tail which, with the yellow line over the eye and the pale flesh-colored legs, is its best field mark. It has a pair of pale to almost whitish outer tail feathers, but these are not conspicuous. Young lack the yellow eyeline, are less sharply streaked, and, like some winter adults, are often quite buffy on the head and neck, where the color occasionally extends faintly to the breast and flanks.

HABITS: The normal home is low, moist areas dominated by tall rank grasses. The bird is common along streams, rivers, and lakes, and in the dry land edge of fresh- and salt-water marshes. It also breeds in uplands when there is dense herbaceous vegetation or, in some cases, low shrubs. Near the coast it nests and winters in grass-covered sand dunes and hayfields adjoining the tidal marshes.

Savannah sparrows spend most of their time on the ground, where they are very active. When feeding they hop, but to escape danger they run with great speed. Not until they are almost stepped on do they flush, and then only to flutter a short distance before dropping down and disappearing in the grass. Weed and grass seeds and a variety of insects, especially beetles, are its chief foods.

VOICE: The song consists of 2 to 5 generally identical short notes followed by 2 buzzy trills at different pitches, one at least very high-pitched and insectlike—*tsit-tsit-tsit, sweee-zeee*. The Savannah is a persistent singer from the highest available perch, usually a tall weed stem or bush, rarely a tree. Sparrow call notes cannot be adequately described, but they are often distinctive and should be learned in the field.

NEST: On the ground in a slight depression in the shelter of dense vegetation; an open cup of coarse plant stems lined with similar finer material. The 4 or 5 pale blue-green

eggs (.75 x .55) are variably and often very heavily
marked with reddish-brown.

RANGE: (P.M.) Breeds from n. Labrador, n. Mackenzie, and
n. Alaska south to s. New Jersey, West Virginia, Missouri,
n. New Mexico, n.w. Sonora, and s. Lower California.
Winters from Cape Cod, s. Indiana, Colorado, and s.
Alaska south to Cuba and Guatemala.

Grasshopper Sparrow*
Ammodramus savannarum—※46

IDENTIFICATION: L. 5⅛. This sparrow is usually recognized
by its song, its habitat, and its low, buzzy, wren-like flight.
Its small size and disproportionately large head and neck,
unstreaked under parts which are pale buffy across the
breast and on the flanks, and its short, bristly tail are useful field marks. The dull white ends of the outer tail
feathers, the yellow bend of wing, and the yellowish line
between eye and bill are hard to see. These markings
are absent on young birds, the breasts and flanks of which
are first streaked, turning later to a deep buff like that on
the upper parts, which are much buffier than those of the
adults.

HABITS: This species occurs in drier areas than the Savannah
sparrow. Its favorite haunts are old pastures, hayfields,
and worn-out farmland sparsely grown up to weeds and
grasses. The bird is not uniformly distributed over its
known range, and what it regards as acceptable habitat
varies greatly. A Florida race inhabits low (1- to 2-foot)
palmetto and oak scrub, while far-northern birds are found
in clearings and sparsely wooded areas.

Away from the open prairie, where it is uniformly distributed and abundant, breeding groups tend to form loose
colonies which shift nesting grounds from year to year. The
bird seldom leaves the ground or the shelter of weeds and
grasses. When flushed it flutters low over the grass with an

erratic twisting flight and soon drops back to earth. The best time to observe it is when it sings. This it does from the top of a weed, a stone, or a fence post, rarely from a low tree. It is probably our most insectivorous sparrow, being very fond of grasshoppers, weevils, and beetles.

VOICE: The male's song is a long, insectlike buzz preceded by a couple of short preliminary notes. It is pitched so high that many older people cannot hear it. Generally the long buzz is on one pitch but a common variation is a broken jumble of squeaky notes. It often sings at night as well as all day.

NEST: On the ground in a depression near or in a clump of grass or other vegetation. The cup of grasses lined with rootlets and hairs is usually more or less arched over to conceal the eggs. The 4 or 5 white eggs (.72 x .55) are speckled with red-brown about the larger end.

RANGE: (P.M.) Breeds from s. New Hampshire, s. Ontario, s. Wisconsin, North Dakota, and s.e. British Columbia south to Florida, the Greater Antilles, and s. Mexico. Winters from North Carolina, s. Illinois, s. Texas, and c. California south to Costa Rica.

Baird's Sparrow*   *Ammodramus bairdii*—✳46

IDENTIFICATION: L. 5½. The best characters are the short, sharp, black breast streaks that form a narrow band or necklace and the yellow-brown ground color of the head and neck, which is closely flecked with black except for a very broad unmarked crown stripe of rich ocher. The outer webs of the outer feathers of the deeply forked tail are white but not conspicuously so. Young are similar but paler and the markings more diffuse. Its song is its only good character at any distance.

HABITS: Although its breeding range is small, this sparrow is reasonably abundant in migration and on its wintering grounds. It breeds in the drier parts of open prairies where low brush or old matted vegetation affords good cover. Singing is from the top of a higher than average dead weed stalk.

VOICE: Fuller and less insectlike than that of the grasshopper and Savannah sparrows. The song starts with a series of chips and ends in a rolling, chattering, almost musical trill.

NEST: A cup of coarse stems and grasses lined with similar finer materials; on the ground under a low plant or grass clump. The 3 to 5 white eggs (.80 x .60) are blotched with brown at the larger end and marked with dark lines.

RANGE: (M.) Breeds from c. Manitoba and s.w. Saskatchewan south to n.w. Minnesota and c. Montana. Winters from c. Texas west through n.w. Mexico.

Leconte's Sparrow*   *Passerherbulus caudacutus*—#46

IDENTIFICATION: L. 5. The yellow-brown throat and under parts (except belly) streaked on the sides, the red-brown speckled hind neck, and the rich, buffy eyeline are distinctive. Young birds lack the neck markings and are more yellow than brown; the streaks on the under parts extend faintly across the breast to the sides of the throat.

HABITS: During the breeding season look for this diminutive and elusive golden-brown sparrow in the dense, matted vegetation of boggy meadows or on the willow-studded upper margins of marsh areas. At other seasons it may occur almost anywhere in grassland where vegetation of previous years forms a matted cover. One may approach very closely without flushing the birds, as they prefer to escape by running instead of flying. When in song, they rise to the top of a weed or low willow, where they can be studied better than at any other time.

VOICE: High-pitched and thin. The song is a short squeak, followed by a grasshopper-like buzz and a final chip.

NEST: A hair-lined grass cup on the ground or a few inches up in a clump of dead grass; usually well concealed in a tangle of rank, old growth in or near a wet meadow. The 4 white to greenish eggs (.71 x .54) are variously marked with brown chiefly at the large end.

RANGE: (M.) Breeds from s. Mackenzie south to s. Minnesota and North Dakota. Winters from s. North Carolina, s. Tennessee, and s. Kansas south to s. Florida, the Gulf Coast, and Texas.

Henslow's Sparrow*   *Passerherbulus henslowii*—※46

IDENTIFICATION: L. 5. The strong greenish tone of the head, hind neck, and face and the dark reddish-brown on the back and wings are distinctive. Unlike the grasshopper sparrow, it has two streaks on the sides of the throat and a necklace of sharp, black streaks across the breast. Most identifications are by song.

HABITS: Open grasslands with varied rank vegetation is the normal habitat. Wet areas are favored, and the birds seem to like a mixture of tall tufted grasses, tall weeds, and scattered small woody growths. Although widely distributed and generally common, their habit of forming loose colonies during the breeding season tends to leave many apparently suitable areas unpopulated. These big-headed, chunky sparrows with their short stubby tails are hard to see unless they are found singing. When flushed the flight is erratic and undulating.

VOICE: The song is a short, explosive, double-noted buzz—*flee-sic*. It lasts about 2/5 of a second and probably holds the record for shortness. It is delivered from the top of a tall weed or fence post and carries well. Night singing is not uncommon and may continue almost all night.

NEST: A loosely woven cup of grasses on the ground in the shelter of a tuft of grass and often partially domed over. The 4 eggs (.75 x .55) are spotted with reddish-brown.

RANGE: (M.) Breeds from c. New Hampshire, s. Ontario, c. Wisconsin, and South Dakota south to North Carolina, c. Missouri, and n. Texas. Winters from South Carolina, c. Alabama, and s. Arkansas south to c. Florida, and the Gulf Coast to e. Texas.

Sharp-tailed Sparrow*   *Ammospiza caudacuta*—♯46

IDENTIFICATION: L. 5¾. The gray crown stripe, nape, and ear patch, in sharp contrast with the rich buff of the face and the white streaks of the back, are distinctive. Breast and flank color varies from dark to pale buff, and the streaks from sharp to dull and indistinct. Since all birds from a given part of the range have similar variations, five distinct subspecies are recognized. Some of these are occasionally identifiable in the field. Birds of the northern coastal region are pale all over, the buffy areas washed out, the breast streaks broad but blurred. Inland birds have deep, rich buff areas and sparingly and indistinctly streaked breasts.

HABITS: Along the coast this pointed-tailed sparrow lives in the salt-hay meadows of the upper salt marshes. Its habitat joins that of the forked-tailed Savannah sparrow along the wrack line, where marsh and upland meet and the sharp-tailed commonly nests. Inland it chooses a similar location along borders of fresh marshes. The birds seem to colonize favored areas, leaving similar near-by areas unoccupied. They are difficult to see, as they seldom leave the ground except for short song flights. When disturbed they run through the grass like mice. Their food consists of insects, seeds, and small aquatic animals like sand fleas and snails.

VOICE: Call note, a short *chuck*. The song is an insectlike hiss or wheezy trill. It is preceded by 2 short, weak notes and may be divided into 2 parts, the second lower in pitch and weaker.

NEST: Concealed in a grass tussock or on a pile of drift debris just above the high-water line; a loosely woven cup of grasses. The 4 or 5 pale bluish eggs (.78 x .56) are covered with fine dots.

RANGE: (P.M.) Breeds in coastal salt marshes from Cape Breton Island to Virginia and fresh marshes from s. Mackenzie and w.c. Alberta southeastward to n. Illinois. Winters in coastal marshes from Long Island, New York, to Texas.

Seaside Sparrow* *Ammospiza maritima*—※46

IDENTIFICATION: L. 6. This is a big, dark gray sparrow with a yellow line between the eye and bill, dusky streaked under parts, and a white throat region with a sharp stripe along the jaw.

HABITS: The seaside is exclusively a bird of the salt marsh, preferring the wetter parts along channels, where tall coarse grass grows in soft mud. Semi-aquatic in feeding, it often wades like a shore bird. It is fond of small crabs and other marine animals of the exposed mudbanks. Like other ground-dwelling sparrows, these birds are hard to see. Often the best way to get a look is to squeak on one's hand in imitation of a bird in distress; if you stand still the birds usually work closer or rise to the top of a reed stalk to see what is going on.

VOICE: The call is a squeaky *zeep*. The song is given from a grass-top perch or as the bird flutters in air. It starts with several short, weak notes followed by a loud, sharply accented buzz, then a lower-pitched trill, becoming weaker toward the end.

NEST: On the ground under shrubs or in patches of drift at the high-tide line; less commonly it is attached to coarse grass stems at a height which keeps it above the tide. It is woven of coarse grasses and lined with finer grasses. The 5 white eggs (.80 x .63) are heavily and coarsely spotted with reddish-brown.

RANGE: (P.M.) Breeds along the coast from s. Massachusetts south to s. Texas. Winters from Virginia (rarely Massachusetts) south.

Merritt Island Sparrow*   *Ammospiza nigrescens*—✳46

IDENTIFICATION: L. 6. The almost blackish upper parts and the heavy black streaks on the under parts set this species apart from its close relative, the seaside.

HABITS: This bird inhabits fairly dry salt marshes where rushes, salt-hay grass, and glasswort are interspersed with open mud flats. There is some uncertainty as to whether this is a valid species or one in the making; i.e., a race or subspecies of the seaside. In the South the seaside is so sedentary that a few miles of unfavorable habitat can effectively cut off a local population, thus producing the geographical isolation which seems necessary for the evolution of a new species. Whether the Merritt Island sparrow has yet developed mechanisms to insure reproductive isolation from its parent species, should its present geographic isolation break down, is not known.

VOICE: The short song is a buzzy trill preceded by a single liquid note.

NEST: In dense salt-marsh vegetation. Some are almost on the ground, others as high as a foot or so above it. The open cup is made of grasses woven around the supporting stems of the grass or rush clump in which it is concealed. The 4 eggs (.80 x .63) are boldly marked with browns.

RANGE: (R.) The salt marshes of the c.e. Florida coast in the vicinity of Merritt Island.

Cape Sable Sparrow*   *Ammospiza mirabilis*—✳46

IDENTIFICATION: L. 6. The ashy-green upper parts and white ground color of the under parts distinguish it from the two preceding species.

Habits: This species, if it is one, lives in small isolated colonies
scattered about the wetter parts of a coastal prairie. It is
separated from the nearest seaside sparrow population by
about 200 miles. As its flat, exposed habitat is swept from
time to time by hurricanes and floods as well as by prairie
fires, the species must often be reduced to a very few individuals—a factor which would tend to speed up genetic
changes. The bird's status as a full species is as doubtful as
that of the Merritt Island sparrow.

Voice: About the same as the Merritt Island bird.

Nest: Like a seaside's. The 5 eggs (.80 x .63) are a pale blue,
evenly and heavily marked with browns and grays.

Range: (R.) About 3 square miles of brackish coastal prairie
at Cape Sable, Florida.

Vesper Sparrow*   *Pooecetes gramineus*—❉47

Identification: L. 6. The white outer tail feathers which give
the dark tail its white sides are diagnostic. When perched,
the chestnut-brown lesser wing coverts and the line of
prominent black spots below them can be seen. The streaks
on the under parts do not tend to run together into stripes
or a central breast patch as on the song sparrow, but end
squarely on the lower breast, where they create a horizontal line of separation from the unstreaked white belly.

Habits: The vesper is a characteristic bird of high, dry uplands. It likes short-grass hayfields or pastures but is often
found along hedgerows and roadsides through croplands.
In northern areas it occurs wherever the forest has been
opened by lumber operating, burns, windfalls, or clearings.
It sings from a low perch or from the top of a small tree,
but most of the time it is on the ground, where it feeds on
insects and weed seeds. The white outer tail feathers make
these the most readily identified of the many sparrows one
flushes up along country roads.

VOICE: The song starts with 2 pairs of loud, clear, and fairly long notes, the second pair higher than the first, then becomes a descending series of short, musical trills. It is more deliberate and in general more melodious than the song sparrow's.

NEST: Grass and rootlets are used to build a neat cup on the ground, usually in a slight hollow or by a grass clump, occasionally up in the center of a tussock of grass. The 4 white eggs (.80 x .60) are thickly marked with brown.

RANGE: (P.M.) Breeds from Cape Breton Island, s. Quebec, c. Ontario, s. Saskatchewan, n.e. Alberta, and s. British Columbia south to North Carolina, c. Missouri, Texas, Arizona, and c.e. California. Winters from the southern part of its breeding range south to s. Florida, the Gulf Coast, and s. Mexico.

Lark Sparrow* *Chondestes grammacus*—✳43

IDENTIFICATION: L. 6¼. The white-bordered tail and chestnut head markings make adults unmistakable. Juveniles are heavily streaked above and below but have the chestnut ear patch and the white-bordered tail.

HABITS: The lark sparrow makes itself at home in treeless prairie but seems to reach its greatest abundance in open pastures with scattered bushes and trees. In many regions it is common about farms, country roadsides, and orchards. Occasionally woodland borders, river-bottom groves, and open woodlands are used for breeding. Although it is abundant over a wide area, the number in any given locality may vary in a most erratic and inexplicable manner. The bird is primarily a ground dweller, feeding on weed seeds and insects. The song is delivered from an elevated perch in a low tree or occasionally as the bird hovers in air.

VOICE: The song is rich and melodious, with a wide range in pitch and volume. Two clear introductory notes are followed by runs of short notes and trills, frequently interspersed with a buzzing or purring *churr*. The call note is a weak *tsip*.

NEST: On the ground in a depression under a plant that shades it or up to about 10 feet in the fork of a bush or low tree. Rootlets, plant stems, and grasses are used to form a substantial cup. The 4 white eggs (.80 x .60) are scrawled and blotched with black and brown.

RANGE: (P.M.) Breeds from s. Ontario, c. Wisconsin, s. Saskatchewan, and s. British Columbia south to c. Alabama, s. Louisiana, and n. Mexico and east to the Appalachians. Winters from s. Mississippi and n. California south to Guatemala.

Rufous-crowned Sparrow* *Aimophila ruficeps*—✳45

IDENTIFICATION: L. 5½. The most distinctive marking is the black streak on the sides of the throat. The bird lacks the strong eyeline of a chipping sparrow. Some races are quite gray above, others more reddish. Immatures have a dull brown, slightly streaked crown and are narrowly streaked with brown across the chest.

HABITS: These sparrows like rocky areas with scattered clumps of brush, small trees, and tufts of grass, preferably near a stream. They often occur in small loose colonies. Few birds stick closer to the ground and are harder to flush. They sing, however, from a perch on top of a low bush. Seeds seem to be their chief food.

VOICE: The call is a sharp double chirp, but when alarmed the bird utters a thin mewing note. The song, after a few introductory mews, becomes a rapid wren-like warble with frequent trilled notes.

NEST: On or near the ground in or under a clump of dense vegetation; a cup of stems, grass, and other fibrous material lined with fine grass. The 4 white eggs (.80 x .62) are unmarked.

RANGE: (R.) Breeds from s.e. Colorado, n. New Mexico, and n.c. California south to s. Mexico and east to e.c. Texas.

Pinewoods Sparrow* *Aimophila aestivalis*—※45

IDENTIFICATION: L. 6. This bird's most prominent characteristic is its lack of striking markings. It is, however, the buffiest below of all sparrows with unstreaked under parts. Immatures resemble adults but are streaked below with dark gray, especially on the chest.

HABITS: Dry open woods of pine or oak, with a ground cover of grass or scrub palmetto, are the favorite home, but the bird occurs in impoverished pastures and fields dominated by oat grass or broom sedge and scattered with shrubs and small trees. It spends most of its time on the ground and is hard to see or flush. The song, delivered from a bush or the lower limbs of a tree, is heard from February to late August. The bird eats insects and seeds.

VOICE: When disturbed the birds give a snakelike hissing as they run off. The rich, clear song, though not loud, carries well. It starts with a trill, then drops in pitch to a series of distinct, abrupt notes. Its quality suggests the song of a field sparrow.

NEST: On the ground in a clump of grass or palmetto or under a vine tangle or brushy growth; usually arched over and entered from the side. Grass tops are a favorite material, but plant stems of all kinds are used. The 4 white eggs (.74 x .60) are unmarked.

RANGE: (P.M.) Breeds from s. Ohio, c. Illinois, and s.e. Iowa south to s.c. Florida, the Gulf Coast to c. Texas, and east to s.w. Pennsylvania, c. Virginia, and the s. Atlantic coast. Winters from s. North Carolina and s. Alabama south to c. Florida.

Botteri's Sparrow*   *Aimophila botterii*—⚹44

IDENTIFICATION: L. 5¾. The upper parts are dull brown and the streaking quite indistinct. In flight the tail is darker and browner than the back and wings.

HABITS: Found in areas grown up to tall grass; e.g., the coastal prairies of south Texas. Dense thickets near water attract them, but the birds can live far from water. The one thing they will not tolerate is overgrazing of their grassland; they disappear if it occurs. They are strictly terrestrial, running along the ground like mice and very hard to see.

VOICE: The call note is much like that of a pinewoods sparrow. The song, which is delivered from a perch, never from the air, is a sweet, almost canary-like tinkling quite variable in form. It generally starts with a few halting notes, increases to a trill, and ends with a few slow notes. A pair of notes in the middle clearer and louder than the rest is often a marked characteristic.

NEST: Very little is known about the nest and eggs of this ground-nesting species.

RANGE: (P.M.) Breeds from extreme s. Texas and Sonora south to Guatemala. Retires in winter from the northern part of its breeding range.

Cassin's Sparrow*   *Aimophila cassinii*—⚹44

IDENTIFICATION: L. 5¾. The pale gray upper parts are sharply marked with sandy-brown and black. The short dusky streaks on the sides of the throat and brown streaks on the flanks are good characters, but they cannot be counted upon, as they are not always present. In flight the tail looks as gray as the wings and back. Young are streaked on the breast.

HABITS: Dry, arid country with sparse short grasses and scattered desert shrubs or cacti is the home of this sparrow. It tolerates hot, gravelly areas and rocky slopes where only a few plants can survive. It also occurs about openings in dense mesquite or other low vegetation. The song period is long and the bird sings at night as well as all day. The song begins as the bird hovers on fluttering wings and ends as it drops to its perch on top of a bush.

VOICE: The song is a long, melodious trill preceded and followed by one to several soft, plaintive notes, the last of which are lowest in pitch.

NEST: On the ground hidden in the base of a cactus, clump of grass, or low dense shrub; a deep cup of grasses, bark, and plant stems lined with rootlets and hair. The 4 white eggs (.74 x .57) are unmarked.

RANGE: (P.M.) Breeds from s.w. Kansas and s. Nevada south to extreme n. Mexico. Winters from s. Texas and s. Arizona south to c.n. Mexico.

Black-throated Sparrow*   *Amphispiza bilineata*—✳️44

IDENTIFICATION: L. 5¼. The head pattern and black throat of adults are distinctive. Young have white throats and breasts streaked with grayish. In any plumage the black tail with white outer edges and tips is a good field character.

HABITS: These birds are most at home in the sparsely vegetated desert uplands and rocky slopes where only scattered cholla cacti and creosote bushes grow. Other plants with which they are frequently associated are dwarf juniper, yucca, agave, catclaw, mesquite, sagebrush, and rabbit brush. They sing from the ground and the tops of the bushes. Foraging is on the ground and in the low vegetation, the birds flying about quite actively.

VOICE: The call is a tinkling *weet* with a rising inflection. The song has a number of variations. One starts with a pair of call notes followed by a short note, then a buzzy trill that varies in pitch. Another is 3 short ascending and 3 descending notes with a characteristic metallic vibration.

NEST: Low, in the center of dense vegetation, often in a thorny shrub; a loosely constructed cup of bark shreds, grass, and stems lined with soft material like wool, hair, or feathers. The 4 white eggs (.71 x .52) are usually unmarked.

RANGE: (P.M.) Breeds from s.w. Kansas, n.w. California, n. Nevada, and n.e. California south to c. Mexico and east to e.c. Texas. Winters from c. Texas, s. New Mexico, and s.e. California southward.

White-winged Junco* $Junco\ aikeni$—❋44

IDENTIFICATION: L. 6½. This is a larger, paler bird than the slate-colored. It has 3 white outer tail feathers and a partially white fourth. The wing feathers are generally but not always margined and tipped with enough white to make them quite light. The wings are crossed by two distinct bars. Females and young are often tinged on the back with brown.

HABITS: These juncos breed in the dry yellow-pine forests of the Black Hills. They favor brushy clearings and recently cutover areas, where they often nest about buildings and even in the tin cans of lumber-camp dumps. In winter they generally associate with other juncos in mixed flocks.

VOICE: Like the slate-colored juncos.

NEST: Under logs, tree roots, or rock ledges, preferably on a hillside above running water. Nest and eggs are like the slate-colored's.

RANGE: (P.M.) Breeds in w. South Dakota, s.e. Montana, n.w. Nebraska, and n.e. Wyoming. Winters from the breeding grounds south to n.w. Texas and n. New Mexico and east to e. Nebraska and e. Kansas.

Slate-colored Junco*   *Junco hyemalis*—✳44

IDENTIFICATION: L. 6¼. Males are dark gray and white while females are slightly paler and occasionally brownish on the back and sides. All juvenile juncos are streaked like sparrows above and below. Immatures are brownish above and washed with cinnamon on sides and chest. In all plumages this species has 2 white outer tail feathers and a third partially white.

HABITS: The summer home is in the northern forests of spruce and fir. A few breed south of the conifer zone in deciduous woodlands where only a few hemlocks or white pines occur. Cutover areas with slash piles often attract them. Many nests are along old roads and the edges of clearings. The male's favorite song perch is usually the top of a forest tree or dead snag.

In winter this abundant species scatters over the whole eastern United States. It frequents woodlands and fields but is generally encountered in greatest numbers along hedgerows and brushy field borders. The birds invade residential areas wherever ornamental plantings are available for cover. Flocks are usually small and include other birds, especially sparrows. In winter juncos feed on the ground, taking weed seeds and wild fruit, but during the breeding season their diet includes insects and summer fruit.

VOICE: Call, a series of snapping or clinking notes. Song, a simple trill like a chipping sparrow's but much more musical and occasionally with some variation in tempo or pitch. The bird also has a rambling, broken song, between a warble and a twitter, composed of short, rather faint notes.

NEST: Well hidden on or near the ground among the upturned roots or under the trunk of a fallen tree, under a steep, overhanging bank, or in dense vegetation; a deep nest cup of moss, grasses, and bark shreds lined with fine materials.

The 4 or 5 pale greenish eggs (.76 x .58) are variably spotted with brown. Two broods are usually raised.

RANGE: (P.M.) Breeds from c. Quebec, n. Manitoba, n. Mackenzie, and n.w. Alaska south to Nova Scotia, n. Georgia (mts.), c. Michigan, n. Minnesota, c. Alberta, and s. Yukon. Winters from Nova Scotia, c. New York, c. Michigan, c. Minnesota, Colorado, and w. Washington south to n. Florida, the Gulf Coast, s. Texas, and n.w. Mexico.

Pink-sided Junco   *Junco oreganus*—※44

IDENTIFICATION: L. 6¼. This highly variable species is currently divided into 8 geographical races, some of which look quite different from others. In males the head varies from almost black to slate-gray, the back from rich walnut to pale drab. In the very dark-headed races the hood of the female is much lighter, and in all races it is more or less brown on top and along the nape. The clear pinkish-brown of the sides (occasionally the breast), stopping sharply at the gray hood, combined with the white outer tail feathers, is the unfailing field mark of this species.

HABITS: This junco differs little except in appearance from the slate-colored. In their mountain breeding grounds these juncos show a preference for small openings in the forest. Here the grass and low growths they need for foraging are near the deep shade they seem to find so necessary. Open stands of mature trees that let through enough light to produce the required low growths are also occupied. In winter they are found in flocks wherever bushy growths are near open feeding areas. As slate-colored juncos winter to some extent throughout the range of the pink-sided, both species are often found in the same flock.

VOICE: Apparently the same as the slate-colored.

NEST: Generally on the ground in sites similar to those of the slate-colored; occasionally higher where a solid support is available on a cliff, cabin beam, or fallen tree trunk. Nest and eggs are like those of the preceding species.

RANGE: (P.M.) Breeds from s.w. Saskatchewan, w.c. Alberta, and s.w. Yukon south to n. Wyoming, s. Idaho, and Lower California. Winters from s. Canada south to n. Mexico and east to e. Nebraska and c. Texas.

Slate-colored x Pink-sided Junco Hybrids
Junco hyemalis x Junco oreganus

COMMENT: There is no general agreement as to the number of species of juncos. They form a wide-ranging group which occurs from the Arctic tree line south to western Panama. Although the 21 currently recognized types are assigned to 10 full species, many ornithologists believe that only 2 species are valid, the dark-eyed and the yellow-eyed. The difference in behavior between the birds in these two groups and the close similarity within each group lend weight to their view. Actually, as juncos are all geographically complementary, each with its exclusive territory, they constitute a good example of a superspecies.

Many of the 10 recognized species do not pass the biological test of a valid species. Interbreeding is common where ranges meet, and intergrades or hybrids are frequent. One must expect occasionally to encounter in the field birds showing almost every possible combination of the supposed species characters.

Tree Sparrow*   *Spizella arborea*—✳45

IDENTIFICATION: L. 6¼. The single dark spot in the center of the breast, the dark upper and the yellow lower mandibles, and the whiter wing bars distinguish this from the field sparrow. Juveniles are duller brown and streaked with dusky above and below.

HABITS: The summer home is in the stunted trees and shrubs that dominate the region just south of the tundra and along the Arctic coasts. Here the birds are abundant in streamside alders and willows and brushy borders of scattered patches of taller timber. In winter weedy fields adjacent to woodlands and thickets are their favorite haunts. Here they feed on grass and weed seeds which have fallen to the ground or snow, frequently jumping up to pick at the seeds in an unopened head. As early as February they give brief snatches of their beautiful song.

VOICE: Calls a thin *tseet*, in flock a clear double whistle—the whole flock producing a musical twittering. The song is metallic in spite of its sweet canary-like quality. The notes vary greatly in pitch and length. The opening is usually several long high notes followed by a rapid warble.

NEST: On or near the ground in the shelter of low vegetation. The bulky nest is made of plant stems and bark and lined with hair or feathers. The 4 or 5 pale greenish eggs (.75 x .60) are evenly dotted with browns.

RANGE: (M.) Breeds from n. Quebec, n. Mackenzie, and n. Alaska south to Newfoundland, c. Quebec, n. Manitoba, and n. British Columbia. Winters from the Maritime Provinces, Ontario, s. Minnesota, Montana, and s. British Columbia south to South Carolina, c. Arkansas, New Mexico, and n.e. California.

Chipping Sparrow* *Spizella passerina*—✳45

IDENTIFICATION: L. 5¼. The bright chestnut-brown cap, the dark line through the eye, and the white one over it, together with the grayish-white under parts and black bill, are distinctive. Juveniles lack the brown cap but are more generally reddish above and buffy with thick streaking below. Immatures are buffy but unstreaked below, and the cap is buffy, streaked with black.

HABITS: The "chippy" is a bird of open grassy woodlands and openings in denser woodlands, especially where the grass is short and rather sparse and open. Such man-made habitats as orchards, parks, and residential areas with lawns and shade trees fulfill its requirements perfectly. It is a very common dooryard bird. Chippys feed mostly on the ground but always sing from an elevated perch. During summer most of their food is insects, chiefly soft-bodied caterpillars. At other seasons weed seeds are staples.

VOICE: The call is a simple *tsip*. A monotonous series of short, dry notes repeated so rapidly as to be almost a trill is the only song.

NEST: In dense shrubbery, very young evergreens, or vines 3 to 5 feet up, less commonly up to 25 feet on the limb of a tree; a cup of grass and rootlets lined with whatever hair the bird can find. The 4 green-blue eggs (.72 x .51) are speckled about the larger end with brown.

RANGE: (P.M.) Breeds from Cape Breton Island, s. Quebec, n. Ontario, c. Manitoba, Mackenzie, and Yukon south to c. Georgia, s. Mississippi, and Honduras. Winters from North Carolina, c. Texas, and c. California south.

Clay-colored Sparrow* *Spizella pallida*—⚹45

IDENTIFICATION: L. 5½. This pale brown- and gray-backed sparrow lacks the reddish cap of most other clear-breasted sparrows. The light streak through the crown and the dark-bordered brown cheek patch are distinctive. Juveniles are streaked on breast and sides.

HABITS: This sparrow inhabits grassland wherever brush and poplars occur along streams and lakes. To the north it occurs wherever fires or lumbering have opened the forest. It is often abundant where shrubs and young trees have begun to restore forest cover. The males sing from low perches, and most feeding is on the ground or in low vegetation.

VOICE: The call is a weak chip, the song a thin, rasping, cicada-like buzz.

NEST: From ground level to about 6 feet up in a grass clump or more commonly a shrub or small conifer. The bulky nest is of grass and stems lined with hair. The 4 blue-green eggs (.65 x .50) are spotted with black and brown.

RANGE: (M.) Breeds from Minnesota, c. Manitoba, and s. Mackenzie south to n.w. Illinois, n. Nebraska, and w. Montana. Winters from s. Texas and s. New Mexico south to s. Mexico.

Field Sparrow*   *Spizella pusilla*—❋45

IDENTIFICATION: L. 5½. The bright pinkish bill, the buffy wash on breast and flanks, and the blurred character of its markings are the best field characters.

HABITS: Shrubs or low trees with some open area are essential. Poorly kept brushy pastures, abandoned farmland, woodland borders, and cut- or burned-over woodlands fulfill these requirements. The bird is a persistent singer and often sings on moonlight nights. Its singing perch is usually the top of a bush or small tree. In summer adults turn to insects for themselves and their young. At other seasons they feed almost entirely on the seeds of wild plants, foraging on the ground along roadsides, hayfields, and weedy croplands.

VOICE: Call note, a *tsip*. The song is clear, sweet, and melancholy. The first piping, whistled notes are long, the delivery slow. As the song progresses the notes are shorter and come faster, until it becomes a trill. Usually the trill rises or falls in pitch until it fades out.

NEST: Generally near the ground in a clump of grass or a low bush; a well-made cup of grasses and stems lined with hair. The 4 pale greenish eggs (.65 x .50) are spotted and penciled with reddish-brown.

RANGE: (P.M.) Breeds from Nova Scotia, s. Quebec, s. Michigan, s. Minnesota, and s.e. Montana south to South Carolina, s.c. Alabama, c. Louisiana, and c. Texas. Winters from s. New Jersey, s. Ohio, and s. Missouri south to c. Florida, the Gulf Coast, and n.e. Mexico.

Harris's Sparrow*   *Zonotrichia querula*—❄43

IDENTIFICATION: L. 7½. The reddish bill and black face make fully adult individuals of this very large sparrow easy to identify. Young in their first fall have a black crown scaled with buffy, but the throat is white. They have very buffy sides to the head and neck and irregularly blotched upper breasts and sides. Fall birds in their second year have a black throat separated from the black of the breast by a light line.

HABITS: The summer home is in the scattered patches of stunted timber characteristic of the transition zone between the Hudsonian forest and the Arctic tundra. The birds migrate through and winter in the region of the old tall-grass prairie, avoiding the once-forested area to the east and the short-grass plains to the west. In coldest weather they stay in dense river-bottom thickets. Generally they also frequent woodland borders, vine tangles, hedgerows, and brush piles. They are vigorous scratchers and do most of their feeding on the ground, where they find seeds and some insects. Their most notable habit is singing in chorus just before sundown through the fall and winter.

VOICE: Call note, a loud, metallic *spink*. The fall and winter song is 1 or 2 drawling notes whistled in a minor key with an occasional third note on a different key. The spring and summer song is 1 to 5 quavering, plaintive notes on the same pitch, followed after an interval by several clear notes higher or lower in pitch.

NEST: On the ground at the base of a stunted spruce or shrub or in the side of a moss hummock in a wet spot; made of moss, leaves, and stems lined with grass. The 3 to 5 pale greenish eggs (.94 x .65) are heavily splotched with brown.

RANGE: (M.) Breeds in n. Manitoba and Mackenzie. Occurs in migration from Illinois to c. Montana. Winters from s. Nebraska to s. Texas.

White-crowned Sparrow*   *Zonotrichia leucophrys*—※43

IDENTIFICATION: L. 7. The bright reddish-brown bill (yellowish in the race *nuttalli*) and the broad white crown are distinctive. In two western races (*gambelii* and *nuttalli*) the white line on the sides of the head continues over and forward of the eye to the base of the bill. Immatures are buffier all over and have a pair of broad reddish-brown stripes on their buffy heads. This species has the distinctive habit of partially expanding its crown to form a low crest which shows off the white feathers.

HABITS: During the breeding season the white-crowned is found where extensive brushy cover is adjacent to more or less open or grassy areas. Dwarf willow thickets along streams or lakes are favored spots in the North. The birds are also found in wind-swept areas along the seacoast where low shrubs predominate. Singing is usually from a high perch on a bush or tree.

In migration and during winter white-crowns seek similar habitats. Most feeding is on the ground, and they travel in flocks with other sparrows. From Illinois west flocks often contain the typical western *gambelii* race.

VOICE: The call is a *chink* note. The sweet, plaintive song is a short refrain of 5 or 6 notes, the first long and clear, the latter shorter and somewhat husky, falling away in pitch and volume.

NEST: On the ground under a bush or close to the ground in a bush; a bulky cup of twigs, grass, and bark with a heavy lining of finer material, often rootlets and hair. The

4 pale greenish eggs (.86 x .62) are thickly spotted with
two shades of brown.

RANGE: (P.M.) Breeds from s. Greenland, n. Quebec, n.
Manitoba, n. Mackenzie, and n.w. Alaska south to s.
Quebec, c. Manitoba, n. New Mexico, and s. California.
Winters from Mississippi, s. Missouri, s. Colorado, and
Oregon south to c. Mexico.

White-throated Sparrow*   *Zonotrichia albicollis*—#43

IDENTIFICATION: L. 6¾. The white throat and the yellow area
between the eye and bill, together with the striped head
pattern, are good field marks except for juveniles. Juveniles
are strong chestnut-brown above and yellowish-white below, with heavy dusky streaks except on the chin and
belly.

HABITS: Wherever an opening in the forest permits the growth
of low shrubs and clumps of small trees one finds the
white-throat. Cut-over areas with slash piles, brushy pastures, and borders of clearing afford ideal habitats. The
birds sing from the ground or a low perch in a bush. Feeding is chiefly on the ground, where they scratch noisily in
dead leaves. White-throats and their close relatives eat
more wild fruits than most sparrows. Wintering flocks are
found wherever there are thickets, brushy field borders,
and weed tangles.

VOICE: Call, a lisping *sst*. The very beautiful but melancholy
song starts with 2 or more long, whistled notes which usually vary a little in pitch. Then the bird repeats a short
3-note phrase from 4 to 6 times, the last 1 or 2 becoming
weaker. Phonetically it sounds like *Old Sam, Peabody, Peabody, Peabody, Peabody* sung in a thin, high-pitched minor
key.

NEST: On the ground sunk into a hollow, often in a moss-
covered hummock under overhanging vegetation, occasionally up a foot or two in a dense conifer; a cup of grass,

moss, and rootlets lined with fine grass and hair. The 4 or 5 pale greenish eggs (.82 x .60) are heavily spotted with brown.

RANGE: (M.) Breeds from Newfoundland, c. Quebec, n. Manitoba, and n. Mackenzie south to Nova Scotia, n. New England, n.e. Pennsylvania (mts.), s. Ontario, c. Wisconsin, s. Montana, and c. Alberta. Winters from Massachusetts, s. Pennsylvania, the Ohio Valley, and Missouri south to n. Florida, the Gulf Coast, and n.e. Mexico.

Fox Sparrow*   *Passerella iliaca*—※47

IDENTIFICATION: L. 7¼. The reddish-brown tail and heavily marked under parts are distinctive. In the West fox sparrows of different areas vary greatly in the relative amounts and tone of gray and brown in their plumage.

HABITS: This large, wary sparrow inhabits dense woodland thickets. On its breeding grounds it is common in streamside growths of willow and alder, brushy burned-over lands, and meadow borders of shrubs and young conifers. The birds do most of their foraging in the leaf litter on the ground. Using both feet at once, they kick it vigorously aside as they dig holes well into the leaf mold and humus— a layer rich in small animal life. They sing from a perch on top of a bush or small tree and are often heard singing south of their breeding grounds.

VOICE: Call, a drawn-out *stssp*. The loud, short song is a variable carol of clear, melodious notes, richer than those of any other sparrow. Generally the song rises in pitch, then falls on the closing notes.

NEST: A few feet from the ground in a tangle of low vegetation or on the ground under a bush. The large nest is made of grass, moss, roots, and leaves and is often lined with feathers and fur. The 4 pale greenish eggs (.90 x .69) are thickly spotted with reddish-brown.

RANGE: (P.M.) Breeds from n. Quebec, n. Ontario, n. Manitoba, n. Mackenzie, and n.w. Alaska south to Newfoundland, s. Quebec, s. Manitoba, Colorado, Nevada, and s. California. Winters from Maryland, s. Indiana, s. Missouri, New Mexico, and British Columbia south to c. Florida, the Gulf Coast, c. Texas, and Lower California.

Lincoln's Sparrow*   *Melospiza lincolnii*—#47

IDENTIFICATION: L. 5¾. The buffy wash across the breast and the numerous fine black streaks on the under parts are the best field marks. Unfortunately the buffy wash is sometimes very faint and the spots on the center of the breast occasionally coalesce into a dark spot similar to a song sparrow's. The buffy-olive upper parts, rich brown only on the crown and wings, are uniformly and sharply streaked with black from the crown to the rump. Young are similar to adults but less strongly marked.

HABITS: Lincoln's sparrow breeds along the borders of frequently flooded wet meadows, swamps, woodland bogs, ponds, and streams. Alders, willows, and other shrubs are used as singing perches, but the birds spend most of their time on the ground. In migration they prefer similar wet places but may be found wherever there are dense thickets and weed tangles. At this season they seldom sing, and their skulking habits make them virtually invisible. They are curious, however, and respond to squeaking on the back of one's hand. Although this is a reasonably common species over much of North America, its regular occurrence on a "birder's" year list is evidence of proficiency.

VOICE: Call note, a low *tsup*. The hurried song is a series of trills and liquid, slightly buzzy notes suggesting a house wren's song, but in sweetness and clearness it is more like a purple finch's. The last several notes are often abruptly louder, harsher, and lower in pitch.

NEST: On the ground or in a swamp tussock, generally well hidden under vegetation; a cup of grass and fine sedges. The 4 or 5 pale greenish eggs (.80 x .60) are heavily spotted with browns.

RANGE: (M.) Breeds from Newfoundland, n. Quebec, n. Manitoba, s. Mackenzie, and c. Alaska south to Nova Scotia, n. New York, n. Minnesota, n. New Mexico, and s. California. Winters from n. Mississippi, s. Oklahoma, s. New Mexico, and c. California south to c. Guatemala.

Swamp Sparrow*   *Melospiza georgiana*—#47

IDENTIFICATION: L. 5¾. This is a notably dark sparrow with rich chestnut on wings and back. Fall adults are often quite buffy below, especially on the sides; the clear reddish crown is often streaked with black and divided by a light stripe. Juveniles are marked below like the adult Lincoln's but are darker above and lack the reddish head stripes.

HABITS: Open fresh-water marshes filled with rank vegetation are the typical home. The bird is also found about the borders of ponds and sluggish streams fringed with marsh plants and alder thickets. When not nesting it is less exacting and may be scattered over broom sedge and weed-grown fields, brush patches, and hedgerows along with other sparrows. Like the other wet-land sparrows, these stay on the ground and are hard to observe unless singing. This they do from an elevated perch on a reed or bush top.

VOICE: Call, a metallic *chink*. A common song is a rapidly repeated or trilled series of short, single notes. A richer song is composed of double upslurred phrases—*peet-peet-peet-peet*. Both songs are long, loud, and fairly musical. Sometimes 2 notes, one higher than the other, are trilled simultaneously at different tempos.

NEST: Close to the ground in a dense tussock or mat of marsh vegetation or a few inches up in a bush; a well-hidden cup of grass, often entered from the side. The 4 or 5 blue-green eggs (.76 x .57) are blotched with brown.

RANGE: (P.M.) Breeds from Newfoundland, s. Quebec, n. Manitoba, c. Mackenzie south to New Jersey, West Virginia, n. Illinois, and n. Nebraska. Winters from about the southern limit of the breeding range south to s. Florida, the Gulf Coast, and c. Mexico.

Song Sparrow*   *Melospiza melodia*—※47

IDENTIFICATION: L. 6¼. The dark spot in the center of the breast is the best field mark. Juveniles are similar to swamp sparrow juveniles but not so rufous on the back and wings. This species is divided into many geographical races, which vary greatly in color. In certain small, lightly marked races all markings are in bright rusty-brown; in other large, heavily marked races they are nearly all in dark sooty-brown. In flight the long rounded tail which is pumped up and down is very characteristic of the species.

HABITS: Wherever there is brushy cover with water not too far away one may expect song sparrows. They commonly occupy cutover lands or abandoned farmland from the time a few shrubs become established until the second growth has formed a closed canopy. They readily accept shrubbery about houses yet are equally at home in wild alder swamps and shrub-fringed woodland lakes. They sing from an elevated perch but do most of their feeding on or near the ground. They give brief snatches of song on sunny days throughout the winter.

Few species have been as intensely studied as this. Mrs. M. M. Nice's reports on the details of its life history are classics in their field. She came to know hundreds as individuals and followed the fortunes of many through an entire life span, which for this species may run more than 7 years.

VOICE: Call note, a loud *tchunk*. The 7- to 11-note song varies greatly in pattern and pitch but usually starts with 3 identical notes. These are usually followed by a trilled note plus a series of short notes differing widely in pitch. The song lasts 2 to 3 seconds—5 to 7 a minute on the average.

NEST: Early nests are usually on the ground, hidden in matted clumps of last year's grass or weed stems. Later nests are more apt to be up to 4 feet in a dense shrub or conifer. The well-built cup is of grass stems and leaves often lined with horsehair. The 4 greenish-white eggs (.80 x .60) are blotched, often heavily, with browns.

RANGE: (P.M.) Breeds from Cape Breton Island, s.c. Quebec, n. Ontario, s. Mackenzie, and s. Alaska south to North Carolina, n. Georgia, Missouri, North Dakota, and c. Mexico. Winters from s. New Brunswick, s. Ontario, s. Wisconsin, Montana, and British Columbia south to s. Florida and the Gulf Coast.

McCown's Longspur   *Rhynchophanes mccownii*—✳48

IDENTIFICATION: L. 6. The black T on the white tail is a distinctive field mark in all plumages. Females and young are otherwise much like those of the chestnut-collared longspur. In winter males are somewhat tawny above, and their black markings are partly hidden by gray feather tips.

HABITS: Dry, short-grass plains dominated by buffalo grass are the home of this bird. In the moister eastern prairie where grass grows taller they are found only on higher, more barren ridges and benches. Here they may be abundant in dry years and virtually absent in wet years. Their commonest associates are horned larks and chestnut-collared longspurs. After breeding they gather into large flocks for their southward travels. Grasshoppers are generally their staple summer food, seeds of grasses and weeds at other seasons.

Voice: Call note, a double *chirrup-chirrup*. The loud, clear song is a sweet, twittering warble poured forth as the bird floats slowly and erratically back to the ground after a steep rise. As it falls the tail is spread and the wings are held aloft, showing their white linings.

Nest: In a hollow in open prairie; made of grass and often lined with hair. The 3 or 4 greenish eggs (.81 x .57) are marked and blotched with black and brown.

Range: (M.) Breeds from s. Saskatchewan and c. Alberta south to n. North Dakota and n.e. Colorado. Winters from Kansas and Colorado south through Texas and Arizona to n.w. Mexico.

Lapland Longspur   *Calcarius lapponicus—*#48

Identification: L. 6¼. The tail is largely black, only the 2 outer feathers being partly white. Breeding females, though duller, have a pattern not unlike the male's, but the black areas are more restricted and more obscured by light feather tips. In winter both sexes are duller because the pale tips and edges of the fresh feathers hide the underlying black and brown. In these dull plumages the parallel buffy lines on the back are good field marks. The legs are black or dusky.

Habits: In the southern part of the Arctic barren grounds south to the tree line this is an abundant land bird. It seems to prefer wet hummocky areas overgrown with dwarf birch and crowberry. As winter darkness comes on the birds move south across the northern forests; most of those in North America head for the open prairies and plains of the Midwest. In other regions only small numbers are encountered in association with snow-buntings and horned larks, usually on bare, wind-swept pastures, plowed fields, and coastal dunes. Grass seed is a staple winter food, and the birds frequently alight on a stalk to pick at the seed head.

VOICE: The harsh, rattling flight call has been put down as *dikerick, dikerick, psu'o, psu'o.* The liquid, gurgling, bobolink-like song is given during a song flight like that of the preceding species.

NEST: On the ground under a tussock of grass or a dwarf shrub; made of grass and moss lined frequently with feathers and hair. The 6 greenish-gray eggs (.83 x .60) are thickly blotched with browns and purples.

RANGE: (M.) Circumpolar in breeding range. Winters in Eastern and Western Hemisphere. In North America breeds from e. Greenland (lat. 75°), the Arctic Islands (lat. 73°), and n.w. Alaska south to the northern limit of trees in n. Quebec, n. Manitoba, n.w. Mackenzie, c. Alaska, and the Aleutian Islands. Winters south to New York, Missouri, Colorado, and n.e. California.

Smith's Longspur *Calcarius pictus*—✳48

IDENTIFICATION: L. 6½. This species has the 2 outer tail feathers largely white. In winter the male resembles the female but retains the distinctive white-tipped, black lesser wing coverts. The bill is slenderer and more pointed and the entire under parts buffier than in other longspurs. The legs are yellow.

HABITS: This longspur has a much more limited distribution than the Lapland. Both species occur in the same area, with this showing a preference for ridge summits and other dry areas. Though the bird is not generally common, enormous flocks are sometimes encountered in fall and winter on the western grasslands, especially where the grass is very short.

VOICE: In flight a strange series of sharp, clicking notes in rapid succession, not unlike the winding of a cheap watch. The song resembles the flight call and is usually given from the ground.

NEST: Sunk in a hole dug by the birds or placed in a mossy hummock or sedge tussock in open tundra, often near a strip of sheltering trees; made of fine grasses lined with willow catkin down and feathers. The 4 to 6 clay-colored eggs (.80 x .65) are lined and spotted with purplish-brown.

RANGE: (M.) Breeds along the southern edge of the tundra from n. Manitoba west to n. Alaska. Winters from Illinois and Kansas south to c. Texas.

Chestnut-collared Longspur   *Calcarius ornatus*—※48

IDENTIFICATION: L. 5¾. The predominantly white tail with a small triangular central wedge of black at the end is distinctive. Females and young are like McCown's but faintly streaked on sides and breast where that species is virtually unmarked. Winter males have the black-and-brown markings obscured by pale feather edges.

HABITS: The chestnut-collared longspur is found in dry, grassy uplands. It ranges farther east than McCown's, occurring in prairie areas that receive more rain and normally support a taller and denser stand of grass than the plains. Where the two occur together the chestnut-collared seeks the moister spots with taller grasses for its nest. In general habits they are much alike. Widespread plowing of the prairie has eliminated this longspur from many areas where it was once abundant.

VOICE: Flight call, a musical twitter. The brief, high-pitched, rather weak, twittery song is uttered at intervals while the bird flutters aloft.

NEST: In a hollow which the birds dig in the ground, usually where it is concealed by tall grass or a low shrub; a grass nest often lined with hair. The 4 greenish eggs (.73 x .56) are marked with brown and lavender.

RANGE: (P.M.) Breeds from Manitoba and s.e. Alberta south to w. Minnesota, e. Nebraska, c. Kansas, and e.c. Wyo-

ming. Winters from Iowa and Colorado south to Texas,
Arizona, and n. Mexico.

Common Snow-bunting   *Plectrophenax nivalis*—✳48

IDENTIFICATION: L. 7. The wings, white except at the end,
serve as the best field mark. The body plumage of young
in their first winter is heavily overlaid with rusty. Winter
adults, though extensively rusty, show more white.

HABITS: The treeless tundra that stretches south in all direc-
tions from the Arctic Ocean is the summer home. In this
land of continuous summer sunlight and teeming insect
life, it is sometimes the only land bird and always one of
the most abundant about cliffs and slopes. Moths, crane
flies, mosquitoes, and other insects are staples at this
season. In winter they depend upon the grass and weed
seed heads that remain above the snow. When snowfalls
bury them the birds are forced farther south. "Snowflakes"
are especially attracted to the trash which the wind piles
up on lake and stream shores, and the first arrivals are
usually found there. On the seacoast they frequent dunes,
salt marshes, wind-swept grasslands, and the open beach,
where they sometimes follow the waves like sandpipers.

VOICE: In flight, a sweet single or double whistle often followed by a musical trill. The most interesting call is a
purring note with a curious trembling quality. The song
is a broken twittering warble given from a rock-top perch
or as the bird flutters in air.

NEST: In a crevice in a ledge or on the ground, as well hidden
among rocks or vegetation as the surroundings permit;
made of moss and earth lined first with sedges, then with
feathers and fur. The 4 or 5 eggs (.91 x .64) have a wreath
of reddish-brown spots.

RANGE: (M.) Breeds in Arctic and sub-Arctic regions all over
the world; in North America from n. Greenland (lat.

83°) and n. Alaska south to n. Quebec, n. Mackenzie, and c.w. Alaska. Winters from c. Quebec, c. Manitoba, and s. Alaska south to Pennsylvania, s. Indiana, Kansas, and e. Oregon.

Bibliography

REFERENCE MATERIAL YOU WILL FIND USEFUL IF YOU WISH TO MAKE A MORE DETAILED STUDY OF ANY SPECIAL PHASE OF BIRD LIFE.

Attracting and Encouraging Birds

Attracting Birds, by W. L. McAtee, published by the United States Fish and Wildlife Service, Washington, D.C., 1940.

The Audubon Guide to Attracting Birds, by John H. Baker, published by Doubleday, Doran and Co., New York, N.Y., 1941.

Birds in the Garden and How to Attract Them, by Margaret McKenny, published by Reynal & Hitchcock, New York, N.Y., 1939.

Methods of Attracting Birds, by G. H. Trafton, published by Houghton Mifflin Co., Boston, Mass., 1910.

Song Bird Sanctuaries, by Roger T. Peterson, published by the National Audubon Society, New York, N.Y., 1937.

Banding Birds

Bird Banding, a quarterly published by the Bird Banding Associations, Cambridge, Mass.

The Log of Tanager Hill, by M. A. Commons, published by the Williams and Wilkins Co., Baltimore, Md., 1938.

Manual for Bird Banders, by F. C. Lincoln and S. P. Baldwin, published by the U. S. Department of Agriculture, Washington, D.C., 1929.

Biology and Attributes of Birds

The Biology of Birds, by J. Arthur Thomson, published by the Macmillan Co., New York, N.Y., 1923.

Birds, by A. Wetmore, published by Smithsonian Institution Series, New York, N.Y., 1931.

Birds and Their Attributes, by Glover M. Allen, published by Marshall Jones Co., Boston, Mass., 1925.

Birds as Animals, by James Fisher, published by W. Heinemann, Ltd., London, England, 1939.

The Bird: Its Form and Function, by C. W. Beebe, published by Henry Holt and Co., New York, N.Y., 1906.

The Book of Bird Life, by A. A. Allen, published by D. Van Nostrand Co., New York, N.Y., 1930.

A Laboratory and Field Manual of Ornithology, by Olin Sewall Pettingill, Jr., published by Burgess Publishing Co., Minneapolis, Minn., 1946.

Conservation and Management of Birds

Adventures in Bird Protection, by T. G. Pearson, published by D. Appleton-Century Co., New York, N.Y., 1937.

Fading Trails, by D. B. Beard, published by the Macmillan Co., New York, N.Y., 1942.

Game Management, by Aldo Leopold, published by Charles Scribner's Sons, New York, N.Y., 1933.

The International Protection of Wildlife, by S. S. Hayden, published by Columbia University Press, New York, N.Y., 1942.

Wildlife Conservation, by I. N. Gabrielson, published by the Macmillan Co., New York, N.Y., 1941.

Wildlife Refuges, by I. N. Gabrielson, published by the Macmillan Co., New York, N.Y., 1943.

Ecology of Birds—Birds and Their Environment

Breeding Bird Censuses, an annual summary published as a supplement to *Audubon Magazine.*

Ecology of the Birds of Quaker Run Valley, by A. A. Saunders, published by New York State Museum, Albany, N.Y., 1936.

How Birds Live, by E. M. Nicholson, published by Williams and Norgate, Ltd., London, England, 1927.

Nesting Birds and the Vegetation Substrata, by W. J. Beecher, published by Chicago Ornithological Society, Chicago, Ill., 1942.

Eggs of Wild Birds

North American Birds' Eggs, by C. A. Reed, published by Doubleday, Page & Co., New York, N.Y., 1904.

Evolution and Classification of Birds

Check-List of North American Birds, 4th edition, published by the American Ornithologists Union, Washington, D.C., 1931.

The Origin of Birds, by Gerhard Heilmann, published by D. Appleton and Co., New York, N.Y., 1927.

The Structure and Classification of Birds, by F. E. Beddard, published by Longmans, Green and Co., London, England, 1898.

Systematics and the Origin of Species, by Ernst Mayr, published by Columbia University Press, New York, N.Y., 1942.

Field Study of Birds

Christmas Bird Count, an annual winter bird count published as a supplement to *Audubon Magazine*.

Daily Field Cards, a handy pocket check-list published by the National Audubon Society, New York, N.Y.

A Field Guide to the Birds, by Roger T. Peterson, published by Houghton Mifflin Co., Boston, Mass., 1939.

A Guide to Bird Watching, by Joseph J. Hickey, published by Oxford University Press, New York, N.Y., 1943.

Modern Bird Study, by Ludlow Griscom, published by Harvard University Press, Cambridge, Mass., 1945.

Record Note-book for Field Trips, a bird attendance book published by the National Audubon Society, New York, N.Y.

Watching Birds, by James Fisher, published by Penguin Books, Inc., London, England, 1940.

Food Habits of Birds

The Practical Value of Birds, by Junius Henderson, published by the Macmillan Co., New York, N.Y., 1927.

Life History of Birds

Birds of Massachusetts and Other New England States (3 volumes), by E. H. Forbush, published by the Commonwealth of Massachusetts, Boston, Mass., 1925–29.

The Birds of Minnesota, by T. S. Roberts, published by the University of Minnesota Press, Minneapolis, Minn., 1936.

The Home Life of Wild Birds, by F. H. Herrick, published by G. P. Putnam's Sons, New York, N.Y., 1901.

Life Histories of North American Birds, by Arthur C. Bent, published by the U. S. National Museum, Washington, D.C., bulletins nos. 107, 113, 126, 130, 135, 167, 170 ,174, 176, and 179; 1919–42.

Natural History of the Birds of Eastern and Central North America, by E. H. Forbush and J. B. May, published by Houghton Mifflin Co., Boston, Mass., 1939.

Studies in the Life History of the Song Sparrow (2 volumes), by M. M. Nice, published by the Linnaean Society of New York, N.Y., 1937 and 1943.

The Watcher at the Nest, by M. M. Nice, published by the Macmillan Co., New York, N.Y., 1939.

Wild Birds at Home, by F. H. Herrick, published by D. Appleton-Century Co., New York, N.Y., 1935.

Migration of Birds

The Migration of Birds, by Alexander Wetmore, published by Harvard University Press, Cambridge, Mass., 1930.

The Migration of North American Birds, by Frederick C. Lincoln, published by Doubleday, Doran & Co., New York, N.Y., 1939.

Problems of Bird Migration, by Arthur L. Thomson, published by Houghton Mifflin Co., Boston, Mass., 1926.

The Riddle of Migration, by W. Rowan, published by the Williams & Wilkins Co., Baltimore, Md., 1931.

The Season, a quarterly report on bird movements from 12 key regions, published as a supplement to *Audubon Magazine*.

Periodicals on Birds

Audubon Magazine, a bimonthly published by the National Audubon Society, New York, N.Y.

The Auk, a quarterly published by the American Ornithologists Union, Lancaster, Pa.

The Condor, a quarterly published by the Cooper Ornithological Club, Berkeley, Calif.

The Wilson Bulletin, a quarterly published by the Wilson Ornithological Club, Ann Arbor, Mich.

Plumage Descriptions

Birds of North and Middle America, by Robert Ridgway, published by the U.S. National Museum, Washington, D.C., 1901-41. Issued in 9 parts.

Color Standards and Color Nomenclature, by Robert Ridgway, published by A. Hoen & Co., Washington, D.C., 1912.

Sequence of Plumage and Moults of the Passerine Birds of New York, by Jonathan Dwight, Jr., published in annals of the New York Academy of Science, New York, N.Y., 1900.

Psychology and Behavior of Birds

Bird Behavior, by F. B. Kirkman, published by T. Nelson & Sons, London, England, 1937.

Bird Display, An Introduction to the Study of Bird Psychology,
by Edward A. Armstrong, published by Cambridge University
Press, Cambridge, England, 1942.

Bird Flocks and the Breeding Cycle, by F. F. Darling, published
by Cambridge University Press, Cambridge, England, 1938.

The Nature of a Bird's World, by H. Eliot Howard, published by
Cambridge University Press, Cambridge, England, 1935.

Territory in Bird Life, by H. E. Howard, published by John
Murray, London, England, 1920.

A Waterhen's World, by H. E. Howard, published by Cambridge
University Press, Cambridge, England, 1940.

Songs of Birds

A Guide to Bird Songs, by Aretas A. Saunders, published by
D. Appleton-Century Co., New York, N.Y., 1935.

American Bird Songs, a collection of 72 recordings on disks, by
the Albert R. Brand Song Foundation of Cornell University, published by Comstock Publishing Co., Ithaca, N.Y., 1945.

World Bird Life

The Birds of the World, by F. H. Knowlton, published by Henry
Holt & Co., New York, N.Y., 1909.

Check-List of Birds of the World, by J. L. Peters, published by
Harvard University Press, Cambridge, Mass., 1931. (5 volumes
published to date.)

Index

THE BOUNDARIES OF THE LIFE ZONES SUPERIMPOSED ON A MAP OF THE NORTH AMERICAN BIOMES

Hudsonian

Canadian

Transition

Upper Austral

Lower Austral

Tropical

Cladonia-Caribou
Biome (Tundra)

Spruce-Moose
Biome (Coniferous
Forest)

Cedar-Sitka Deer
Biome (Moist Con.
Forest)

Adenostoma-Brush Rabbit
Biome (Chaparral)

Shadscale-Kangaroo Rat
Biome (Cool-Desert)

Creosote Bush-Desert Fox
Biome (Hot Desert)

Juniper-Rock Squirrel
Biome (Pinyon-Juniper Woodland)